IMAGES
of America

Kansas City's Historic Midtown Neighborhoods

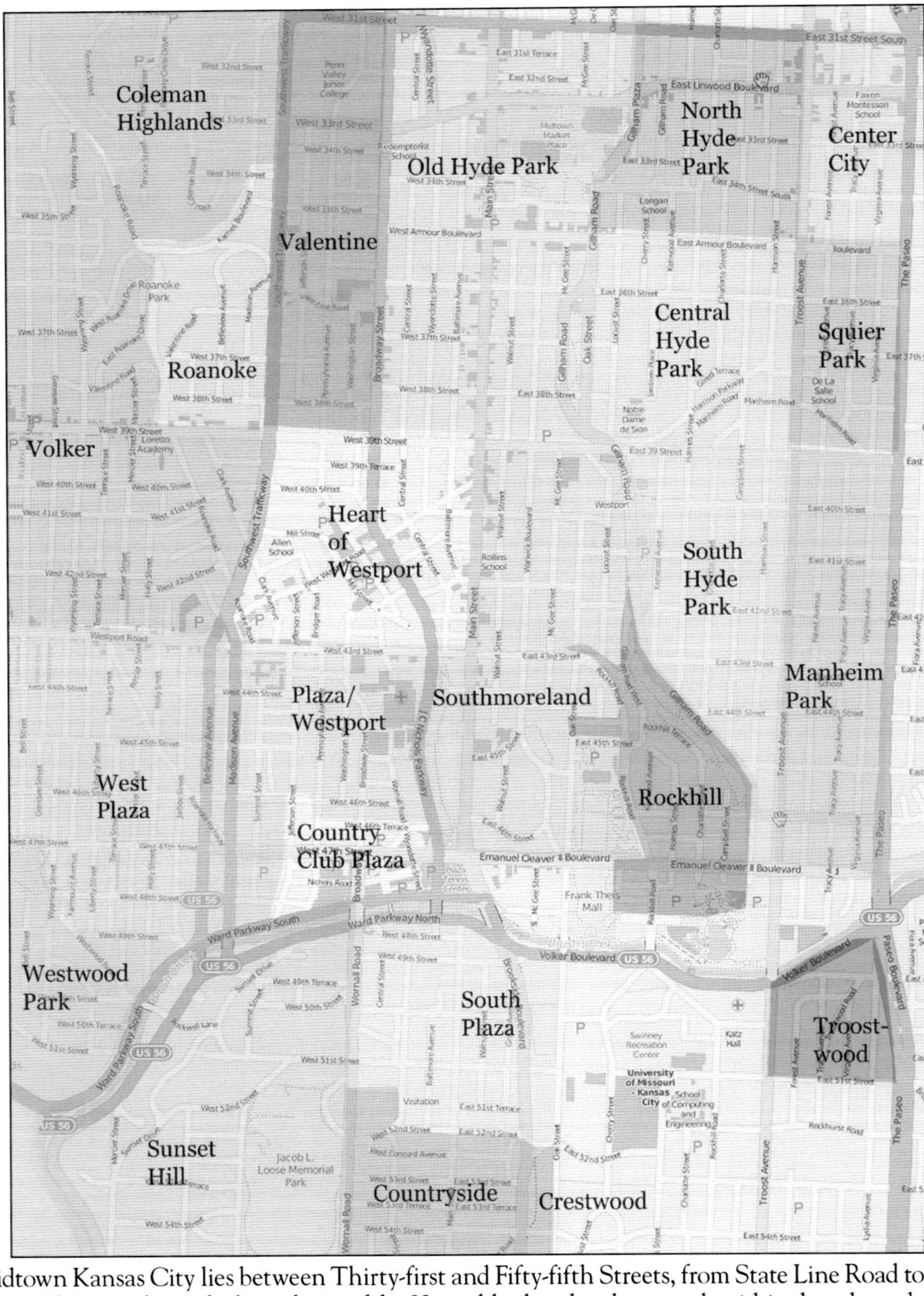

Midtown Kansas City lies between Thirty-first and Fifty-fifth Streets, from State Line Road to the Paseo. This map shows the boundaries of the 22 neighborhoods at least partly within those boundaries. (Map by the author, based on official City of Kansas City, Missouri, neighborhood boundaries.)

On the Cover: Streetcar tracks and automobiles helped Midtown Kansas City neighborhoods grow and thrive from 1900 to the 1950s, and the neighborhoods continue to attract residents and businesses today. The Troost streetcar line carried people from the newly created residential districts to the south to jobs downtown. As neighborhoods grew, businesses flourished on Troost Avenue, as did entertainment venues like the popular Isis Theater. (Courtesy of Wilborn and Associates.)

IMAGES
of America

KANSAS CITY'S HISTORIC MIDTOWN NEIGHBORHOODS

Mary Jo Draper

ARCADIA
PUBLISHING

ISBN 978-1-4671-1342-7

Published by Arcadia Publishing
Charleston, South Carolina

Printed in the United States of America

Library of Congress Control Number: 2014947176

For all general information, please contact Arcadia Publishing:
Telephone 843-853-2070
Fax 843-853-0044
E-mail sales@arcadiapublishing.com
For customer service and orders:
Toll-Free 1-888-313-2665

Visit us on the Internet at www.arcadiapublishing.com

To all the people who now call Midtown home,
and all of those we hope someday will.

Contents

ACKNOWLEDGMENTS

Many people shared their interest in Midtown Kansas City and its neighborhoods. Without their help, this book would not have been possible.

The researchers who have spent countless hours digging out the history of Kansas City have done a great service to all of us, and they do not often get the thanks they deserve. The applications to the National Historic Register, with their careful documentation of specific neighborhoods and their houses and businesses, are an important repository of information. The Historic Kansas City Foundation has also helped to document, and advocate for saving, historic Midtown buildings. The Westport Historic Society has helped to continue to add to our knowledge of early Westport.

For assistance in finding information and photographs, thanks must go first to Jeremy Drouin at the Missouri Valley Room of the Kansas City Public Library. I am also grateful to Diane Burnette at the Main Street Development Corporation, who shared that organization's archives, as well as the Westport Historical Society.

Kansas City's strong neighborhood associations work every day to preserve Midtown and keep the history alive. I would especially like to thank Joe Montanari of the West Plaza neighborhood, who has researched the history of that area and shared it generously in the neighborhood newsletter over the years.

Julie Tenenbaum offered invaluable help in proofreading and generous moral support.

I would also like to thank the readers of the *Midtown KC Post*, who share a passion for Kansas City neighborhoods and history and who treasure the homes, buildings, and streets that make Midtown such a unique place to live.

Photographic sources are abbreviated as follows: Missouri Valley Special Collections, Kansas City, Missouri Public Library (MVSC-KCPL); University of Missouri–Kansas City Libraries, Dr. Kenneth J. LaBudde, Department of Special Collections (UMKC–LaBudde); Library of Congress Prints and Photographs Division, Washington, DC (Library of Congress); photographs taken by Mary Jo Draper (author's collection); *Midtown KC Post* Uncovering History Collection (*Midtown KC Post*); Westport Historical Society (Westport Historical); Main Street Corridor Development Corporation (MainCor); and Wilborn and Associates Photographers (Wilborn and Associates).

Introduction

Visitors to Kansas City and longtime residents alike often tend to lump the area of the city from Thirty-first to Fifty-fifth Streets, from State Line Road to the Paseo, into a general category: Midtown Kansas City. Yet Midtown actually contains 22 distinct neighborhoods, each with a unique history, character, and flavor.

Much has been written about some of the Midtown neighborhoods. Others are less well known. The idea behind this book was to bring together the histories of the neighborhoods that have been discovered by professional and neighborhood historians and to inspire additional digging into the past.

These neighborhoods are defined by their history, the buildings within their borders, the major and minor streets, the parks and green spaces, and the schools and commercial areas that have served their residents. In most cases, these neighborhood "bones" were built between 1880 and 1930, creating the structure of the Midtown neighborhoods known today.

Midtown grew out of two towns: Kansas City, incorporated in 1853, and Westport, the outfitting center for the Oregon, California, and Santa Fe Trails, incorporated in 1857. Mrs. G.H. Wheeler, who grew up at Ninth and Main Streets, recalled taking a trip to Westport as a child in the mid-1800s. The horse passed only two houses along the way. It took the riders over steep and hilly terrain, through orchards and fields. The homes she passed were simple and utilitarian.

When Wheeler recounted her trip near the turn of the 20th century, things had changed in many ways. Kansas City was a center of commerce for the railroad, grain-handling, and meatpacking industries. After the Civil War, a growing number of middle-class men and women had arrived in the city. Wealthy people had moved away from downtown, and the homes they erected were large and fancy.

"In the mid-1880s, real estate speculation in Kansas City reached near-hysterical proportions. Land south of the city, extending to the town of Westport, three miles distant, was sold and resold at fantastic profits," Ray Ellis wrote in *A Civic History of Kansas City*. Those changes helped to shape Midtown.

Midtown's growth began when the wealthiest captains of industry moved to "the south side"—the area called Hyde Park, along Troost Avenue—and to the new Roanoke district. After their mansions went up, middle-class folks followed, building smaller homes or purchasing them from a developer. Their Prairie-style and Kansas City shirtwaist homes, along with rows of bungalows, give Midtown much of its distinct image today. Immigrants and workers filled in the remaining spaces.

Nothing had a greater impact on Midtown development than Kansas City's vibrant streetcar system. Early horse-drawn cars connected the Central Business District to Westport. In the 1880s, cable lines installed on Troost Avenue, Grand Boulevard, and Prospect Avenue greatly sped up travel and made it possible to live farther from downtown. Streetcars and the building boom they triggered also transformed major streets such as Broadway Boulevard, Troost Avenue, and Main Street into bustling commercial districts serving the needs of new residents.

Streetcars continued to run in Kansas City until 1957, but photographs of Midtown neighborhoods over the years show increasing signs of dependence on automobiles. By the 1940s, photographs show cars lining the curbs, and neighborhoods are dotted with gas stations, auto-repair shops, and car dealers. The fabric of each neighborhood was also woven from the movie theaters, drugstores, and grocery stores where residents met and shared their leisure time.

Some neighborhoods had restrictions against multifamily units, but where those restrictions were not in place, working-class and middle-class apartment buildings began to fill in these new Midtown neighborhoods, especially along the streetcar lines. The colonnade-style apartments built after 1900 added a distinct character to the neighborhoods and, even now, provide housing for many residents.

The high-rise luxury residential hotels of the 1920s, built for the wealthy during a housing shortage, are another legacy of this era. Armour Boulevard, once a quiet residential street, was transformed in the 1920s into a boulevard of residential apartment hotels. Many are currently being used for middle-class or low-income housing.

Maps of Midtown neighborhoods reveal that some were built on a strict north-south city grid, while others were designed around curving streets or parks. William Rockhill Nelson and J.C. Nichols, among others, believed in following the natural contours of the land, allowing streets to curve, as streams and ravines had done before the area was developed.

Another major influence on the structure of these neighborhoods was the city's park-and-boulevard system, which was being built at the time Midtown was developing. The principles of the City Beautiful movement had a profound impact on the development of Kansas City's parks and boulevards, which continue to differentiate Midtown neighborhoods and influence the land use around them.

Churches, schools, and social clubs followed residents as well. The school district built elementary and secondary schools, and Kansas City's major universities were established during this period. In many cases, these institutions have long since moved to new residential areas, but their substantial buildings remained, to be repurposed as part of Midtown's landscape.

Interwoven into the story of Midtown development are issues of race and class. In his book *Race, Real Estate and Uneven Development: The Kansas City Experience, 1900–2010,* Kevin Gotham Fox explains that, before the 1900s, city neighborhoods were generally mixed, both by race and class. But, beginning in the 1920s, a number of factors led to increasing segregation in Midtown. Neighborhood developers, including J.C. Nichols, began to use racial covenants to restrict ownership in some subdivisions. As Fox explains, real estate industry practices and federal housing policy also promoted racial division in neighborhoods. Practices of the Kansas City School District further exacerbated the problem. Many white families left Midtown for the new suburbs in Kansas, and Troost Avenue became a racial dividing line.

By the 1930s, Midtown's buildings were in place. For the most part, they remain today. The area has seen periods of decline, including the splitting of large homes into apartments after World War II and white flight in the 1950s and 1960s. Some areas were renovated by urban pioneers in the 1970s and 1980s, and some are still awaiting renewal. Today, many neighborhoods and residents are working to break down historical racial barriers and continue to preserve the housing stock that makes them special.

An important note about the photographs in this book: As Midtown Kansas City was developing and changing, the most elaborate buildings and the homes of the most prominent Kansas Citians were extensively recorded by photographers and postcard companies. What has been lost, in part, is a pictorial record of the homes of average people. There is, however, a very important record of the city's buildings. In 1940, the Work Projects Administration, in conjunction with the Jackson County Tax Assessors Office, sent photographers out to take a snapshot of every building in the city. These "tax photographs" record the condition of every piece of property in that post-Depression year. This book makes ample use of these photographs for two reasons: First, because they are the only record of some of the properties in Midtown; second, because they provide a baseline of comparison among the neighborhoods in Kansas City. The man in the hat holding the sign with the property identification has become a familiar sight to many people in Kansas City who research the history of their homes. These photographs are now available at the Missouri Valley Room of the Kansas City Public Library, which makes this valuable resource available to everyone.

One

Neighborhoods between Broadway and Troost

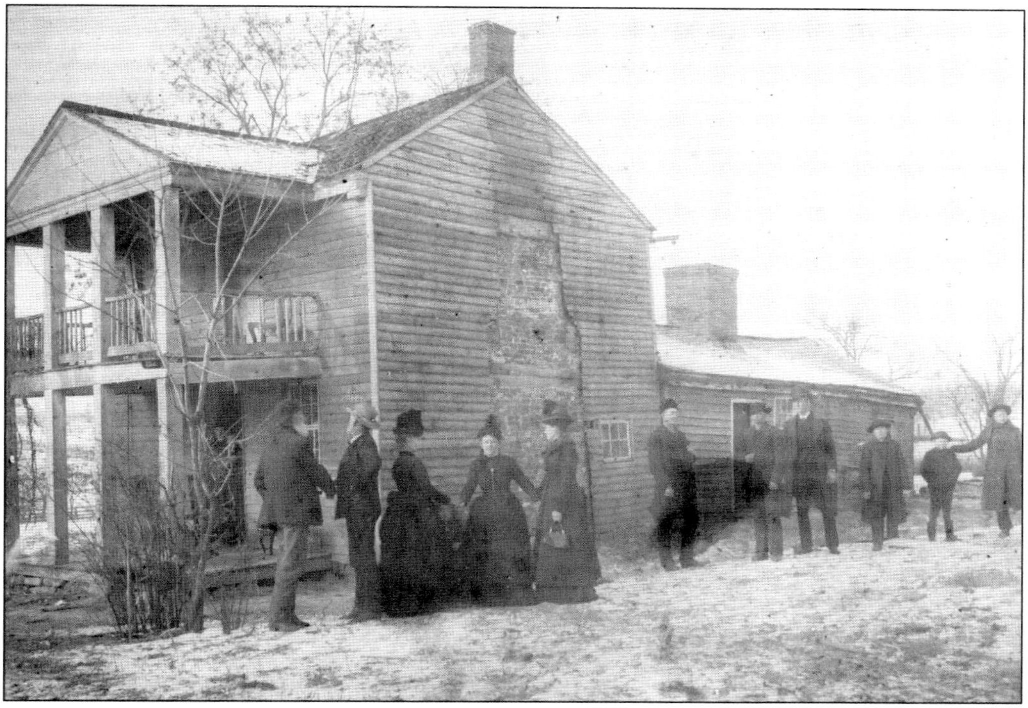

Moving South from Downtown, 1886. Between Broadway Boulevard and Troost Avenue—where the neighborhoods of Old Hyde Park, Hyde Park (Central, North, and South), Southmoreland, and Rockhill would later develop—early Kansas City and Westport settlers built farmsteads in the early 1800s. For several decades, a handful of owners lived on large tracts spread out over the hills. It is not known exactly when the home shown here was built, but the Jacob Ragan family moved into the house and 60-acre farm near the current intersection of Armour Boulevard and Gillham Road in the 1830s. Nearby was a large spring where people camped during their trips west on the Santa Fe Trail. The Ragan family moved away in 1886, and the farm was platted as the Kenwood subdivision. (Courtesy of MVSC-KCPL.)

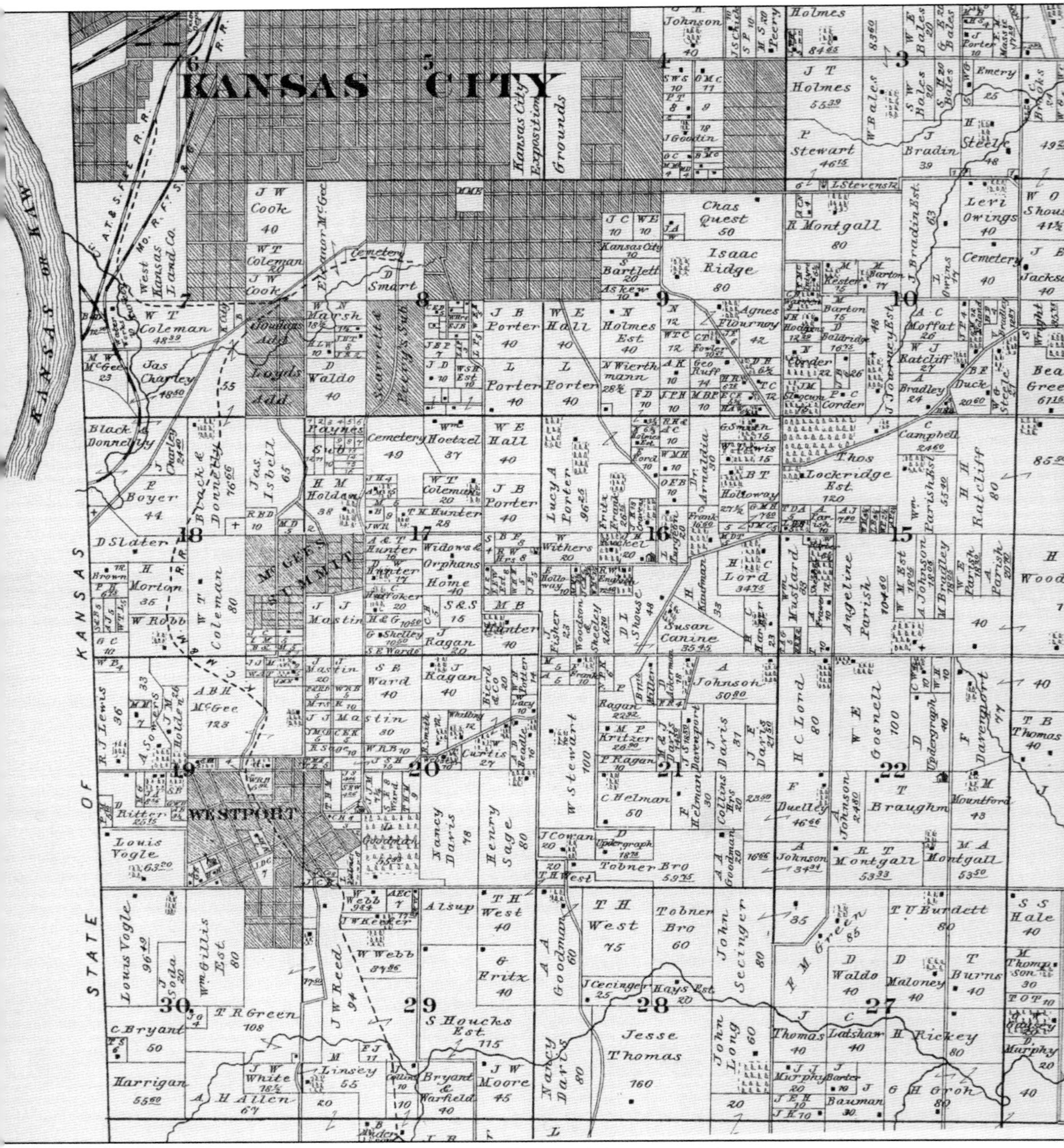

Early Settlers. This page from the 1887 *Illustrated Historical Atlas of Kansas City* shows Kansas City, Westport, and the early residential area called McGee's Summit. Besides these areas, most of what is now Midtown was made up of large farms owned by early settlers. The Ragan, A.B.H. McGee, Louis Vogel, and Webster Withers farms, among others, can be seen. Note the orchards on either side of Westport. Many of these farms would be sold and platted as subdivisions that became Midtown neighborhoods. (Courtesy of *Midtown KC Post.*)

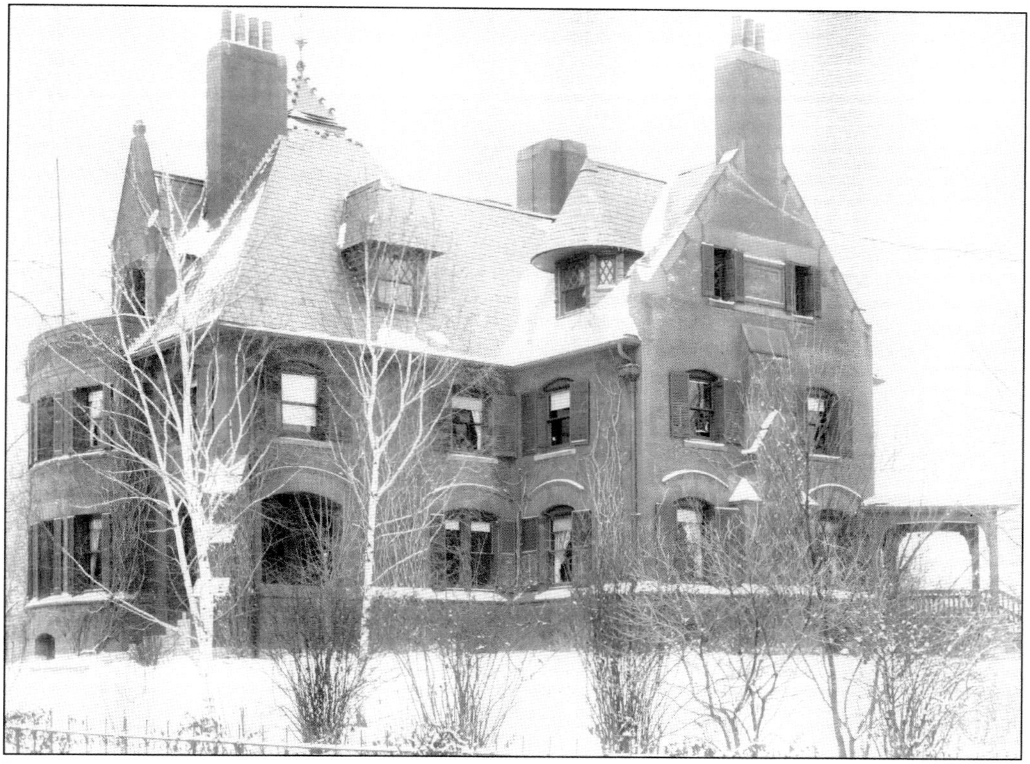

Development Begins, 1880s. Downtown was getting crowded, and by the late 1880s, the movement south began. Charles Morse, general manager of the Kansas City stockyards, built his home at Thirty-sixth Street and Warwick Boulevard, and others soon followed. The Morse home was demolished in the 1930s. Before the neighborhoods had fully developed, the area between Broadway Boulevard and Troost Avenue was referred to as Hyde Park in general. Today, smaller areas are designated as Old Hyde Park, Central Hyde Park, North Hyde Park, and South Hyde Park. (Courtesy of MVSC-KCPL.)

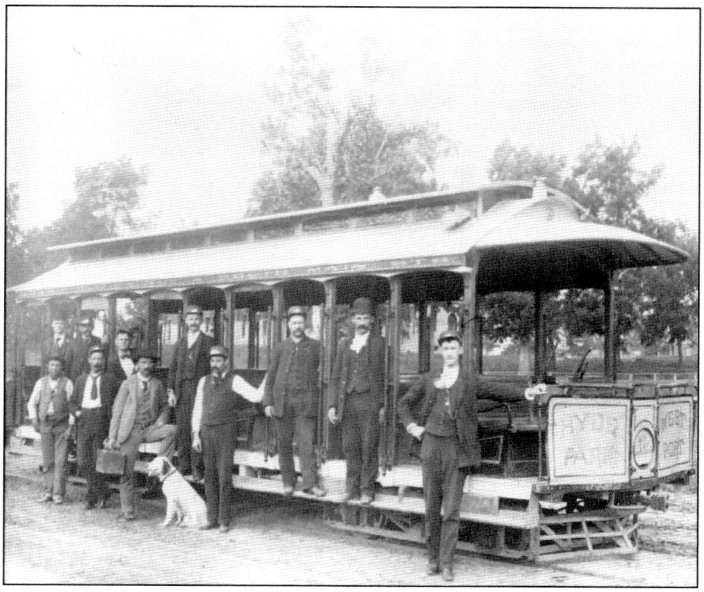

Hyde Park Streetcar. Until the 1880s, the only public transportation connecting Hyde Park and downtown was mule-drawn streetcars. But with the advent of new cable-car lines, development of the south side opened up. In 1899, Kansas City annexed Westport, adding additional steam to a single-family housing boom in the Hyde Park area. (Courtesy of Westport Historical Society.)

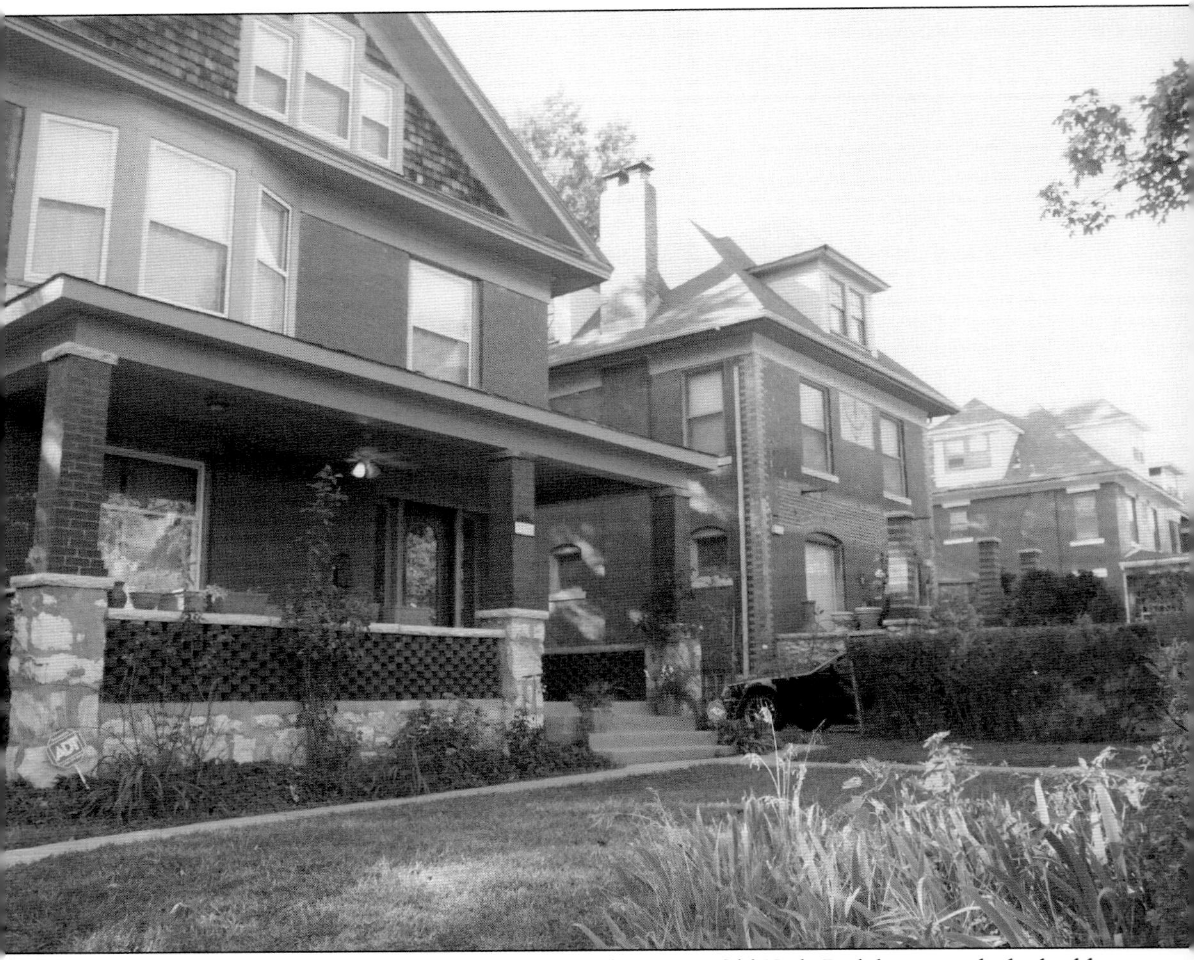

Old Hyde Park. Construction of the area now known as Old Hyde Park began with the building boom before 1900, but the majority of the construction took place between 1900 and 1909. Old Hyde Park today contains several historic districts and buildings in the National Register of Historic Places. According to the register's nomination statement for the Old Hyde Park West Historic District, the area developed during a period of great architectural variety; the popularity of exuberant Victorian architecture was waning as the early 20th century "witnessed the return of more subdued Classical and Colonial Revival styles, the exploration of traditional Craftsman themes, and the development of the uniquely Midwestern Prairie Style." These styles are scattered throughout the neighborhood, creating what the nomination form describes as a "neighborhood of substantial residences, eclectic in design, that represents a streetscape largely unchanged since the 1920s." (Author's collection.)

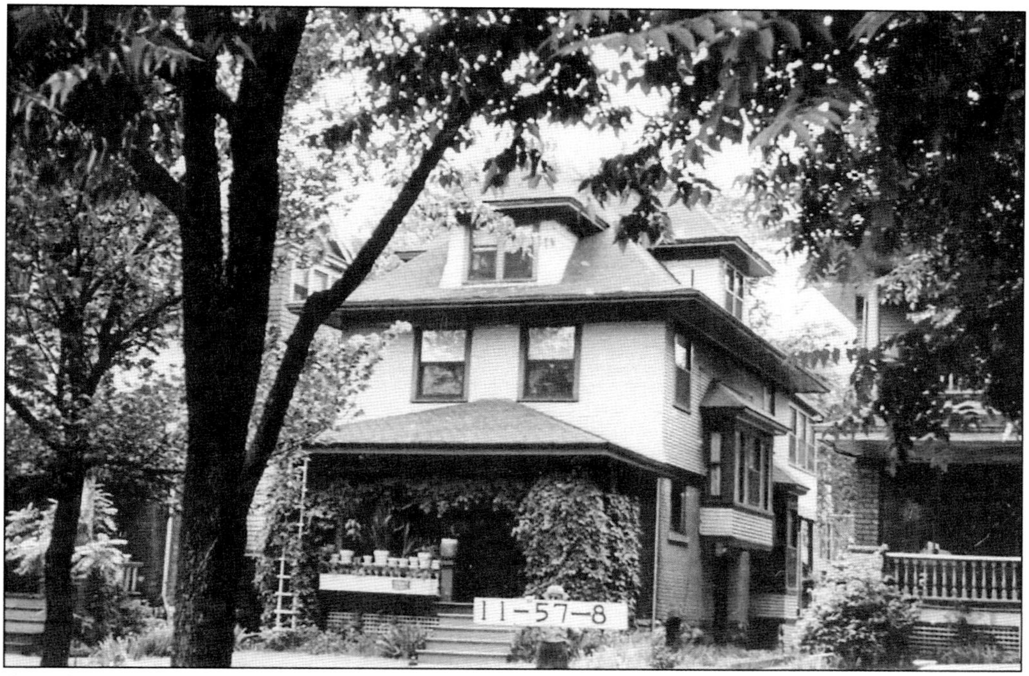

OLD HYDE PARK, 1940. Old Hyde Park is typical of many Midtown neighborhoods where homes were built with high-quality construction materials that continued to make them attractive to residents over the decades. Most of the single-family homes in Old Hyde Park are one to two and a half stories. Multifamily dwellings in the neighborhood include two- to four-story apartment buildings, although there are a few taller apartments. In the 1940s, many of the large homes in Old Hyde Park, similar to those in other Midtown neighborhoods, were broken up into multiple units. There has been a movement to return these homes to single-family residences. (Both, courtesy of MVSC-KCPL.)

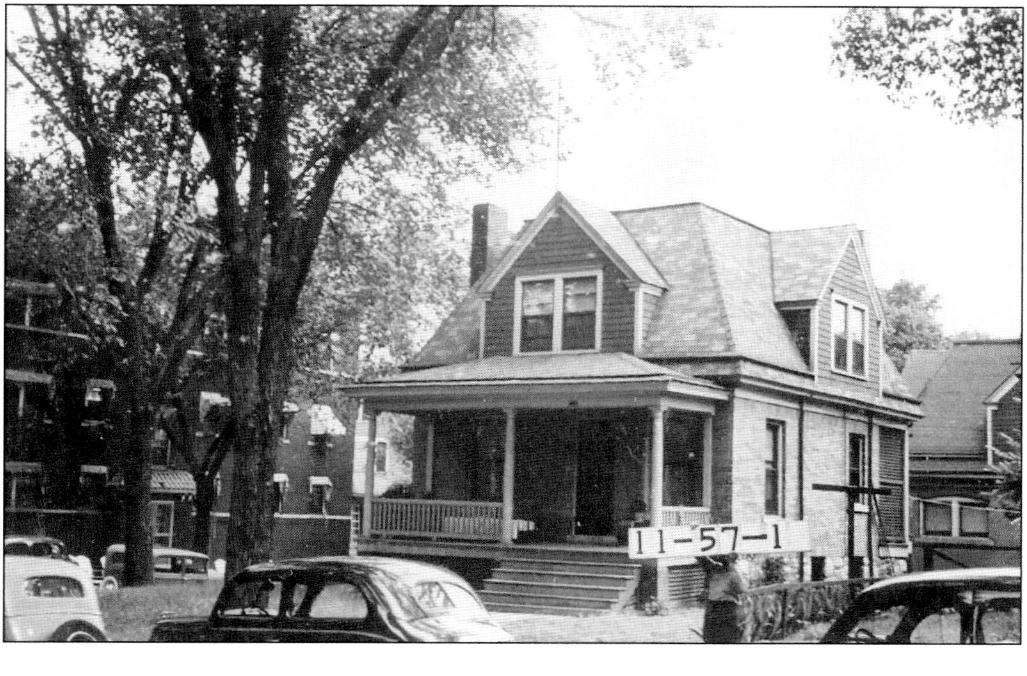

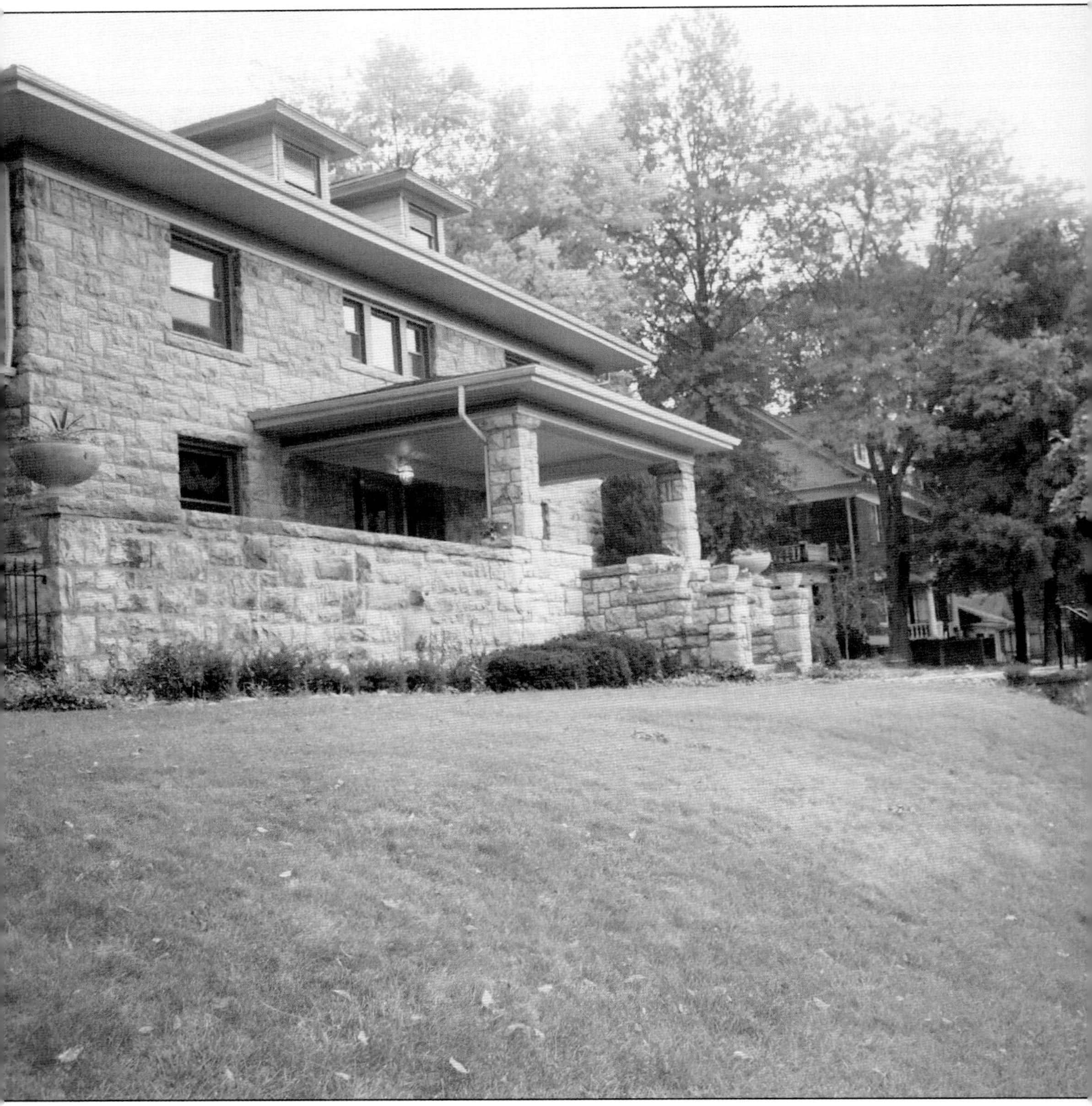

CENTRAL HYDE PARK. The large Hyde Park neighborhood is divided into three sections: Central Hyde Park, North Hyde Park, and South Hyde Park. Central Hyde Park is described by historians as a well-preserved turn-of-the-century residential neighborhood that has retained its unique character. Its homes display a mixture of architectural styles, and many were designed by leading architects of the day. Central Hyde Park was home to some of the wealthiest and most prominent city fathers, and, according to its historic register nomination, it "reflects their taste for conservative, but excellent design and craftsmanship." A handful of Hyde Park homes were built before the turn of the 20th century, but the major construction boom took place in Central Hyde Park between 1900 and 1907. By the end of World War II, many of the original owners of Hyde Park homes had died or moved away. Similar to the pattern in other neighborhoods, the big houses were often converted into apartments or sleeping rooms. In the last several decades, a move to renovate and restore the homes has taken many back to single-family occupancy. (Author's collection.)

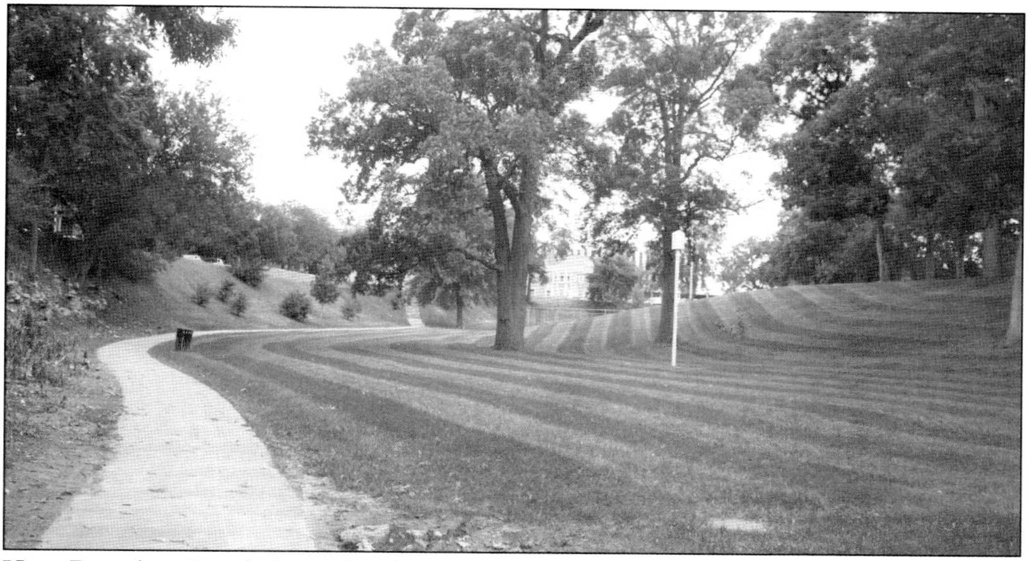

Hyde Park (the Park). Central Hyde Park contains a unique city park, also named Hyde Park, in between the lanes of Gillham Road between Thirty-ninth Street and Brush Creek Boulevard. Designer George Kessler hoped building a park in the steeply sloped valley would both provide a neighborhood recreation area and encourage development along Gillham Road. In the 1890s, Hyde Park became an informal country club with tennis courts, croquet grounds, and the first golf course in Kansas City. (Author's collection.)

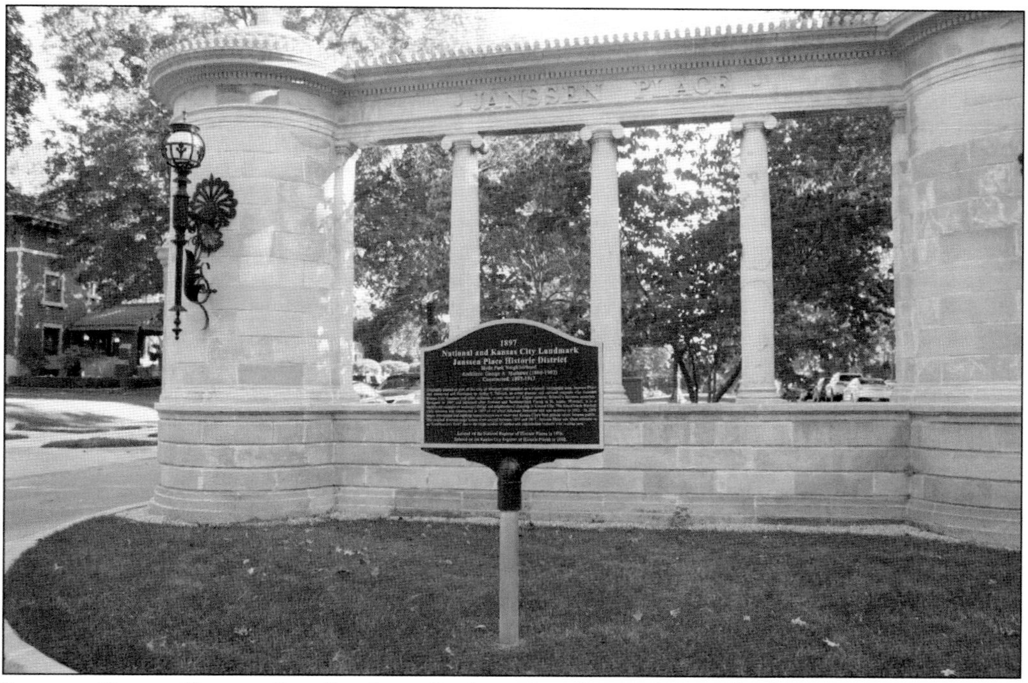

Janssen Place. Kansas City Southern Railway founder Arthur Stillwell conceived of an elite private street within Hyde Park in 1897. Stilwell's Janssen Place became known as "Lumberman's Row" as owners profiting from the lumber and construction industries moved in. All homes had servants' quarters, and some homes were built on more than one lot. Today, the entrance to Janssen Place looks much as it did when the area was developed. (Author's collection.)

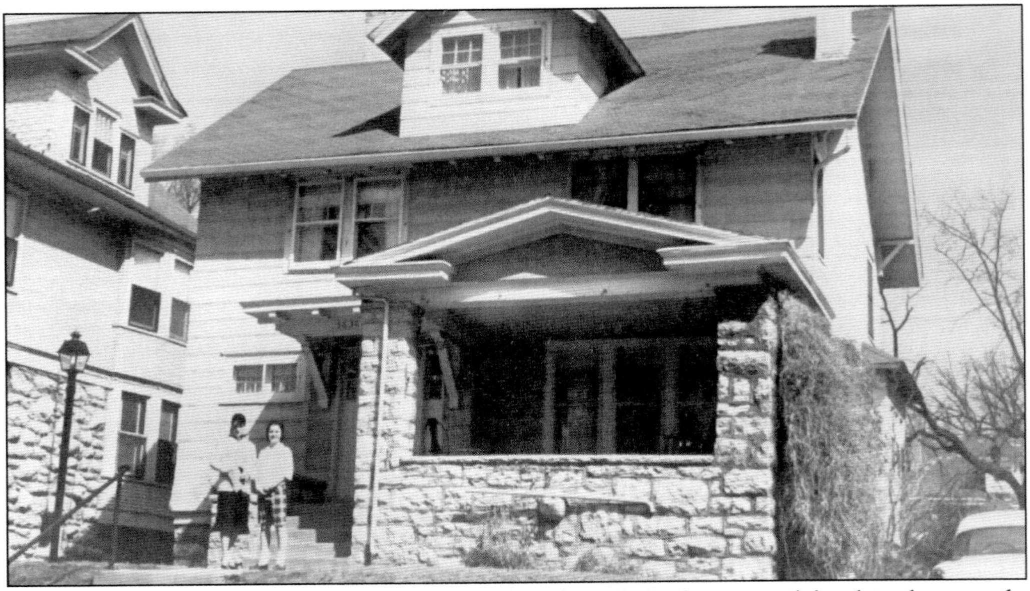

Central Hyde Park, 1959. When Judy (left) and Linda Latham posed for this photograph, their parents, William S. and Genevieve, had just purchased this home at 3631 Charlotte Street. F.E. Danielson built the house in 1920. Like other developers across the city, he bought and built on an unimproved lot. From 1920 to the 1950s, Judge Albert Reeves, who helped bring down the Pendergast machine, lived in the house. The Lathams' other daughters Sharon and Carolyn remember growing up in a quiet, middle-class neighborhood, attending Westport High School, and going shopping and to the movies on Troost Avenue. (Courtesy of Sharon Easley and Carolyn Londerholm.)

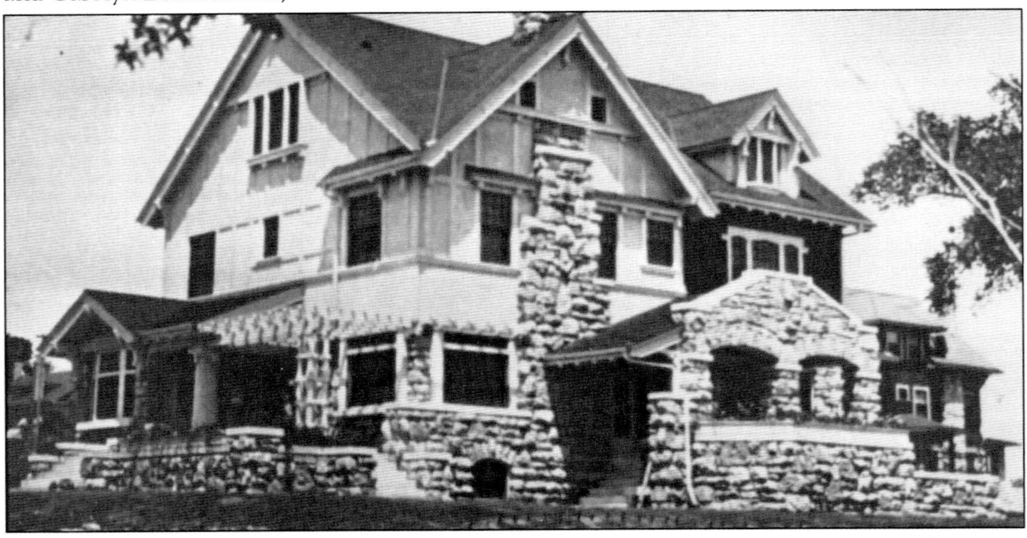

Central Hyde Park, 1940s. This Central Hyde Park home was built in 1907. Like many other Midtown homes, city renumbering changed its official address at some point from 3711 Charlotte Street to 3659 Charlotte Street. G. Bryant Brachman, who lived in the home until 1914, remembered the porches' magnificent red rambler roses and wisteria. He also recalled that a cave under the house ran down to a small creek in the park below, where he gathered watercress for salads. The cave was rumored to be the occasional hideout of Jesse James (as were most caves in Kansas City). (Courtesy of Susan and Doug Borge.)

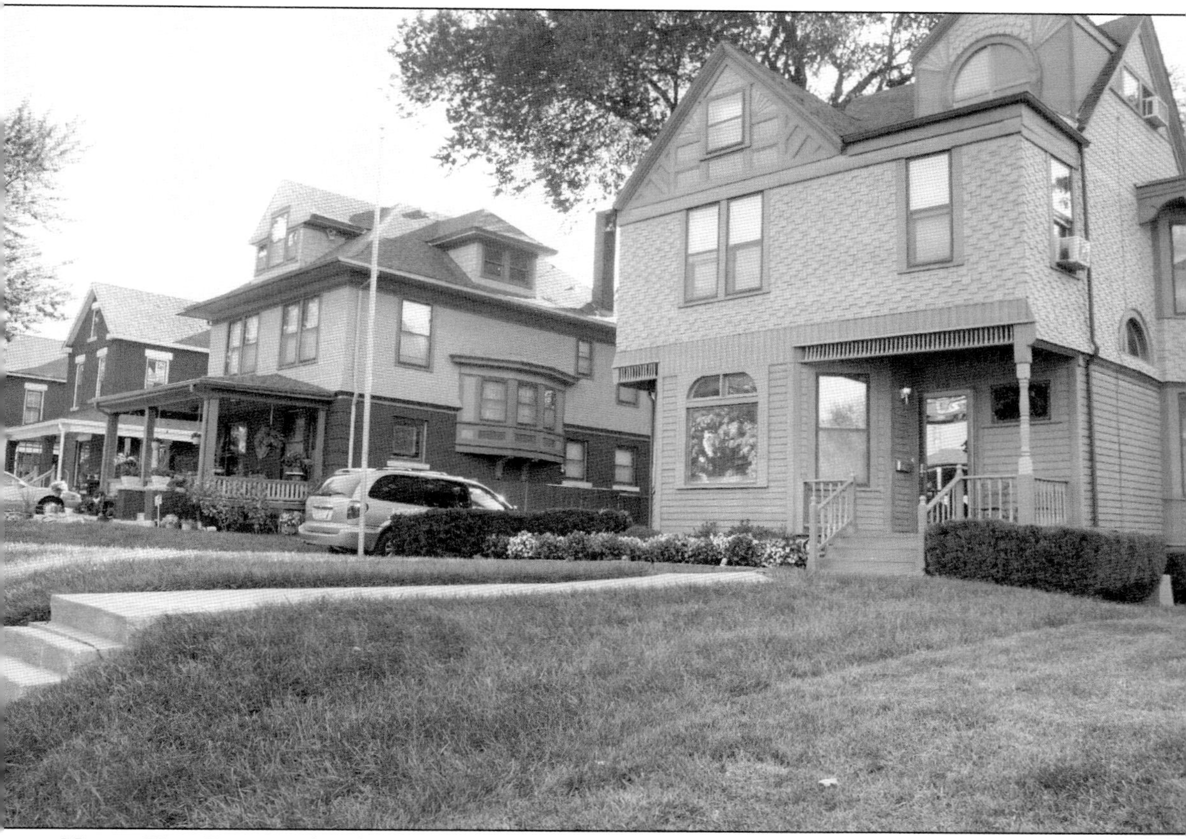

NORTH HYDE PARK. Today, the area of Hyde Park north of Armour Boulevard is called North Hyde Park. Part of North Hyde Park is recognized as a historic district for its homes built from 1880 to the early 1900s. Several homes on the 3300 and 3400 blocks of Harrison Street are among the earliest buildings, constructed for wealthy residents when the Hyde Park area and nearby Armour Boulevard were the most fashionable addresses in town. Most of the homes were built between 1890 and 1911, with several constructed between 1890 and 1899 that show evidence of the slightly different style of that period. Queen Anne, Victorian, and Kansas City shirtwaist homes are the predominant architectural styles, with decorative touches such as fish-scale shingles, Palladian windows, and oriel windows. North Hyde Park also contains some significant apartment buildings along Armour Boulevard. The Central Presbyterian Church, Trinity M.E. Church, and Longan School are located within North Hyde Park. (Author's collection.)

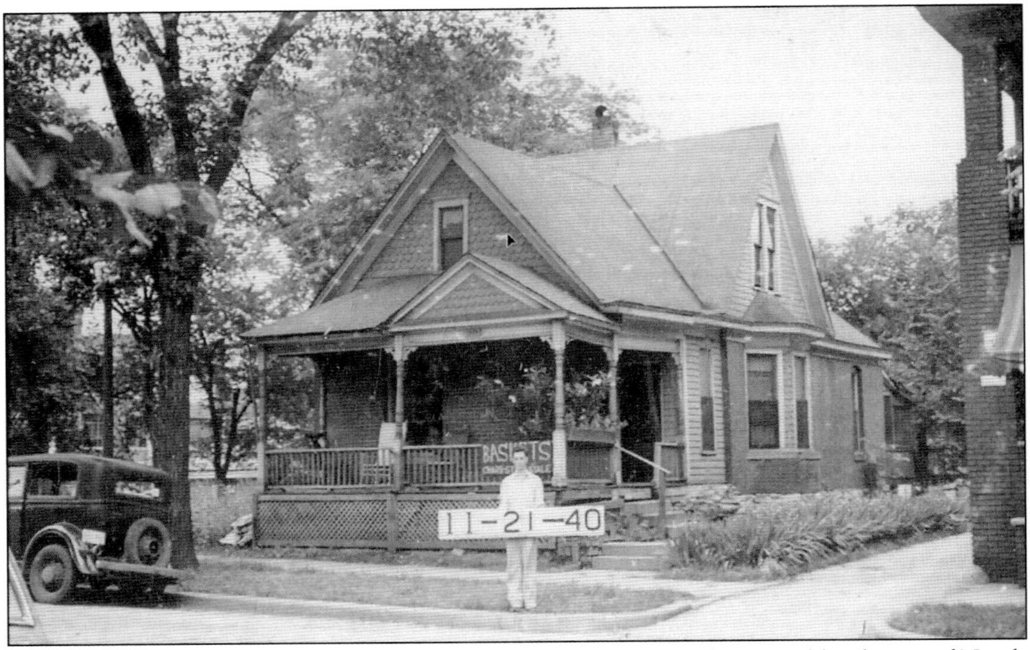

NORTH HYDE PARK, 1940. Smaller homes are also part of the architectural landscape of North Hyde Park. The district contains a significant number of residences built by the Cowherd Brothers, a leading builder-realtor that was active in several Midtown neighborhoods. Because of the proximity to streetcar lines, small apartment buildings are also an important part of North Hyde Park's makeup. As the neighborhood filled in with smaller homes, these apartments were often built between two houses, as seen below. Typical apartments of the era had large front porches to catch the evening breeze. Awnings were a popular addition at the time the photograph below was taken. (Both, courtesy of MVSC-KCPL.)

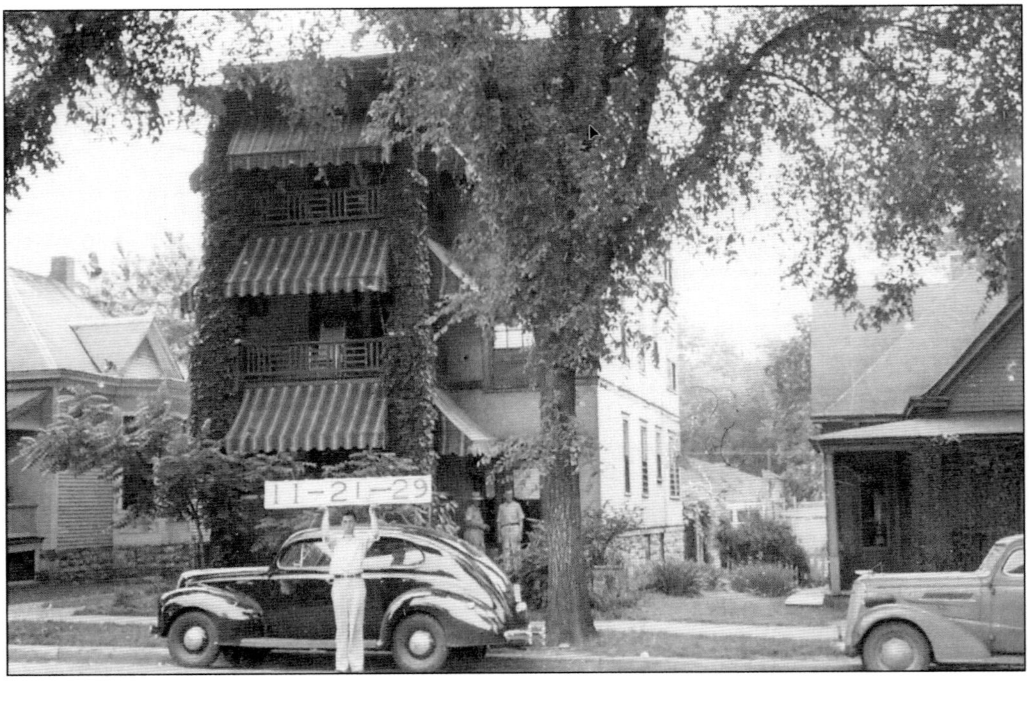

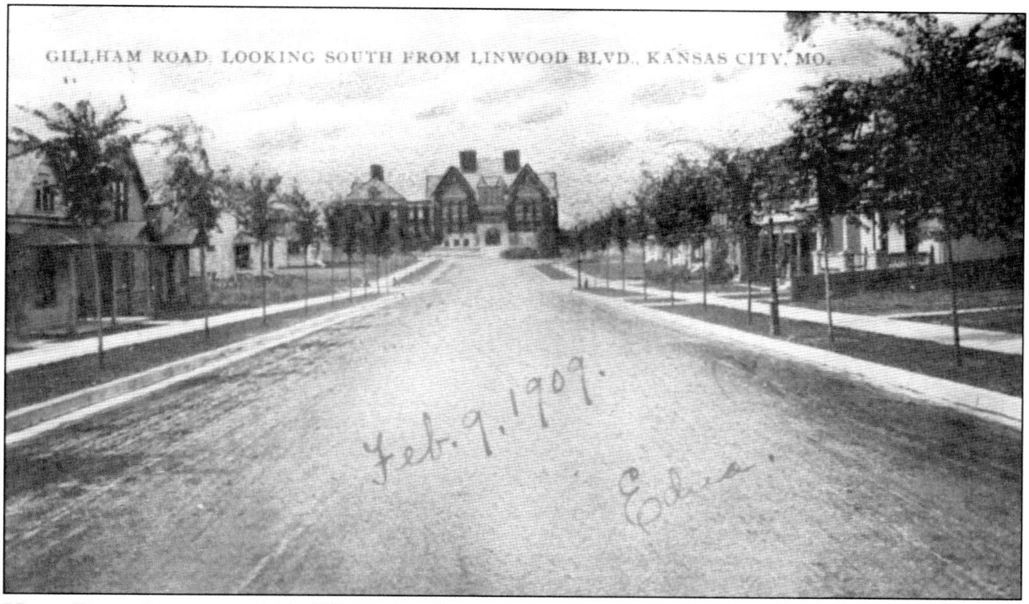

Hyde Park School, 1909. This school, at Thirty-third and McGee Streets, was part of the Westport School District before it was annexed by Kansas City. The school replaced an earlier eight-room frame schoolhouse. The school was razed in 1955, replaced by the "modern" George B. Longan School. Hyde Park also had a Catholic school, Notre Dame de Sion, which opened its four-story brick building in 1927 at 3823 Locust Street. Some of its classes were taught in French. (Courtesy of *Midtown KC Post*.)

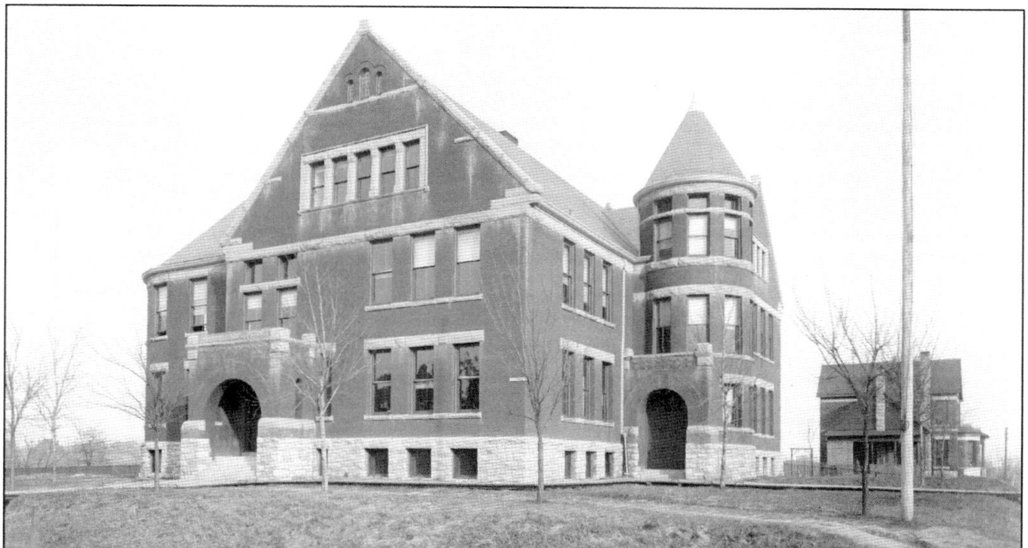

Westport High School, 1885. The first Westport High School, at Thirty-ninth Street and Warwick Boulevard, burned in 1885 and was replaced by another school by the same name at Thirty-ninth and Locust Streets in 1908. Both Westport High School, at 315 East Thirty-ninth Street, and Westport Junior High, across the street at 300 East Thirty-ninth Street, are examples of Progressive-era schools, shaped by reform movements of the period. Their large windows allow ample light and air into classrooms. The junior high school was closed in 2009, and the high school was closed in 2010. (Courtesy of MVSC-KCPL.)

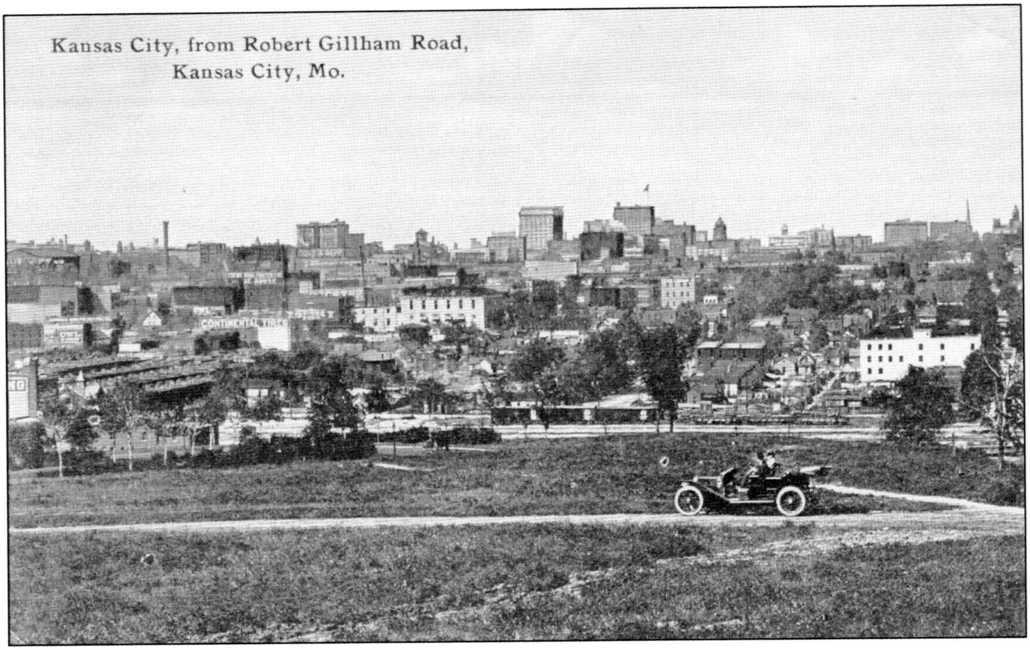

View from Gillham Road, 1910s. Around the turn of the century, many postcards featured Kansas City parks and boulevards, showing them off to the world. One measure of the popularity of the Hyde Park area is the number of postcards that celebrated its homes and streets. The downtown Kansas City skyline, as seen from Gillham Road (above), is evidence of downtown's development. The boulevard, in contrast, provided open space and green grass. The postcard below shows Gillham looking south from Thirty-seventh Street, still a dirt road with scattered houses and plenty of large trees. The boulevard was graded and paved between 1903 and 1906. (Both, courtesy of *Midtown KC Post*.)

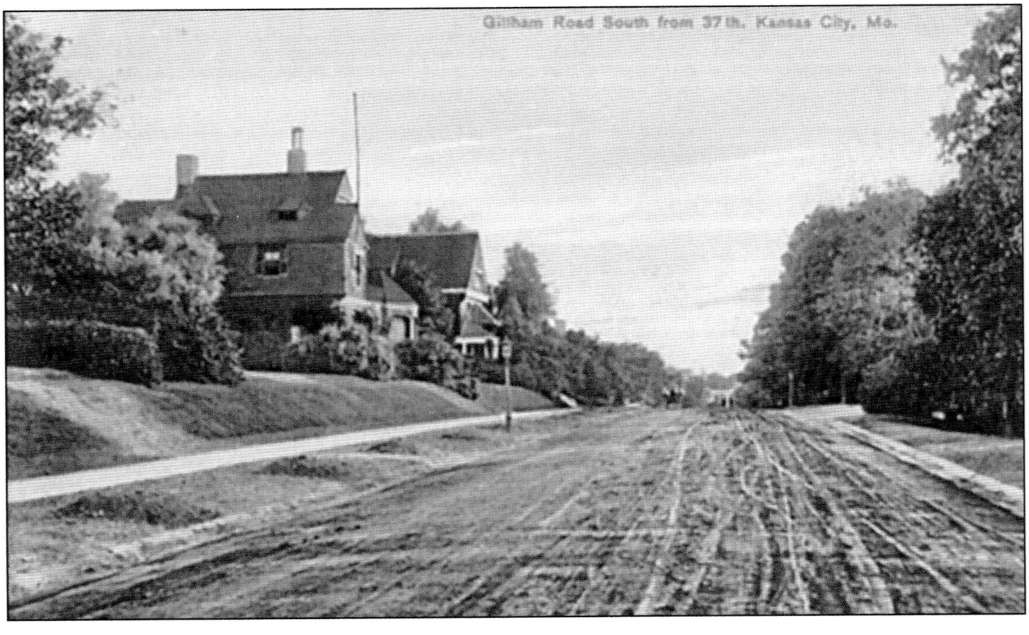

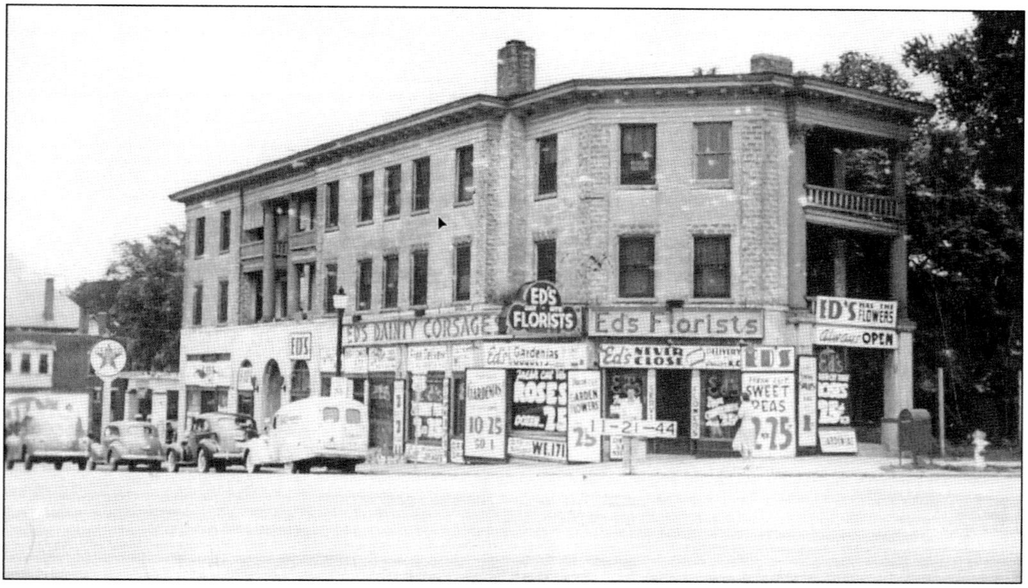

Gillham Road Businesses, 1940. Although the area between Broadway Boulevard and Troost Avenue is generally residential, with most of the commercial business along Main Street, another small commercial area grew up on Gillham Road. In the 1940s, Kansas Citians from all over town shopped for flowers at Ed's Florist (above) at Linwood Boulevard and Gillham Road. The Gillham Pharmacy (below) at 3269 Gillham Road was one of two drugstores serving the area. Other businesses along Gillham Road and Linwood Boulevard included car dealerships and gas stations, as well as the Anheuser-Busch Brewing Company. (Both, courtesy of MVSC-KCPL.)

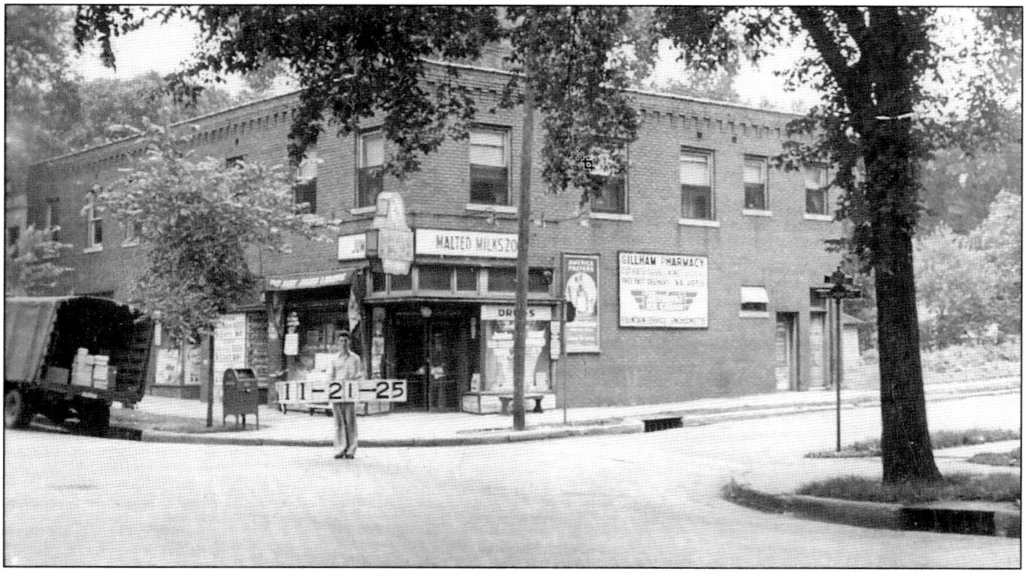

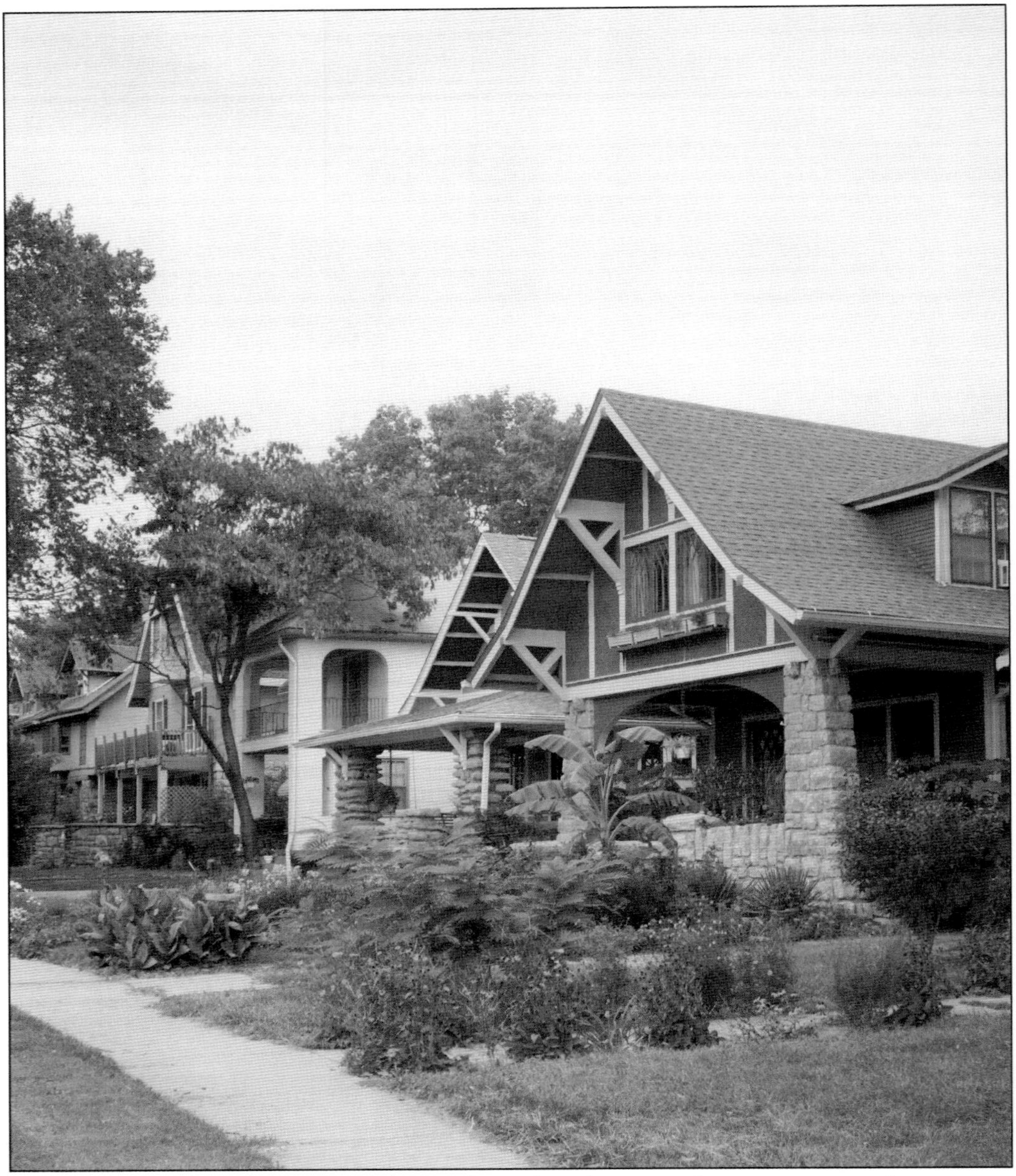

South Hyde Park. This area was designed to take advantage of its proximity to the streetcar lines on Troost Avenue. The majority of homes in this neighborhood are modest working-class houses; there are also a few larger residences and multifamily apartment buildings. South Hyde Park was platted in 1885, and the neighborhood was almost completely built up by 1935. Much of the land was platted during the land boom of the 1880s, although James Squier, a cattle dealer, held on to his 40 acres between Forty-third and Forty-fifth Streets and from Holmes Road to Troost Avenue, until he died in 1900. The major period of development came after city water became available in South Hyde Park in 1905. It is common in the neighborhood to see rows of identical houses with slight variations in details. Neighborhood shopping was available along Troost Avenue. Residents also enjoy access to Gillham Park, which forms the western edge of the neighborhood. (Author's collection.)

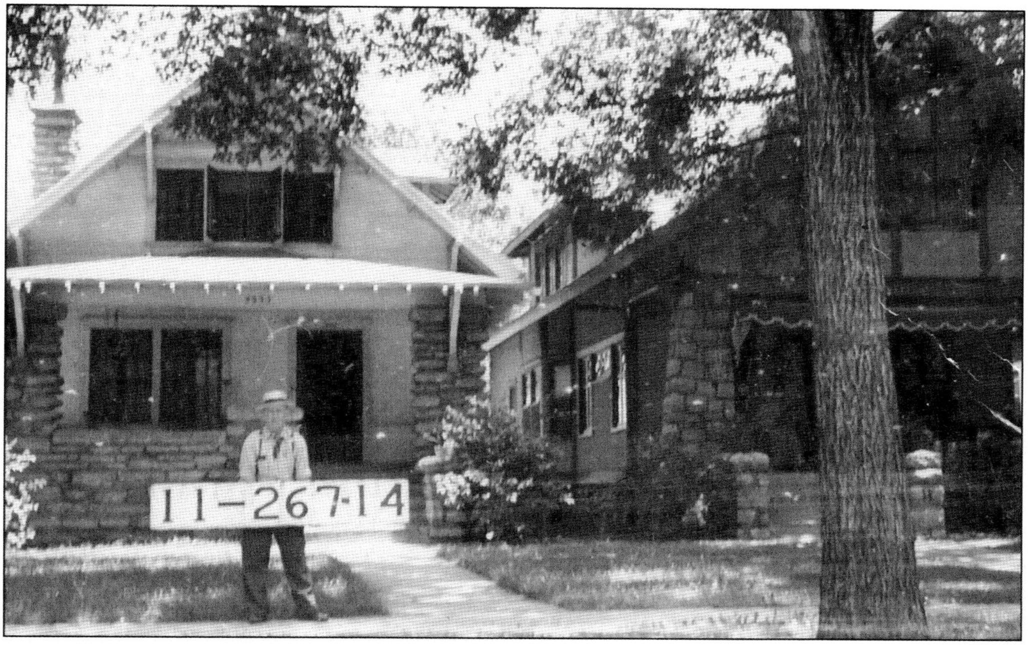

SOUTH HYDE PARK, 1940. By the time these photographs were taken, construction of homes in Hyde Park was completed, and the residents had settled in. Along with single-family homes, South Hyde Park saw the construction of 40 apartment buildings in the 1920s. According to the National Register of Historic Places nomination for South Hyde Park, the apartments generally filled in the spaces not claimed by the first wave of homeowners and speculators. The colonnade style of apartment continued to be popular, as were smaller apartment buildings. (Both, courtesy of MVSC-KCPL.)

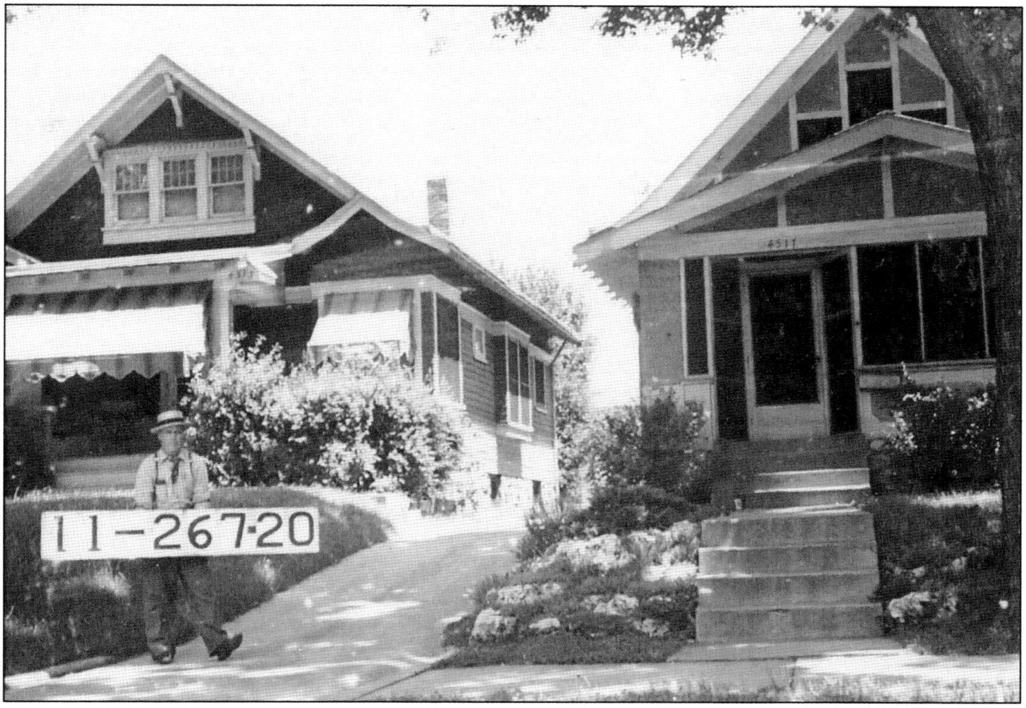

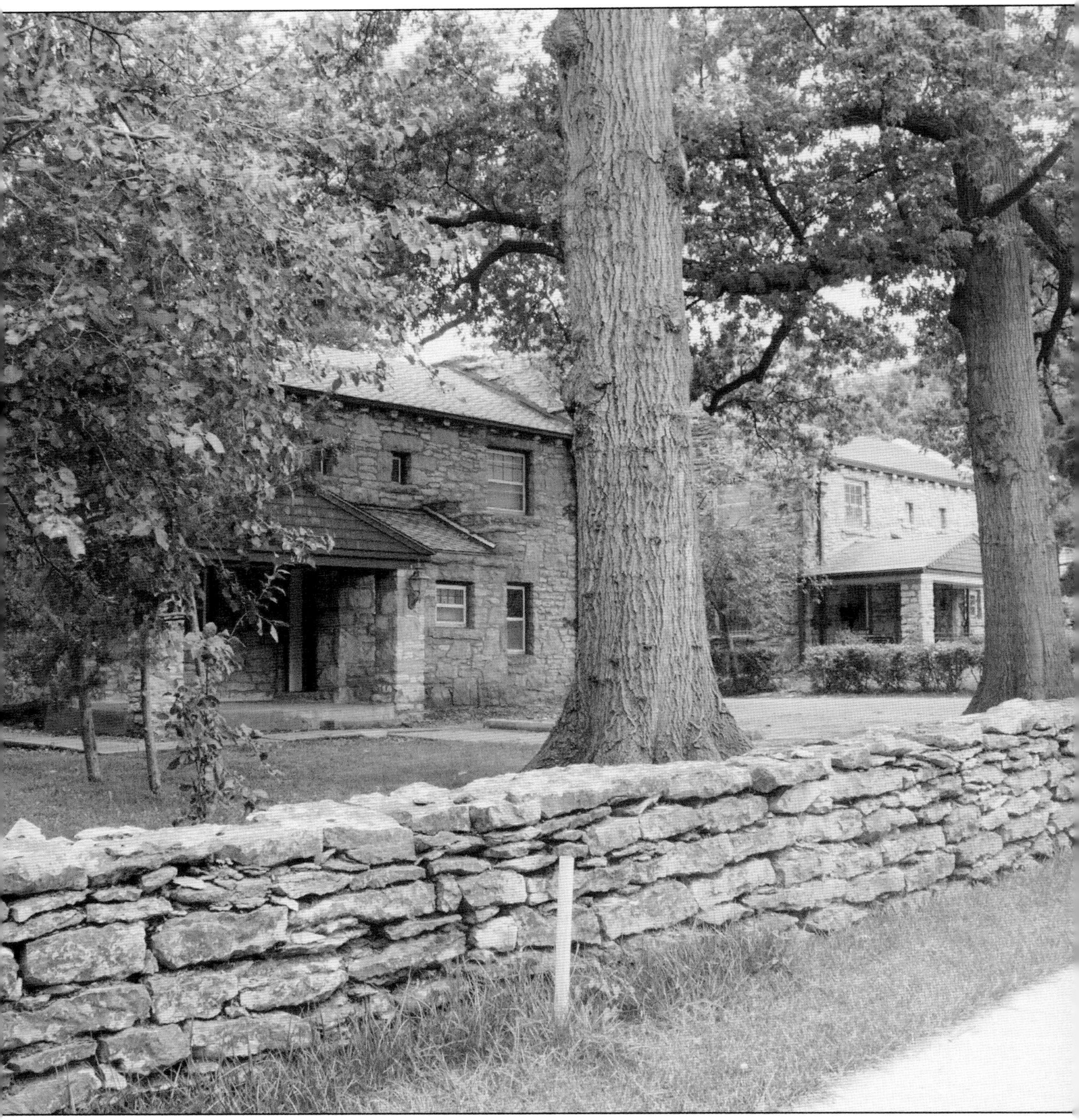

Rockhill. As the Hyde Park neighborhoods developed to the north, there was activity farther south, between Broadway Boulevard and Troost Avenue. The Rockhill and Southmoreland neighborhoods of today grew out of the Rockhill district, built by *Kansas City Star* publisher William Rockhill Nelson from 1904 to 1909. Nelson, a newspaperman, was also a developer. He had developed two small areas of homes for working people in today's Union Hill area, and Nelson began laying out the plans for an area south of the Hyde Park district that would include both large estates and smaller groups of homes. The Rockhill area, which includes today's Rockhill and Southmoreland neighborhoods, would be characterized by the stone walls Nelson constructed from a quarry on his property. Some parts of the original Rockhill district were lost over the years due to the building and expansion of the Nelson-Atkins Museum of Art, the University of Missouri, and the Troost Avenue commercial corridor. (Author's collection.)

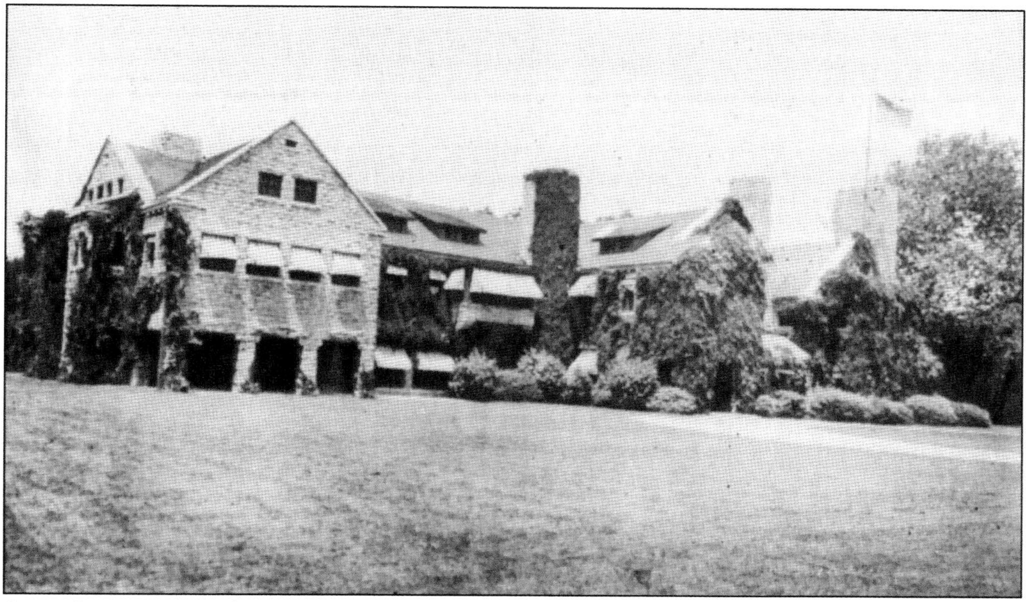

Oak Hall, 1890. The vision for the Rockhill residential area began with William Rockhill Nelson, the publisher of the *Kansas City Star,* who built Oak Hall in 1890 on the land that is now the grounds of the Nelson-Atkins Museum of Art. Nelson realized that Kansas City had come to expect boulevards in its new neighborhoods, so he built Rockhill Road in 1901 at his own expense. (Courtesy of MVSC-KCPL.)

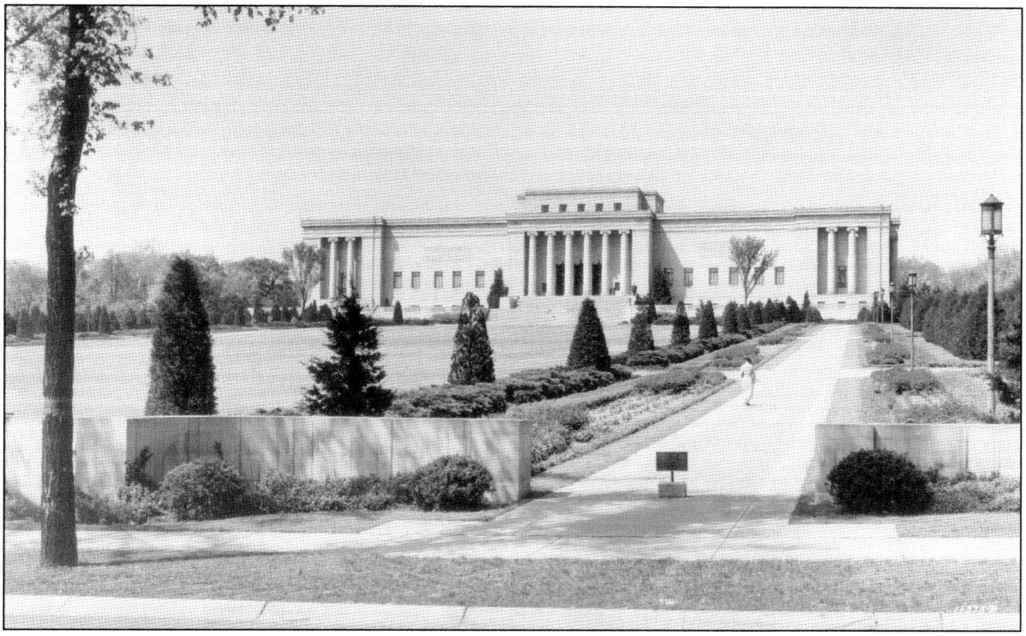

Nelson-Atkins Museum of Art, 1936. Nelson wanted to improve the neighborhood around his home; he thought Kansas City needed an art gallery to help it lose its cowtown image. When Nelson died in 1915, his will stated that the proceeds of his estate go to acquiring paintings. Meanwhile, the estate of former schoolteacher Mary McAfee Atkins contained a bequest to establish an art museum. Ground breaking for the Nelson-Atkins building was celebrated in 1930. (Courtesy of Nelson-Atkins Museum of Art.)

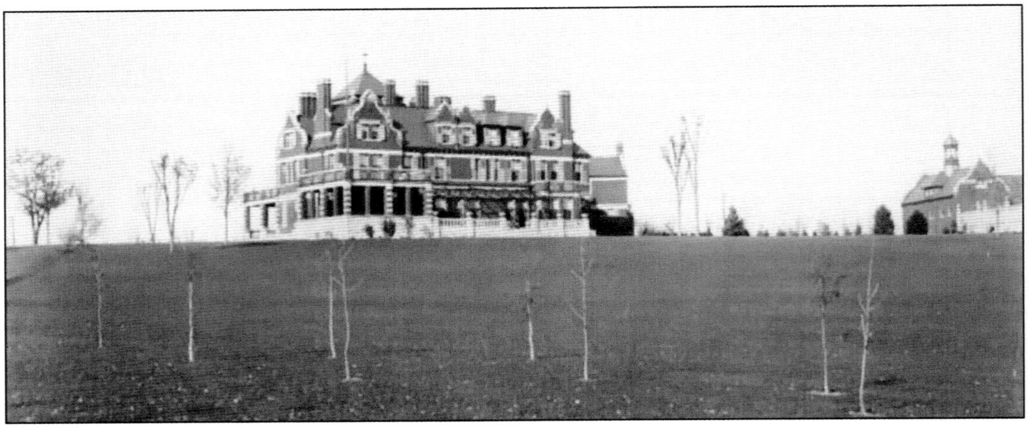

Meyer Home/Vanderslice Hall and Art Institute, 1896. August Meyer built his large home in what is today the Southmoreland neighborhood, next to Nelson's estate. Meyer, president of the Consolidated Kansas City Smelting and Refining Company, is best remembered for his role as president of the Board of Parks and Boulevard Commissioners during the time the city's park system was conceived. Meyer clearly felt he had room to spread out far from city life when he built his mansion on 8.5 acres at 4415 Warwick Boulevard between 1895 and 1896 (above). Only 30 years later, in 1928, his home became the first building of the Kansas City Art Institute. (Both, courtesy of MVSC-KCPL.)

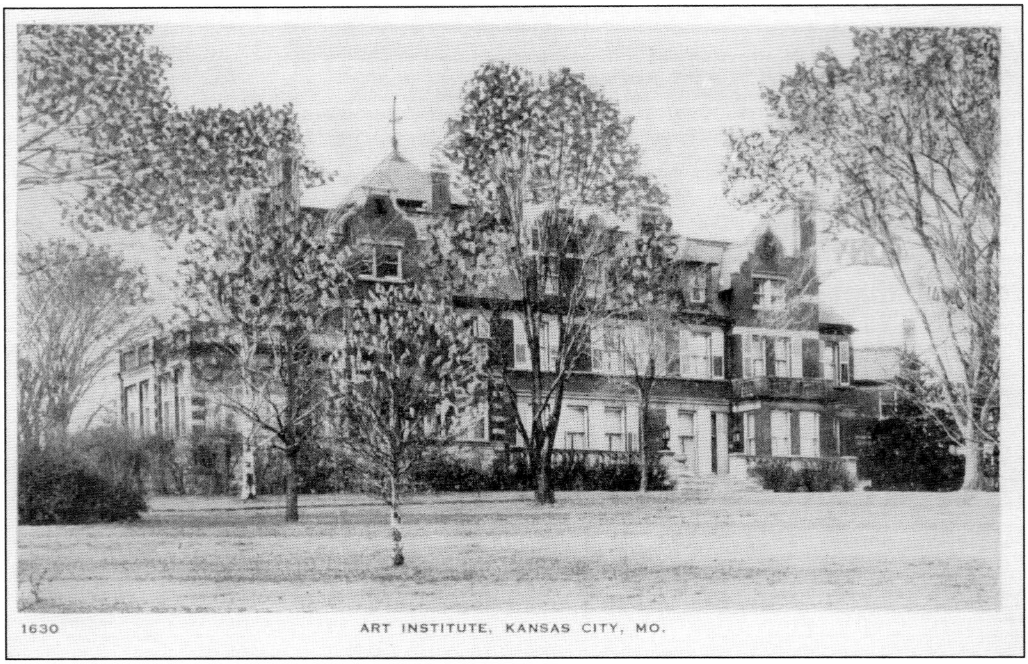

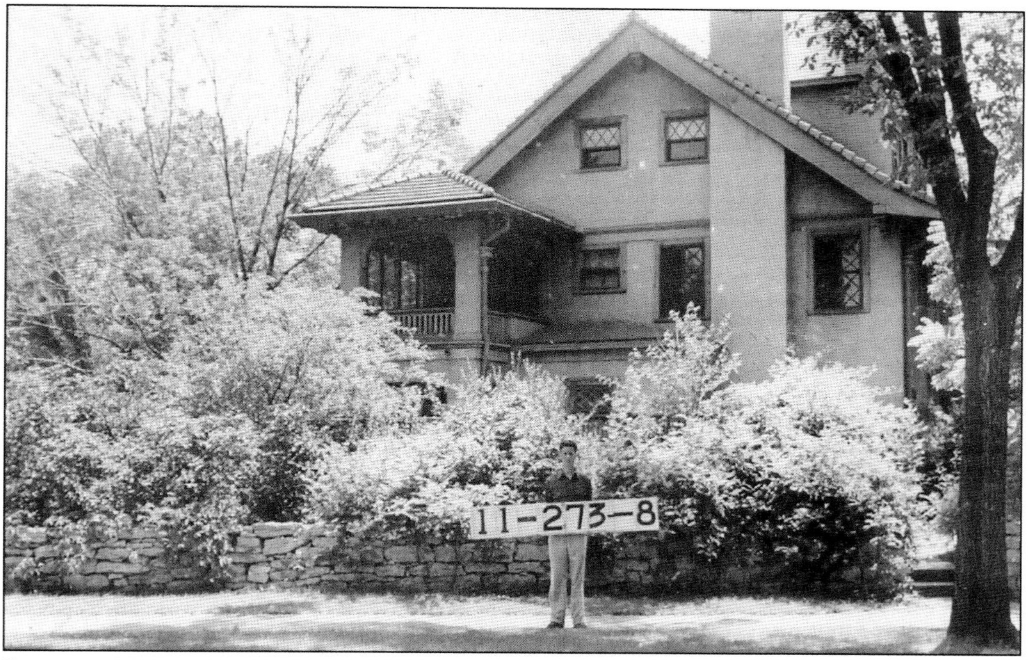

ROCKHILL NEIGHBORHOOD, 1940. Nelson's vision for the area included large mansions like Meyer's, but he also wanted to continue to experiment with building smaller, well-landscaped homes for working people. He landscaped the area with miles of crimson rambler roses. A limestone quarry provided a source of stone used in many of the homes and for walls. Nelson was a proponent of the City Beautiful movement, believing beauty and clean air would bolster neighborhood land values. By the time these photographs were taken in 1940, Rockhill was a stable neighborhood of homeowners and renters from Nelson's company, for whom he reserved some of the homes for lease. (Both, courtesy of MVSC-KCPL.)

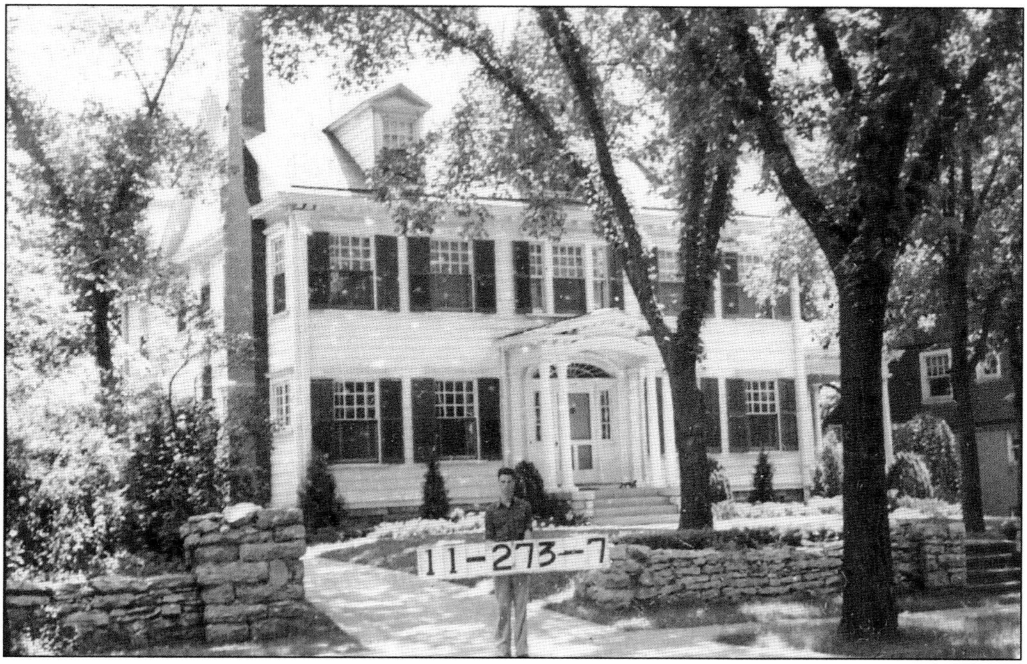

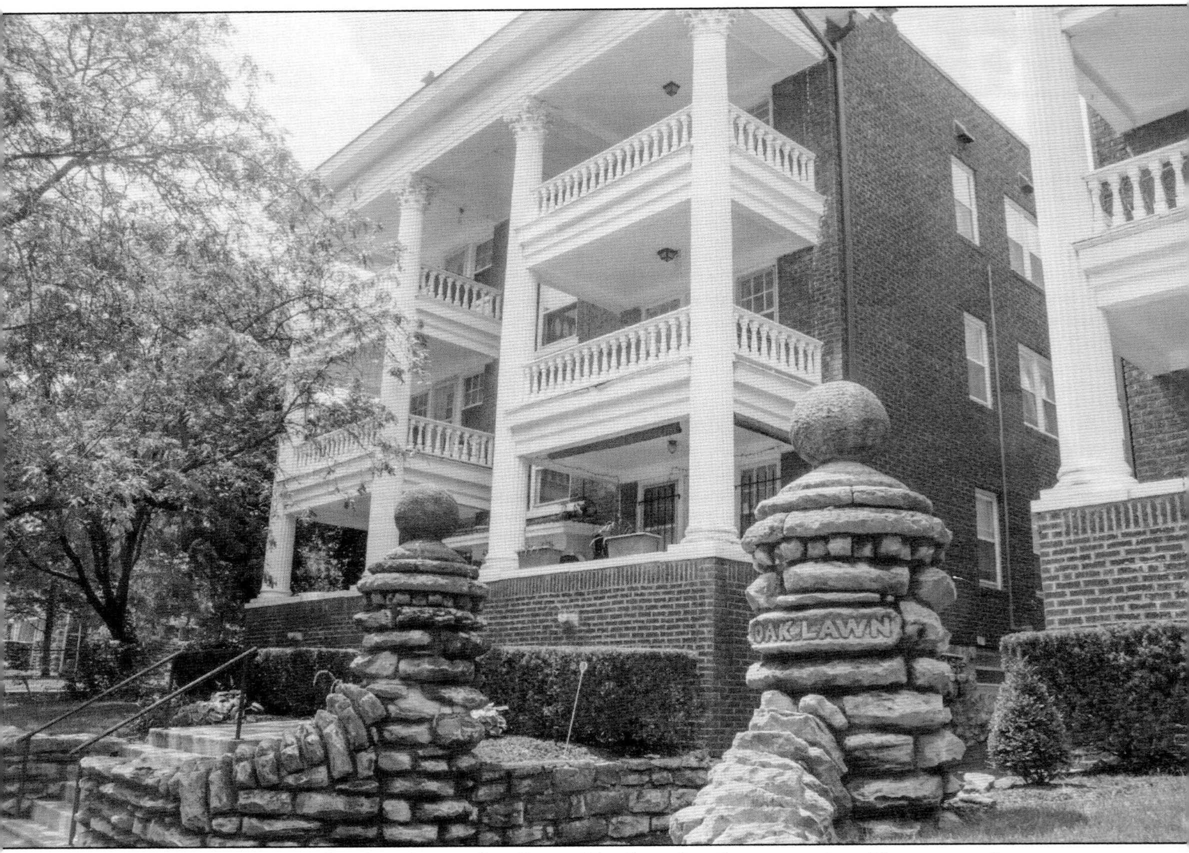

Southmoreland. The Southmoreland neighborhood today is a mix of homes and apartments surrounding the Nelson-Atkins Museum of Art and the Kansas City Art Institute. As was the case in other Midtown neighborhoods, wealthy businessmen were the first to move into the area and build their large homes. They were followed by middle-class and working-class families, who liked the easy access to streetcar lines. At Forty-third and Oak Streets, the W.A. Rule home once stood on 40 acres, a "great stone house" facing Oak Street. In 1922, the *Kansas City Star* reported that a real estate company had bought the property and was busy constructing apartment buildings on the site. The stone walls that surrounded the mansion were left intact. The Southmoreland neighborhood also includes a city park called Southmoreland. Its limestone retaining walls may date to Nelson's original design. He gave the park to the Town of Westport, and it was later incorporated into the growing park-and-boulevard system. (Author's collection.)

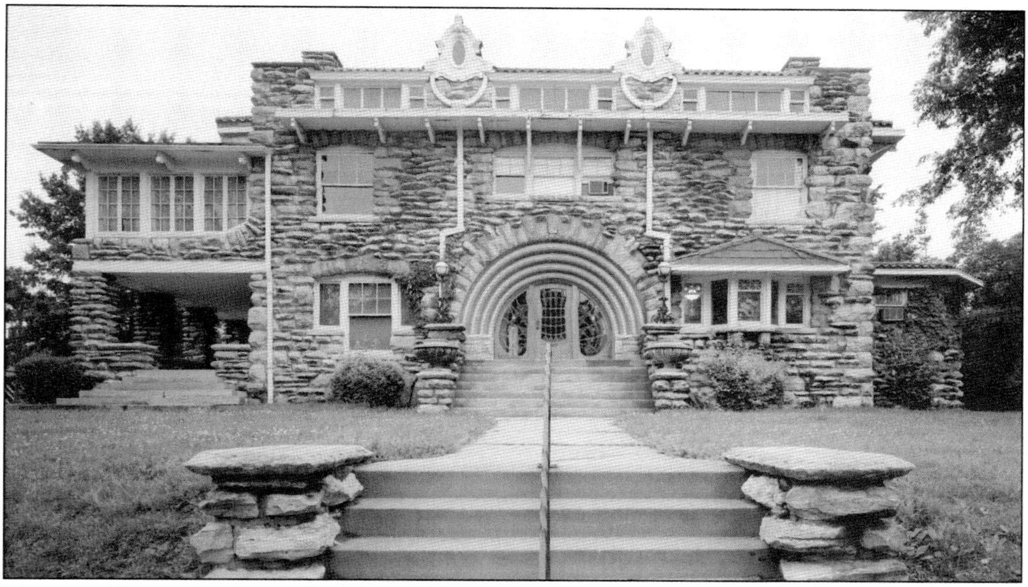

Mineral Hall. This home, built by R.E. Brunner in 1904, is in the National Register of Historic Places. Brunner was a mining magnate who embedded mineral samples into the interior stone walls of his first-floor library. This building and Vanderslice Hall are just two examples of late-19th and early-20th-century mansions that have been put to a new use. They have continued to contribute to Midtown's unique flavor for more than a century. (Courtesy of Library of Congress.)

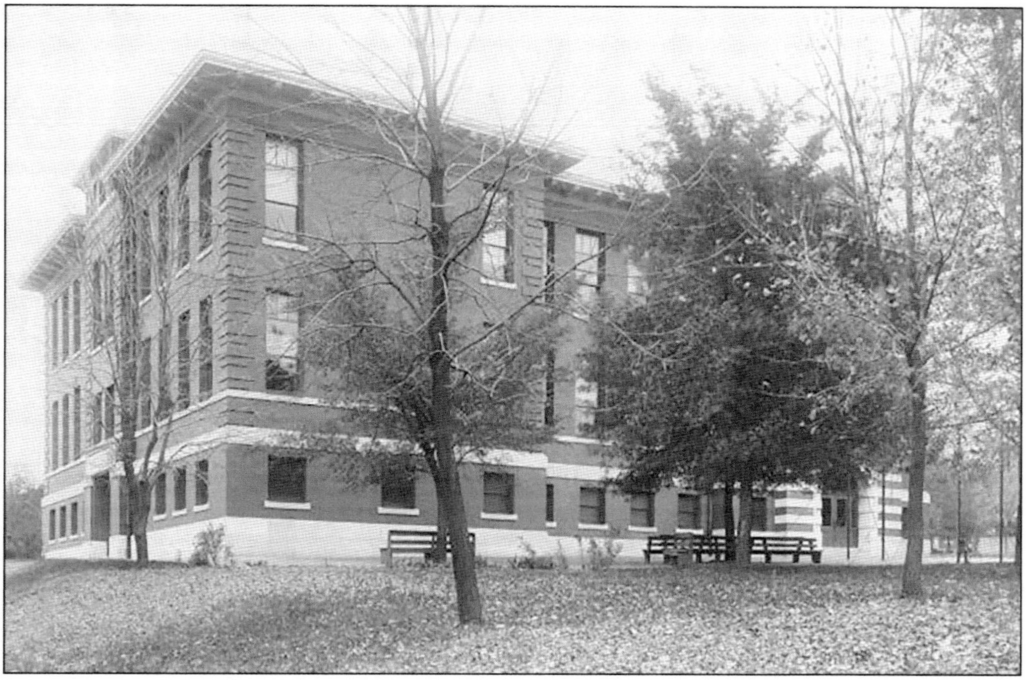

Rollins School. This school at 4043 Main Street served the children of the Hyde Park neighborhoods. Before the school district constructed the school in 1903, this property was the farm of Westport School District president Lowell Goodman and the site of a beloved apple orchard. As the area grew and the need for a school developed, Goodman sold the land to the district. A fire destroyed the school in 1992. (Courtesy of MVSC-KCPL.)

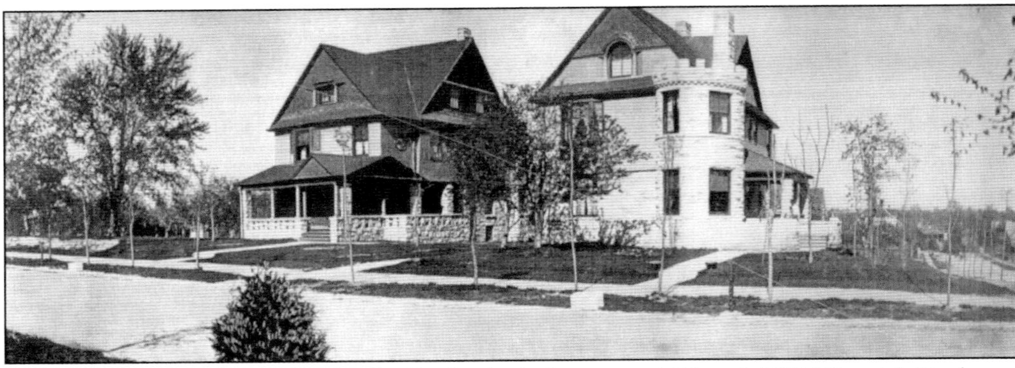

SOUTHMORELAND, 1900. Charles Findley built the homes at 4031 and 4033 Warwick Boulevard around the turn of the century. He was among the developers advertising lots and homes for sale as a streetcar line attracted residents to Southmoreland. The Lee K. Mooney Company advertised lots in 1894, promising a fine suburb surrounded by palatial homes at $500 to $1,250 an acre. (Courtesy of MVSC-KCPL.)

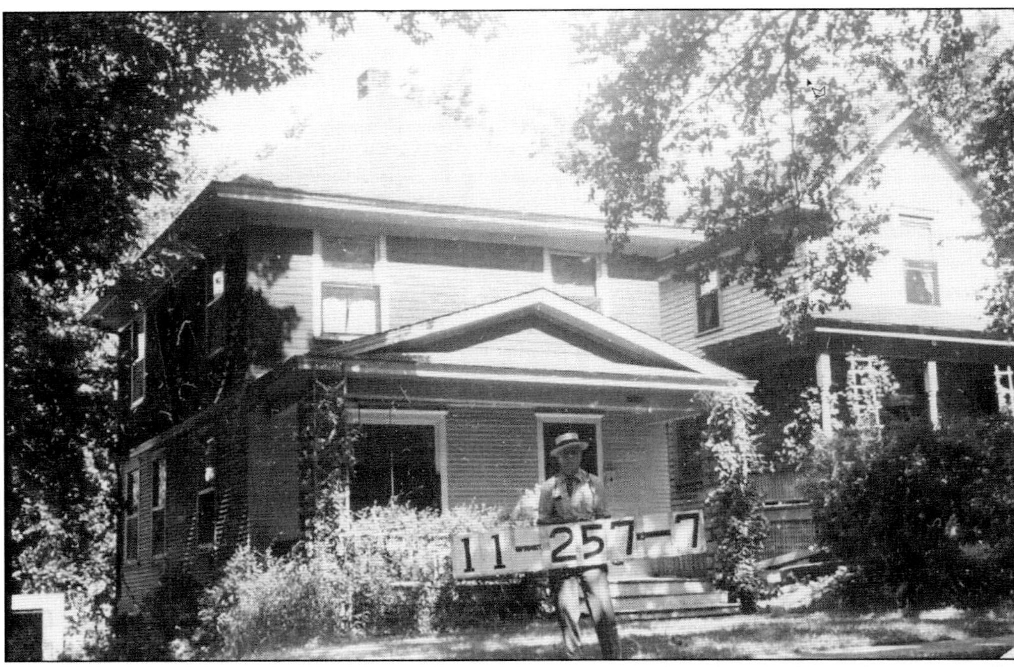

SOUTHMORELAND, 1940. By 1940, Southmoreland was a neighborhood of large homes, smaller residences, and apartments. Families could count on the convenience of nearby shopping on Main Street. Newspaper advertisements touted the proximity to the Country Club Plaza, art museum, and university. (Courtesy of MVSC-KCPL.)

Two

THE MAIN STREET COMMERCIAL DISTRICT

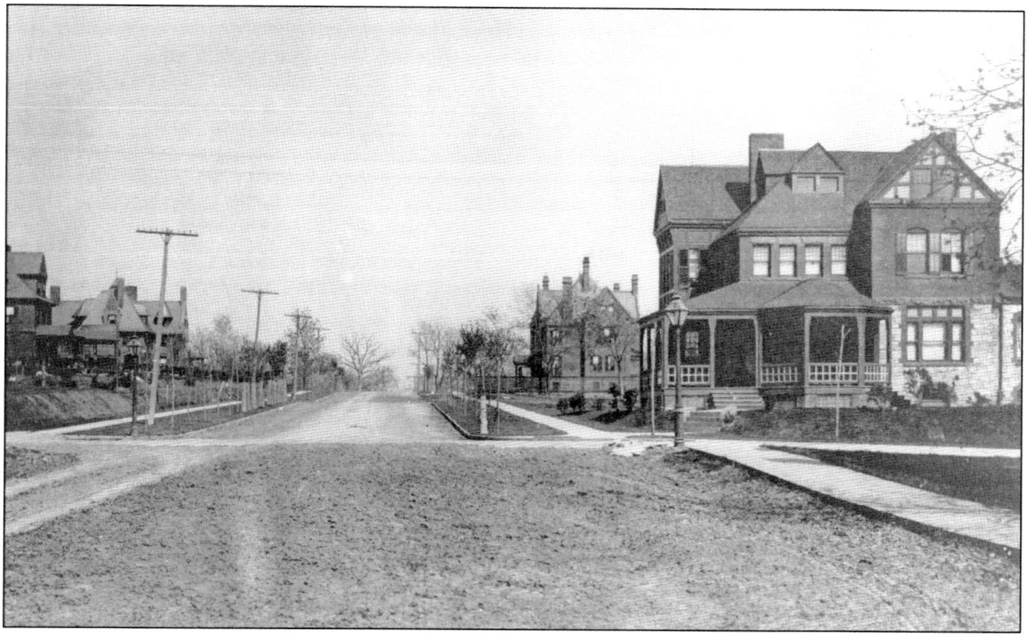

MAIN STREET, 1880s. Before Main Street became a major business corridor, it was a posh residential district. The mansions of well-to-do Kansas Citians fleeing the crowded downtown area began to line Main Street. The William McLeod residence at 3601 Main Street was surrounded by other large homes on wide lots dotting Humbolt Avenue (now Thirty-sixth Street). But between 1910 and 1930, Main Street would become a major commercial route connecting downtown to the Country Club Plaza. (Courtesy of MVSC-KCPL.)

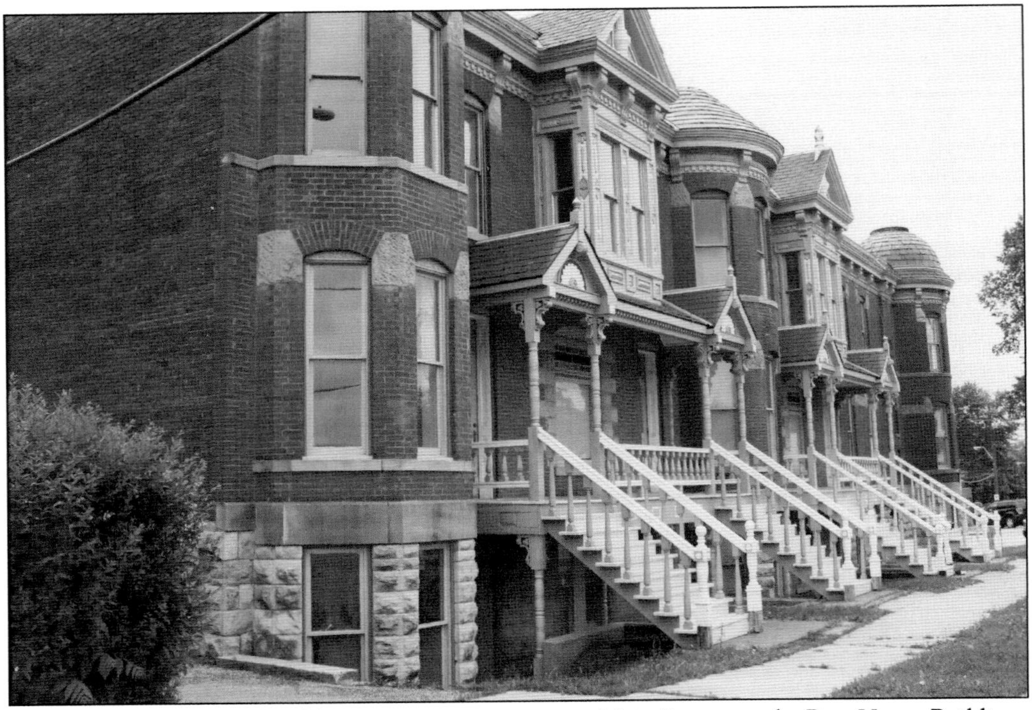

Row Houses. Some of the oldest surviving structures on Main Street are the Row House Buildings at Thirty-fourth and Main Streets. These buildings, listed in the National Register of Historic Places, are rare examples of row houses in Kansas City. They were constructed during the building boom of the 1880s. Originally, there were seven along Main Street and these four along Thirty-fourth Street. Today, only the Thirty-fourth Street portion remains. (Author's collection.)

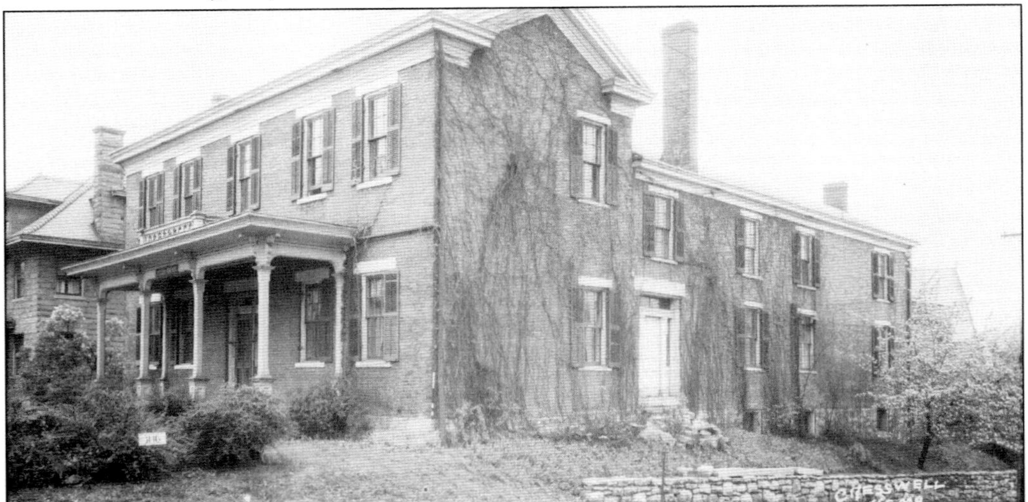

Harris-Kearney Home. The corner of Westport Road and Main Street was always a key intersection in Kansas City. Westport pioneer John Harris built a brick home here in 1833, and his family watched the Battle of Westport from its roof during the Civil War. Elmer Williams, a businessman who saw commercial potential for the site, bought the corner in 1921, and the Harris home was moved to its current location at 4000 Baltimore Avenue in 1922. (Courtesy of Library of Congress.)

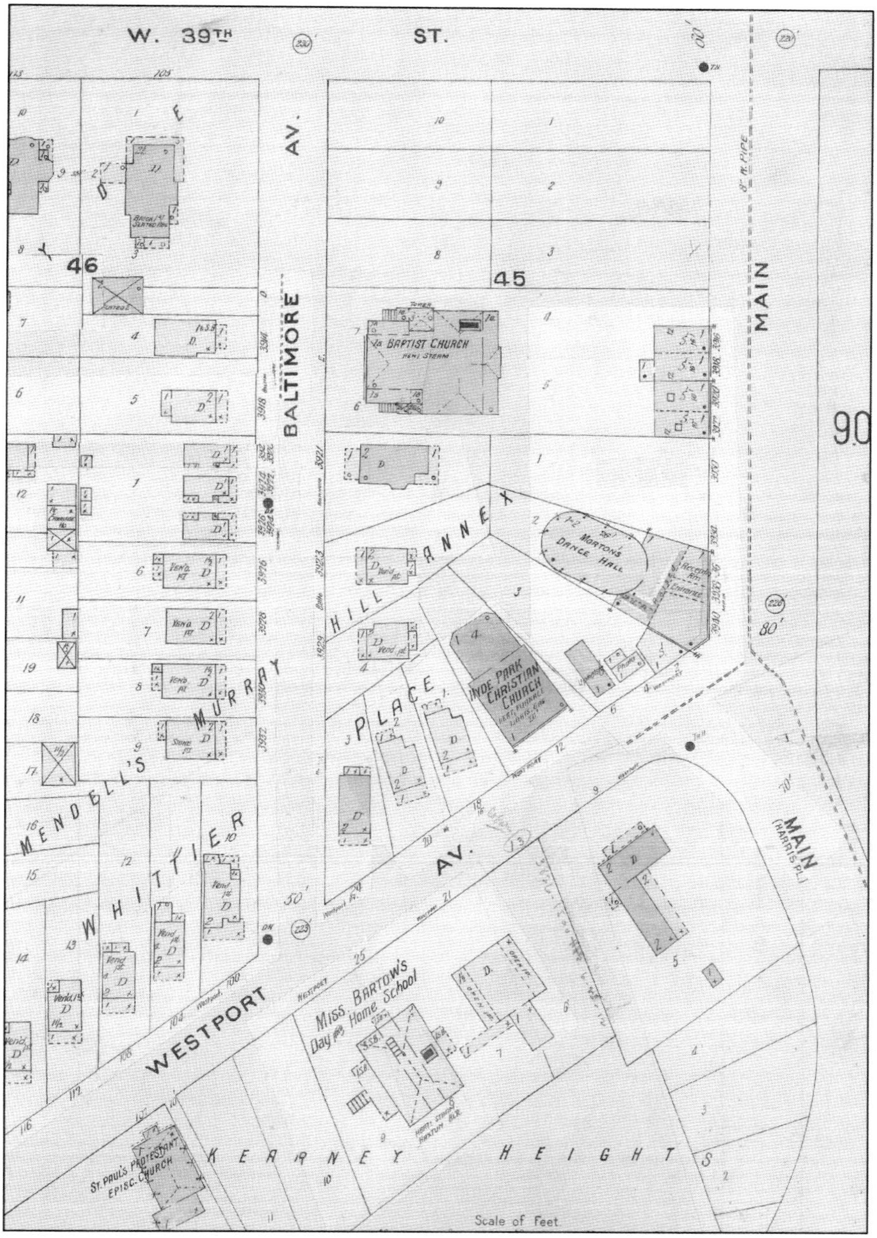

MAIN STREET AND WESTPORT ROAD, 1895. This Sanborn Fire Insurance map shows the corner of Westport Road and Main Street before the transition from residential to commercial use. Already this key corner was attracting major businesses and institutions. The building with the circular room on the corner was Morton's Hall and Confectionery, the de facto country club at the turn of the century. When Morton's opened, Kansas City patrons and those from surrounding neighborhoods arrived in horse-drawn carriages for lunch, dinner, teas, and wedding receptions. People also rode the cable car to "the end of the line" just to visit the confectionery, known for its ice cream and candy. The building later became the Jack O'Lantern, a popular dance hall. The corner also housed three churches and the Miss Barstow Day and Home School. In 1926, Main Street was widened and straightened, eliminating the curve seen on this map. (Courtesy of MVSC-KCPL.)

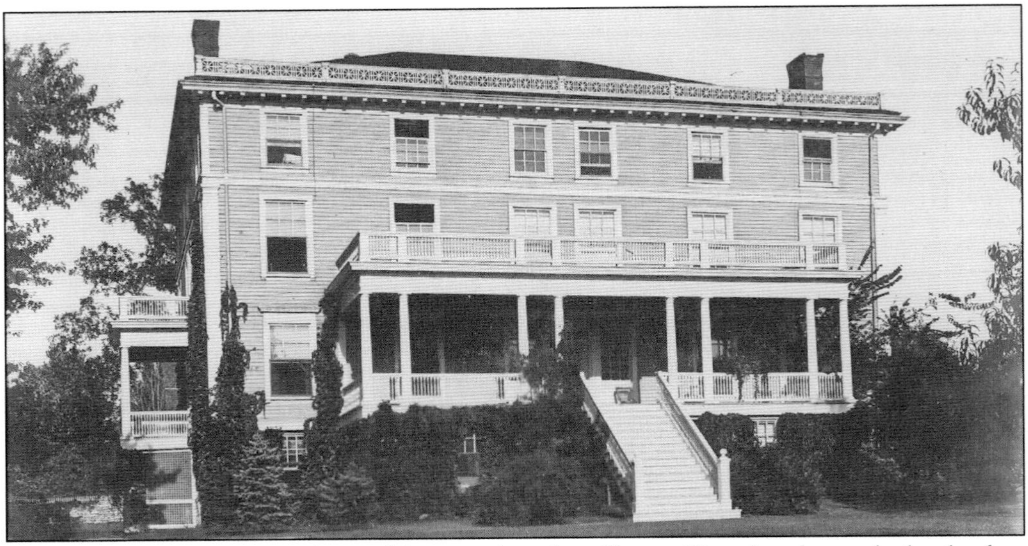

Miss Barstow School. As the wealthy moved south in Kansas City, churches and schools often followed. The Westport Presbyterian Church originally met in a log church at Forty-second Street and Pennsylvania Avenue, moving to 706 Westport Road just after the Civil War. A stone church on Westport Road, southeast of Main Street, was opened in 1904. The Miss Barstow School was founded in 1884 by two Wellesley College graduates, Mary Barstow and Ada Brann, in response to the need for a local school comparable to East Coast schools. It moved from Quality Hill to Westport Road and Main Street around 1900 and again followed the movement south to Forty-ninth and Cherry Streets in 1924. (Courtesy of *Midtown KC Post*.)

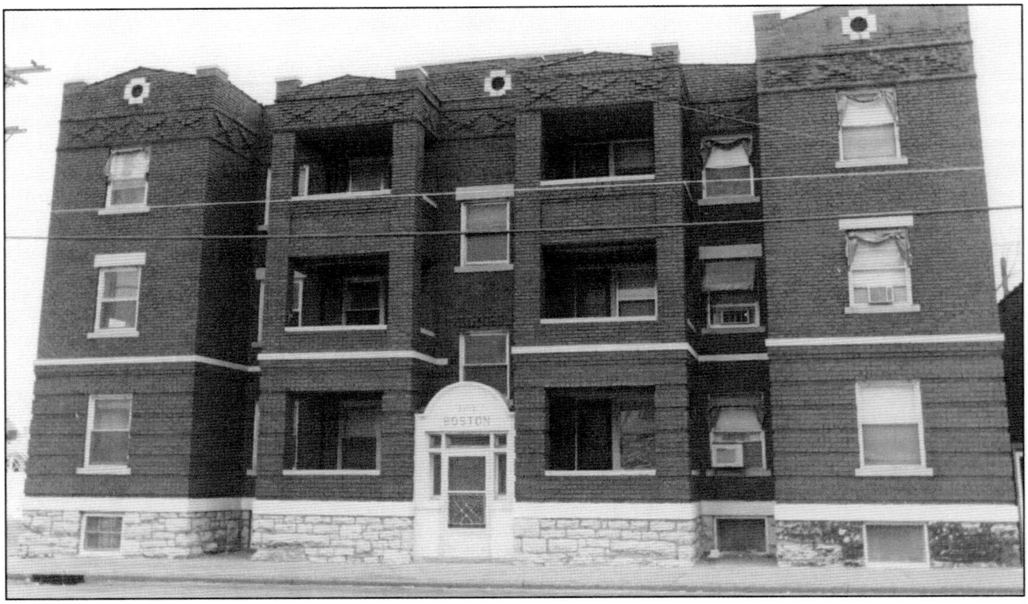

Boston Apartments. While Main Street once had a number of small apartments, not many of these have survived. The Boston Apartments at Thirty-eighth and Main Streets is among the few buildings still in existence. It was built in 1907 with 21 apartments of four to seven rooms each. Like many other properties on Main Street, this one was often bought and sold, always at a greater profit to the seller, between its construction and 1920 during the Kansas City land boom. (Courtesy of MainCor.)

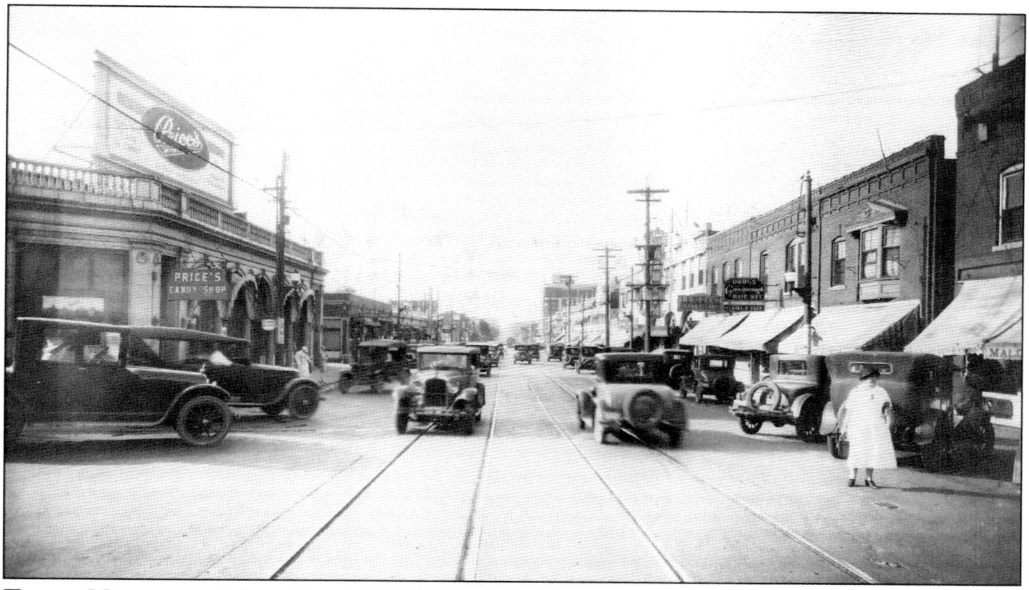

Thirty-Ninth and Main Streets. This intersection blossomed in 1920; automobiles brought shoppers to a wide array of shops and services. The intersection also served as a busy transfer point for streetcar lines. The booming Main Street corridor included the popular Price's Candy Store as well as dressmakers, beauty shops, dry cleaners, and cafeterias, all serving the new south side neighborhoods. (Courtesy of MainCor.)

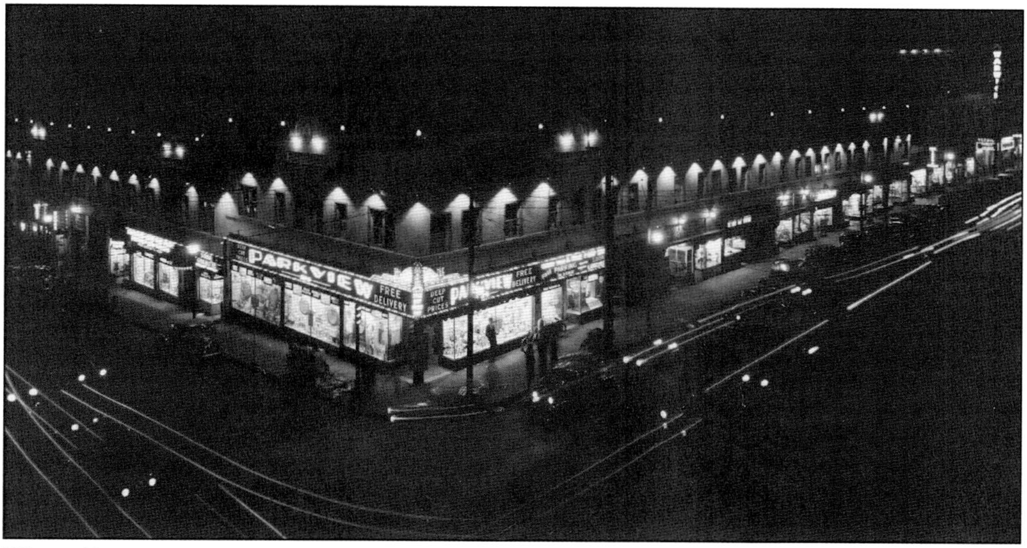

Werby Building at Night. One of the people who breathed life into Main Street over the years was David Werby, a real estate broker who helped to develop Thirty-ninth and Main Streets. In the 1920s, one of the major anchors of that intersection was the Werby Building, seen here at night in its full glory. The building had 50 suites that housed 25 stores. It was demolished in the 1970s. (Courtesy of MainCor.)

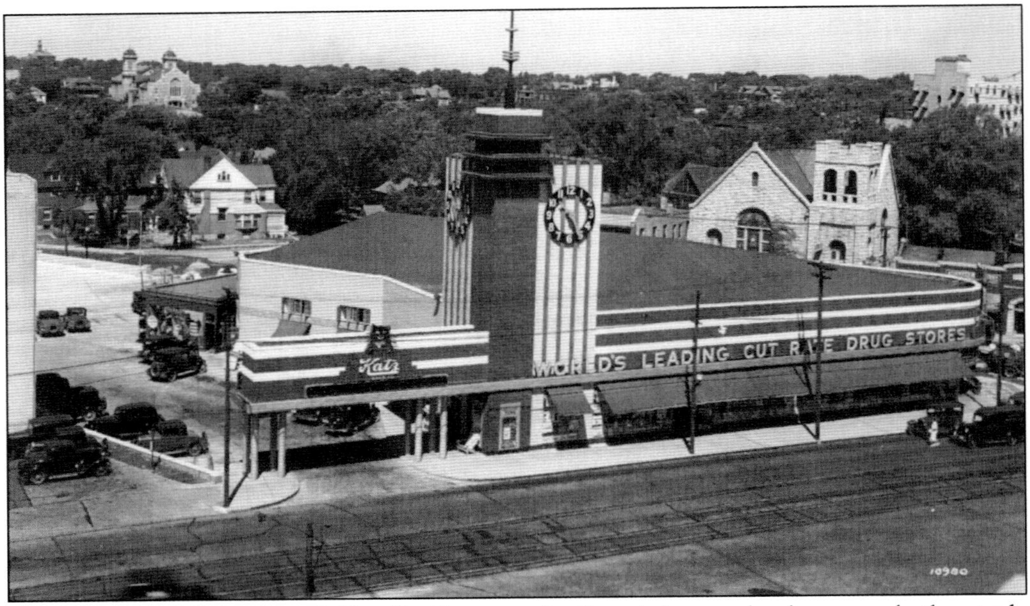

Katz Building. Main Street's Katz Building was the first of the popular drugstores built outside the central business district in the 1930s. Clarence Kivett, an important Kansas City architect, was unknown when he designed the building in a mix of Art Deco and Art Moderne style. It stands on the site where the Harris-Kearney House originally stood. (Courtesy of MainCor.)

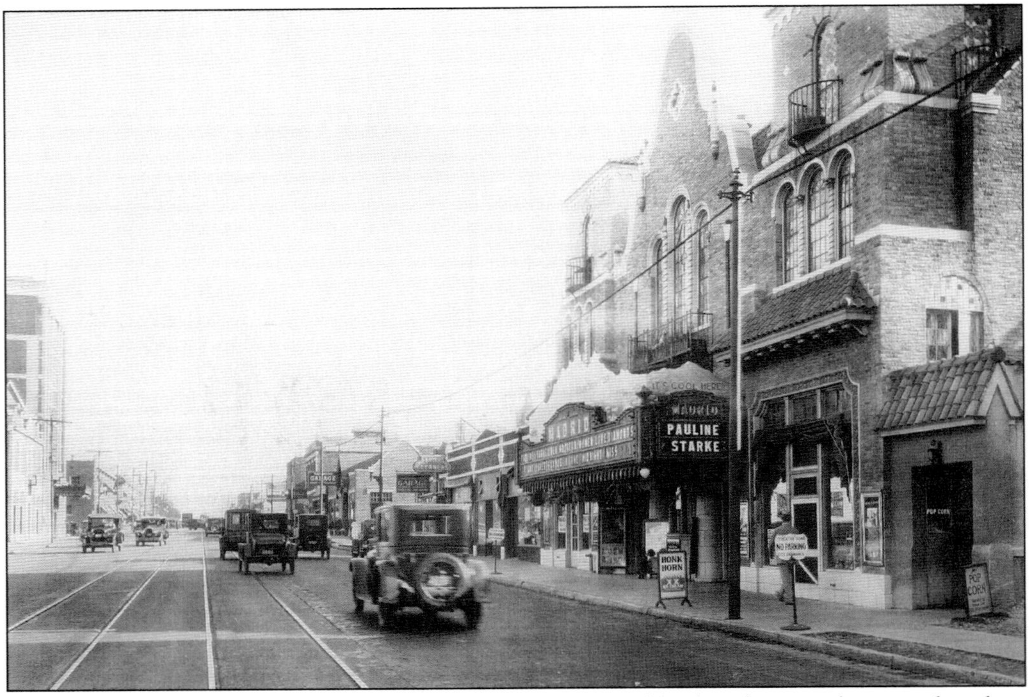

Madrid Theater. The new residents of the south side neighborhoods not only wanted to shop and work, they had a big appetite for entertainment. One of the places they flocked to in the 1920s was the 1,500-seat Madrid Theater, built at a cost of $400,000. It competed with the Warwick Theater a few blocks to the south. (Courtesy of MainCor.)

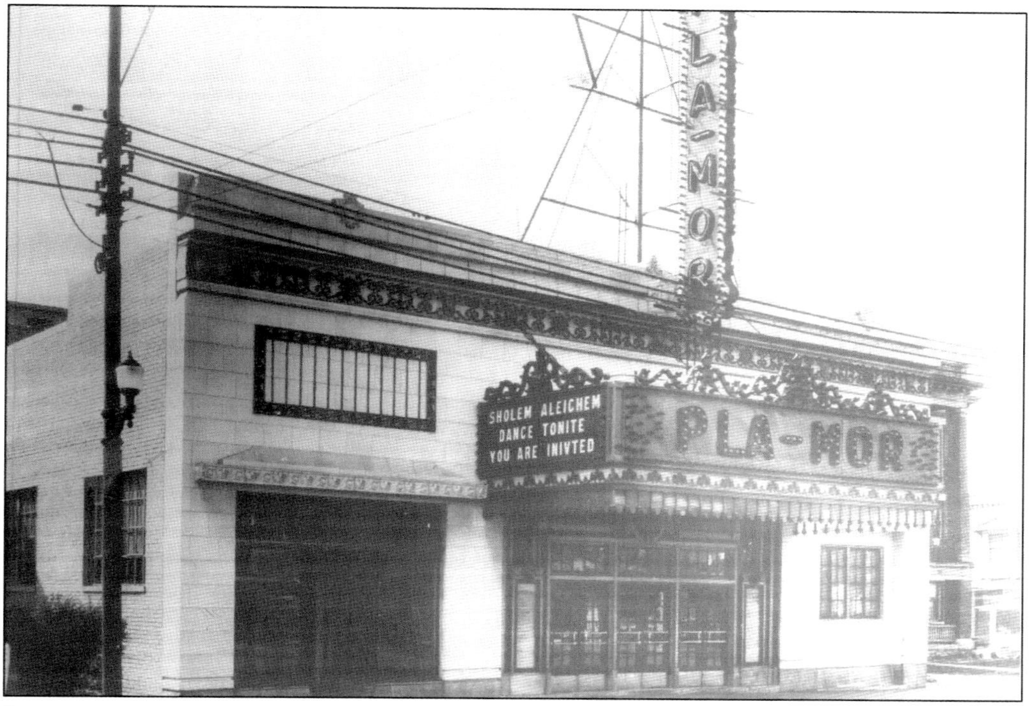

PLA-MOR BALLROOM. This venue at 3142 Main Street opened in 1927 to thousands of people ready to dance on its wooden floor, which had more than 7,000 springs to give it extra bounce. It was the height of the jazz era in Kansas City, which was becoming known for music, booze, and overall sin. The list of famous jazz musicians who played there for the next two decades reads like a who's who: Tommy and Jimmy Dorsey, Bix Beiderbecke, Frankie Trumbauer, Stan Kenton, and Ella Fitzgerald, among others. The ballroom was just one lure to what was said to be the nation's largest entertainment center, an amusement complex in three big buildings between Main and Wyandotte Streets. It included a bowling alley, billiards tables, and an ice-skating rink. In 1931, the largest swimming pool west of the Mississippi River was added. The ballroom closed in 1951, and the building was demolished in 1972. (Courtesy of UMKC–LaBudde.)

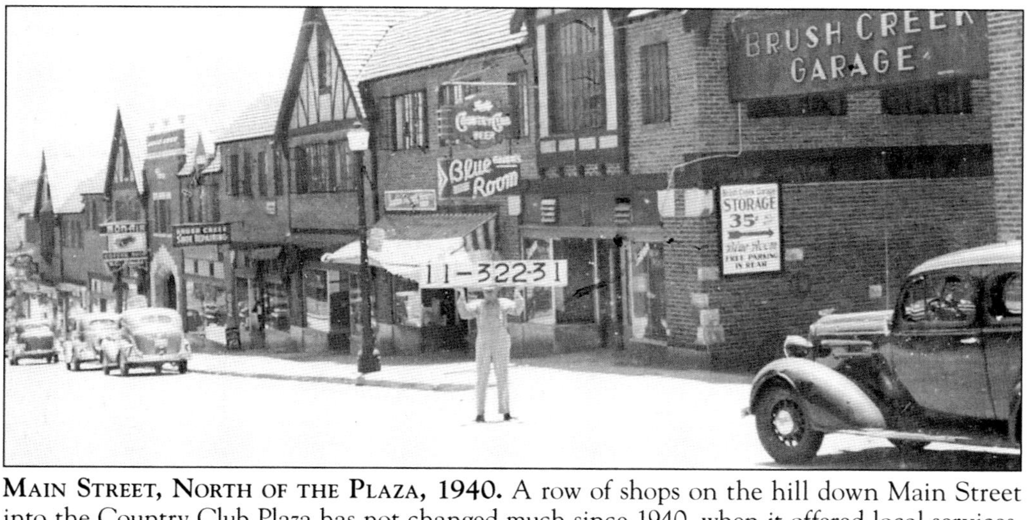

MAIN STREET, NORTH OF THE PLAZA, 1940. A row of shops on the hill down Main Street into the Country Club Plaza has not changed much since 1940, when it offered local services, entertainment venues, and parking spots. (Courtesy of KCPL-MVSC.)

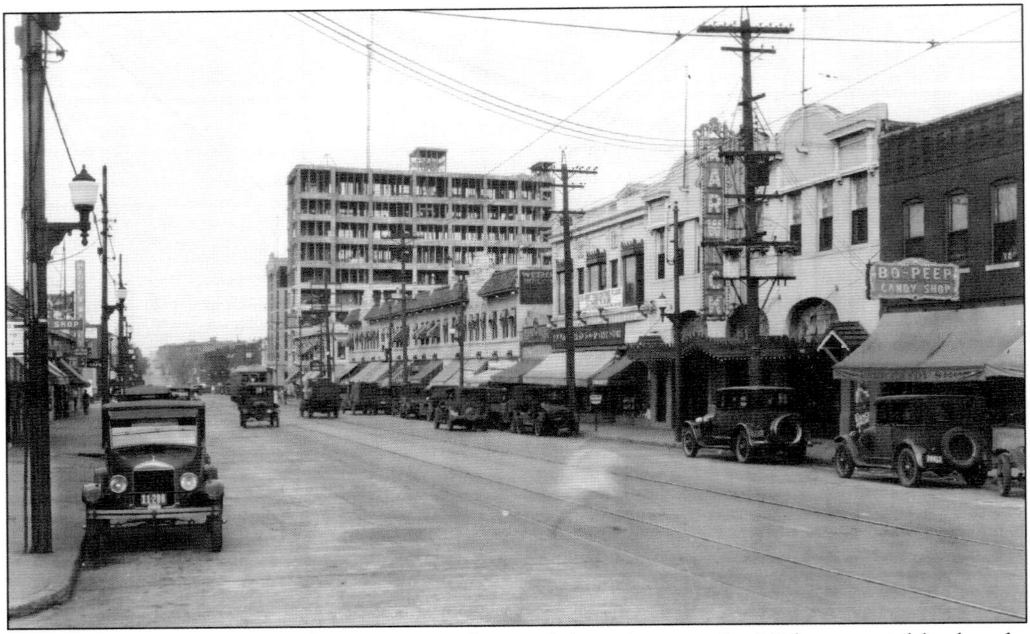

MAIN STREET, 1927. Main Street remained a vital shopping area for Midtown neighborhoods. One of the major attractions was the Warwick Theater, built in 1912. It had a seating capacity of 2,200. The Warwick (right) closed as a theater in 1953, but it continues to be used as a commercial building. Also seen here is the Netherlands Hotel under construction. (Courtesy of MainCor.)

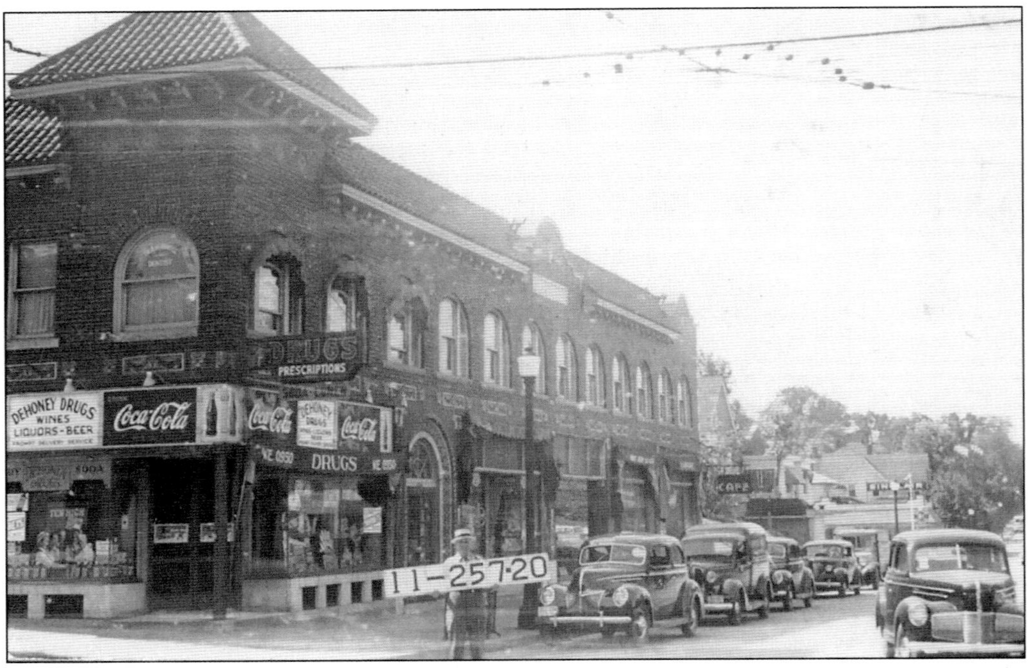

MAIN AND FORTY-THIRD STREETS, 1940. Small drugstores served Kansas City neighborhoods, well within walking distance or a quick stop between the streetcar and home. The residents of the nearby neighborhoods also had easy access to cafés, restaurants, and gas stations. (Courtesy of MVSC-KCPL.)

Three

Neighborhoods West of Broadway

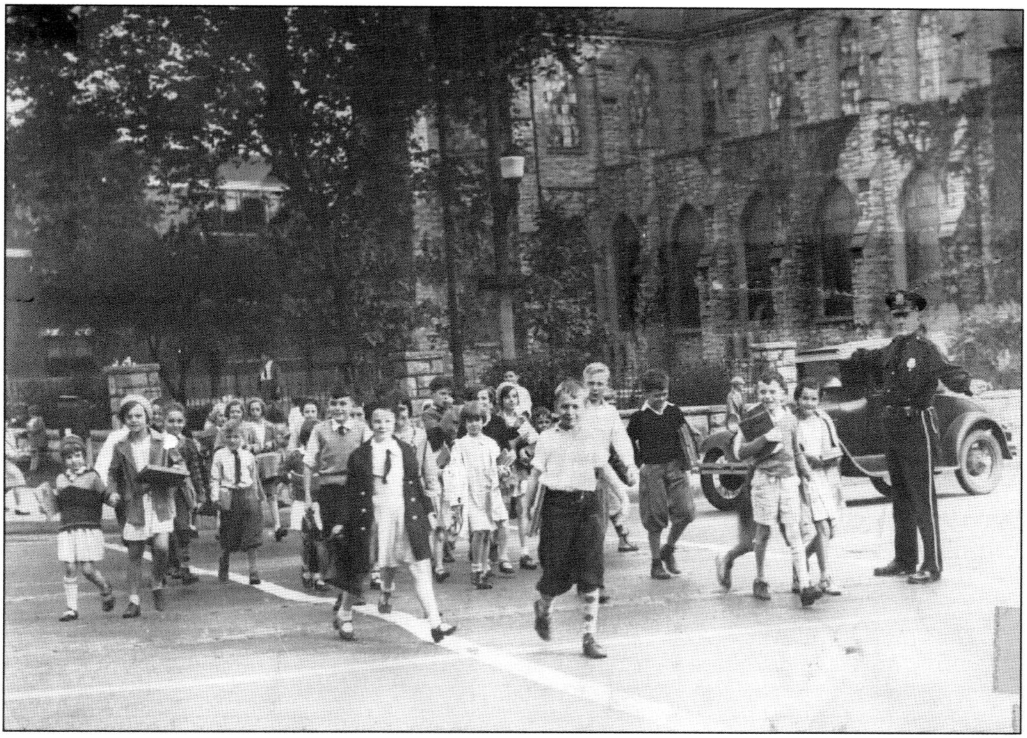

Redemptorist Students, 1920s. As the Hyde Park area developed in the center of today's Midtown Kansas City, another set of neighborhoods was growing to the west of Broadway Boulevard. Valentine, Coleman Highlands, Roanoke, Volker, West Plaza, Plaza/Westport, and the Heart of Westport grew in a similar way—wealthy residents moved south and built huge homes. They were followed by the middle class, and, as streetcar lines extended from Westport and downtown, these new neighborhoods opened up to everyone. Redemptorist Church, built in 1912, was called the "center of the Catholic universe" in Midtown. Students from surrounding neighborhoods streamed across Broadway when Redemptorist School let out for the day. (Courtesy of Redemptorist Church Archives.)

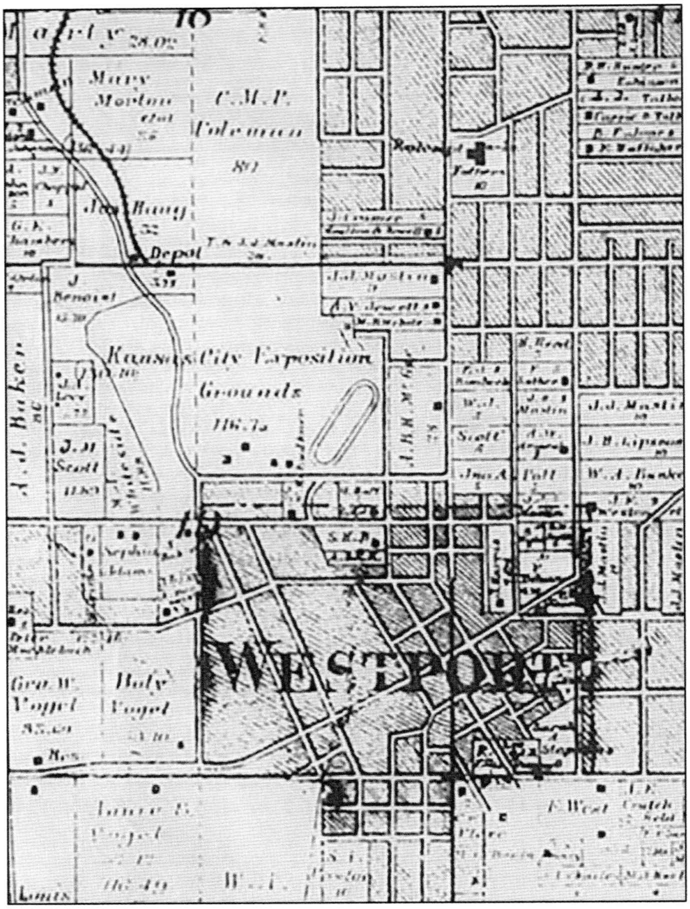

INTERSTATE FAIRGROUNDS, 1887. The Interstate Fairgrounds played an important role in the history of the northwestern Midtown neighborhoods. A.B.H. McGee, the biggest landowner in what would become the Valentine and Roanoke neighborhoods, formed the Interstate Fair Company in 1882. From 1882 to 1887, all of Kansas City flocked to the fair, which featured horse races, concerts, and fireworks. But by 1887, with Kansas City's building boom in full steam, the owners sold the fairgrounds for 15 times more than they had paid for it. The 1887 map (left) shows the fairgrounds with its oval-shaped racetrack. Today, the route of Valentine Road (below) is said to follow the curve of the fairgrounds' racetrack. (Both, courtesy of *Midtown KC Post*.)

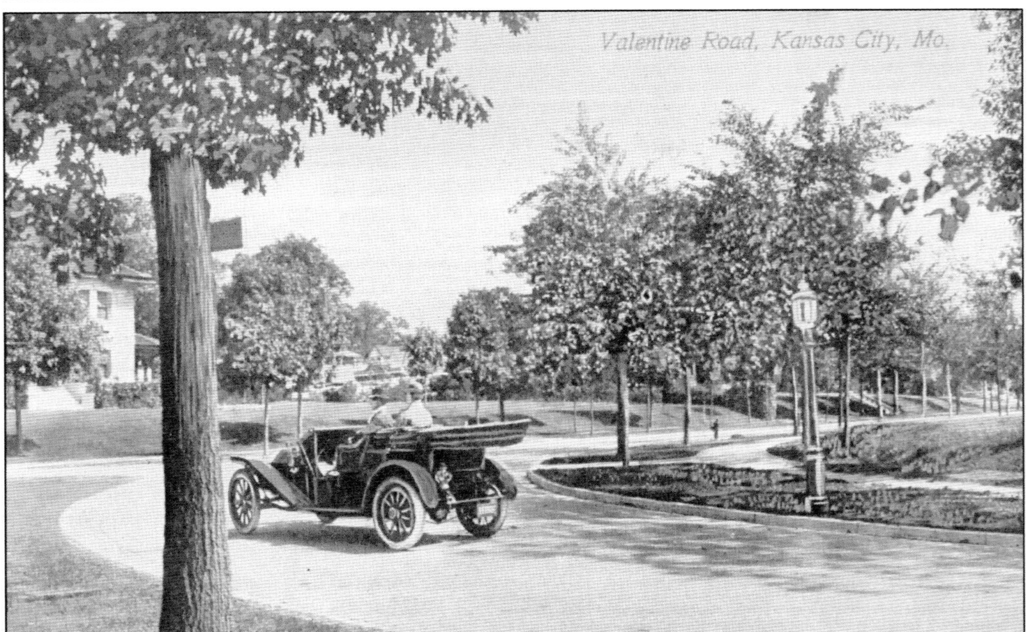

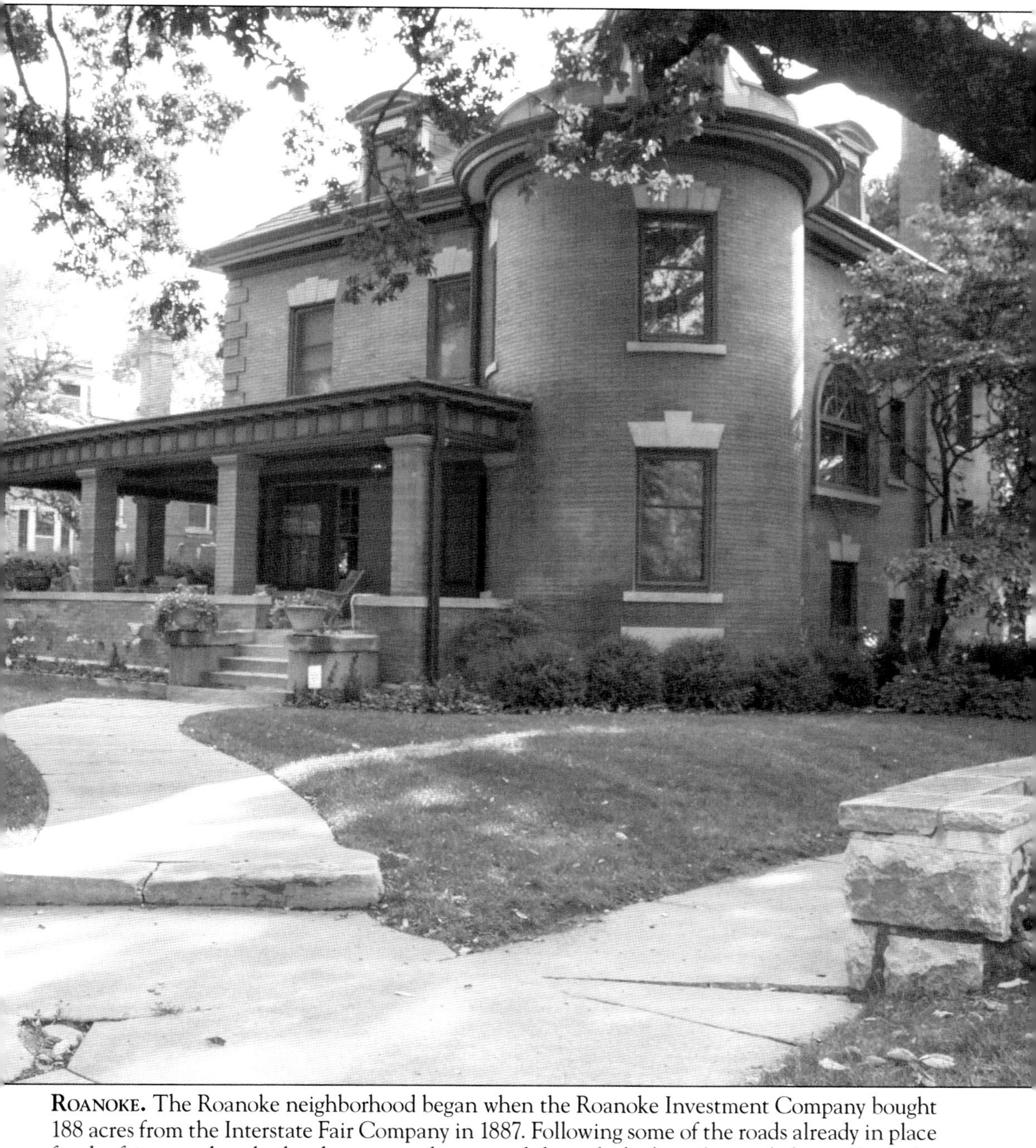

ROANOKE. The Roanoke neighborhood began when the Roanoke Investment Company bought 188 acres from the Interstate Fair Company in 1887. Following some of the roads already in place for the fairgrounds, it built other streets that wound through the heavily wooded area. From the beginning, the developers and residents of Roanoke decided it would be entirely residential, "without flats, unhandsome architecture or the disconcerting contrast between a cheap home and a costly home," according to the *Kansas City Star* in 1907. Restrictions required houses to be of sufficient cost and on large lots at least 30 feet from the street. Roanoke attracted well-off owners who built homes in the popular styles of the late 19th and early 20th centuries. Residents valued the wooded nature of the area and had their architects design homes that fit the natural terrain. The wide roads contribute to the parklike quality of the neighborhood. (Author's collection.)

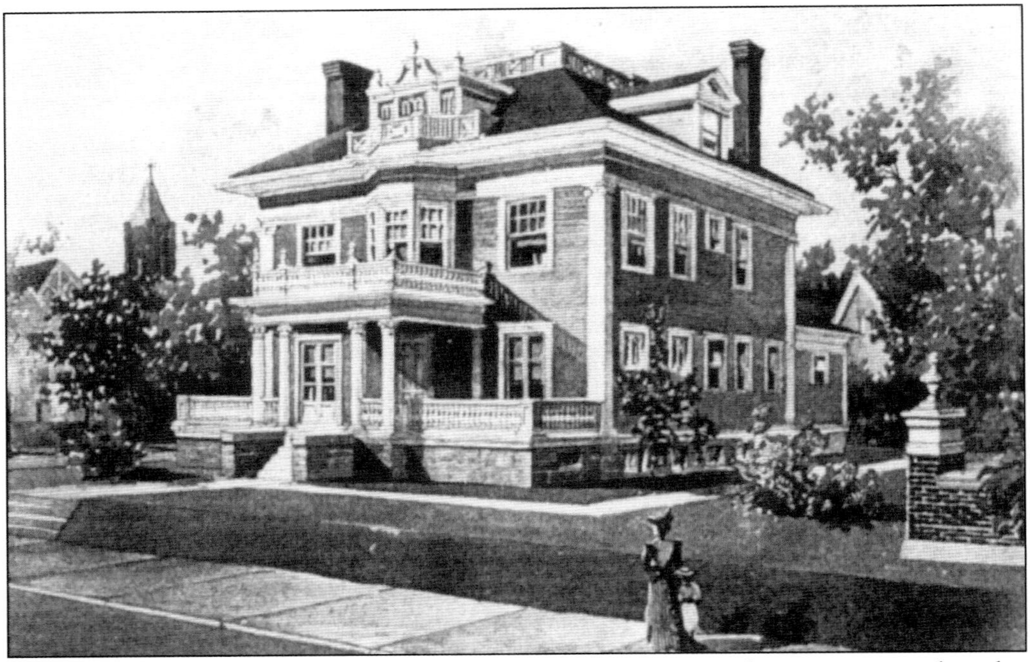

Roanoke, 1901. Kansas City's best architects began planning Roanoke's mansions, such as this one for A.E. Holmes, which was designed in 1901. By 1907, the *Kansas City Star* was extolling the virtues of this "exclusive residence district bounded on one side by Penn Valley Park and on the other by broad streets that furnish an outlet by streetcar lines to any part of the city." (Courtesy of MVSC-KCPL.)

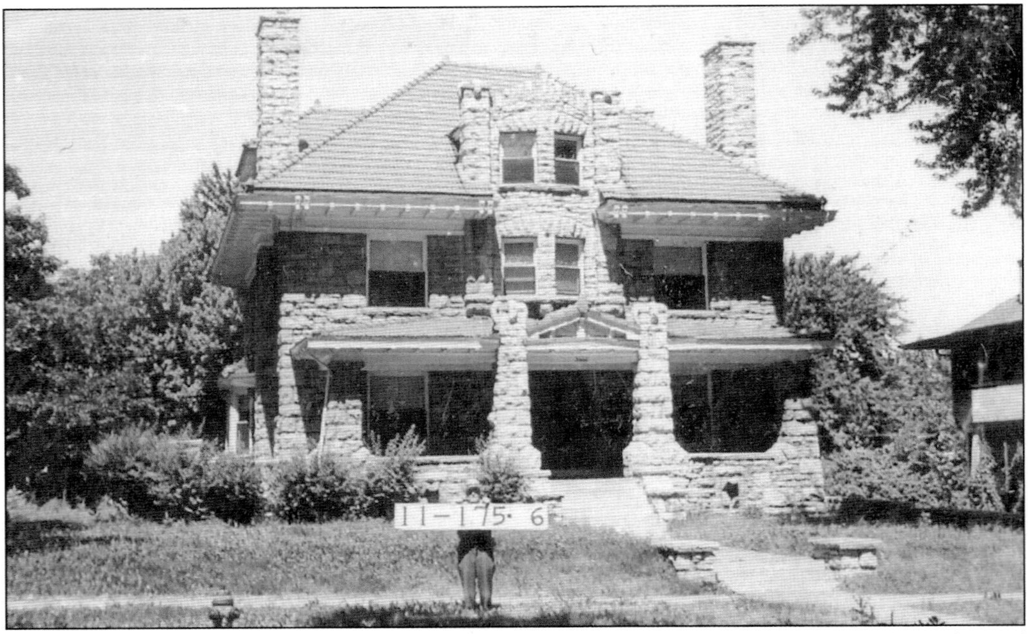

Roanoke, 1940. In 1921, there were no city zoning codes in place, so the new residents formed the Roanoke Protective Homes Association and gave it teeth to enforce single-family requirements for the neighborhood. In the 1940s, when many Midtown homes were divided into apartments, Roanoke homes remained single-family dwellings. (Courtesy of MVSC-KCPL.)

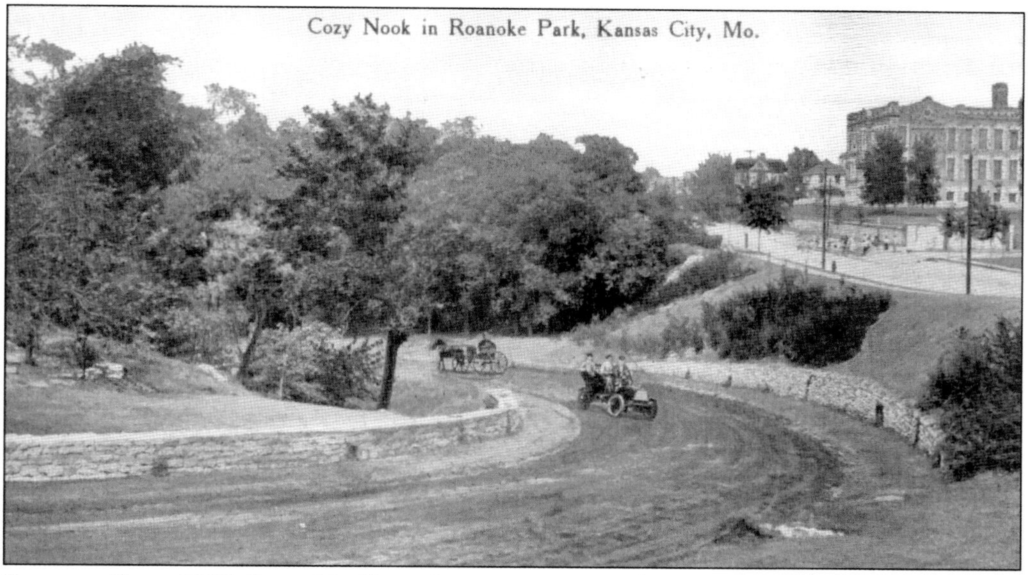

ROANOKE PARK, 1909. Part of the Roanoke area was a rugged ravine surrounded by steep hillsides with limestone outcroppings. The limestone from a quarry in the area that became the park was used to build the homes and stone walls in the neighborhood. Residents soon determined that the rugged strip of land would be difficult to develop. To prevent undesirable growth and to protect property values, landowners donated land to create Roanoke Park. This postcard shows the park at the turn of the century. The Mellier (later Volker and then Gordon Parks) school in Volker can be seen on the hill. (Courtesy of *Midtown KC Post*.)

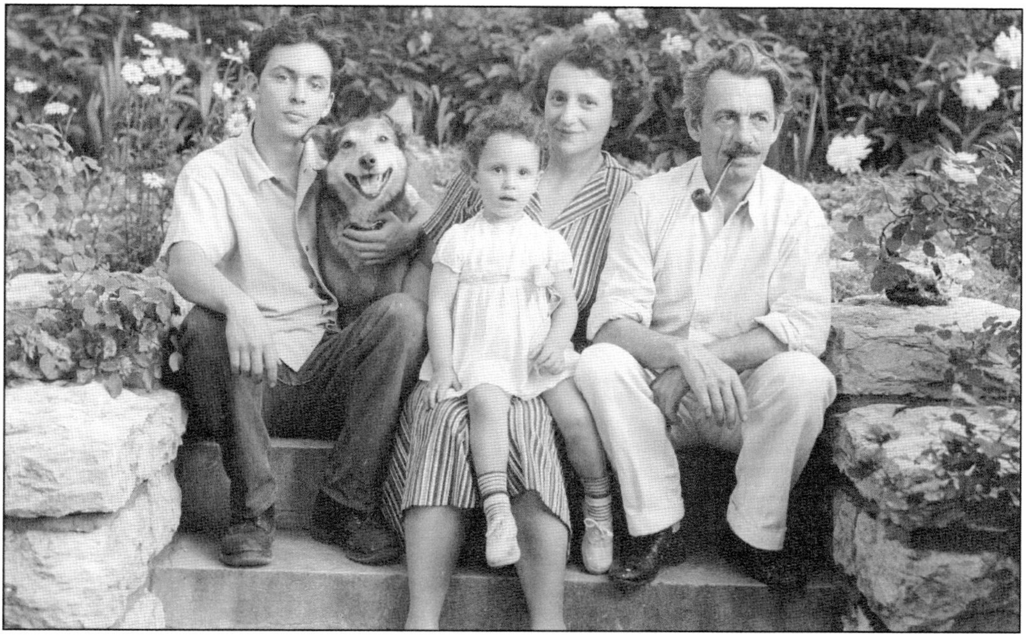

THOMAS HART BENTON FAMILY, 1939. Noted American painter Thomas Hart Benton, who lived in the Roanoke neighborhood, taught at the Kansas City Art Institute in the 1930s. His home at 3616 Belleview Avenue is now a state historic site. The members of the Benton family are, from left to right, T.P., dog Jake, Jessie, Rita, and Thomas. They are sitting on the steps leading to the garden area. (Courtesy of Missouri State Parks.)

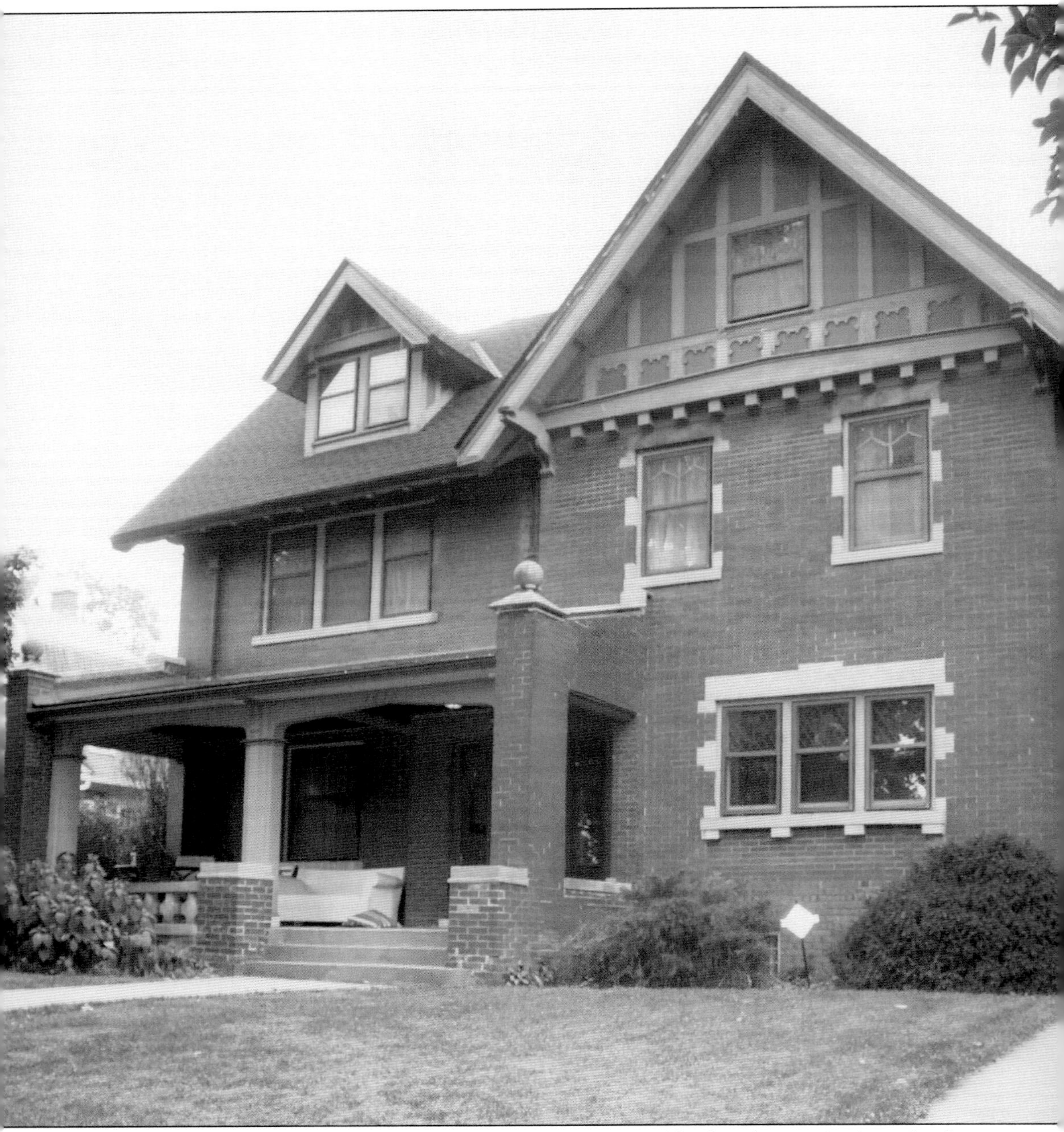

VALENTINE. The present-day Roanoke and Valentine neighborhoods were built on land once owned by A.B.H. McGee, son of one of the founders of Kansas City. McGee's original tract of land included everything from Thirty-fifth to Thirty-ninth Streets and from Broadway Boulevard to State Line Road. McGee used some of the land for crops and pastures. Eventually, he sold some of the property to individuals and then sold a large piece to the Interstate Fair Company. During his 71 years on the "farm," McGee and his family lived in a cabin, then built a more elaborate house and a locally renowned barn on the property, a grand hotel on Broadway Boulevard, and, finally, the house that currently stands at 3758 Washington Street. A block of today's Valentine neighborhood was originally part of the Roanoke subdivision, but when Southwest Trafficway was built in the 1950s, the new freeway split the two neighborhoods. (Author's collection.)

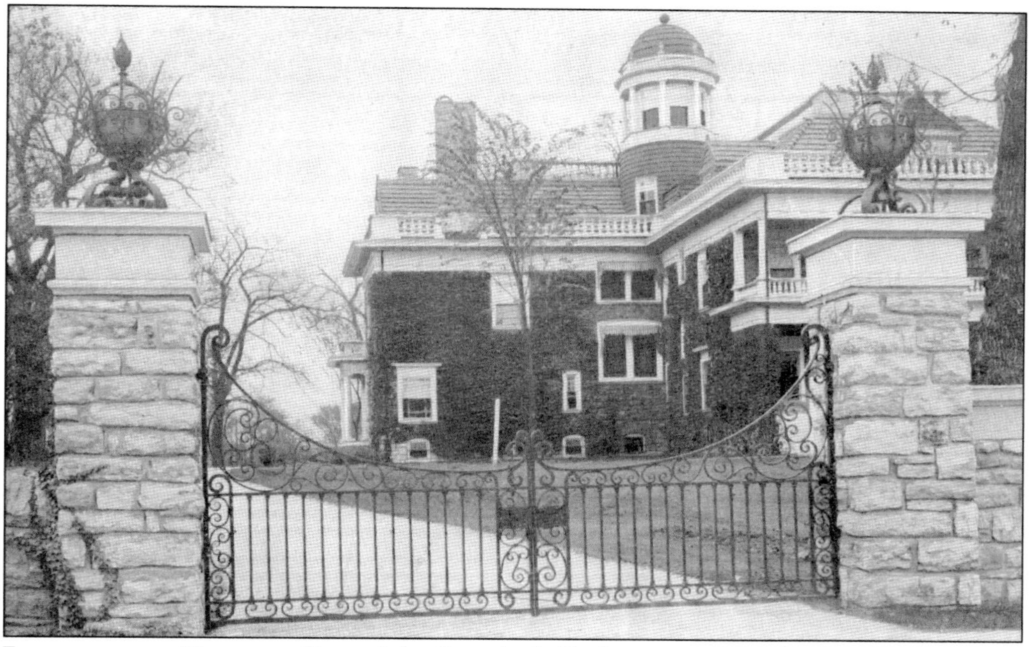

Broadway and Valentine Road. John Perry built Elmhurst in 1898 at the corner of Broadway and Valentine Road as a surprise for his wife and children, who were traveling in Europe. But after their ship sank on their return journey, Perry sold the house. Annie Ridenbaugh Bird, widow of Emery, Bird, and Thayer founder Joseph T. Bird, lived at Elmhurst for many years. The stone wall still surrounds the Uptown Shopping Center. The house was razed in 1937. (Courtesy of MVSC-KCPL.)

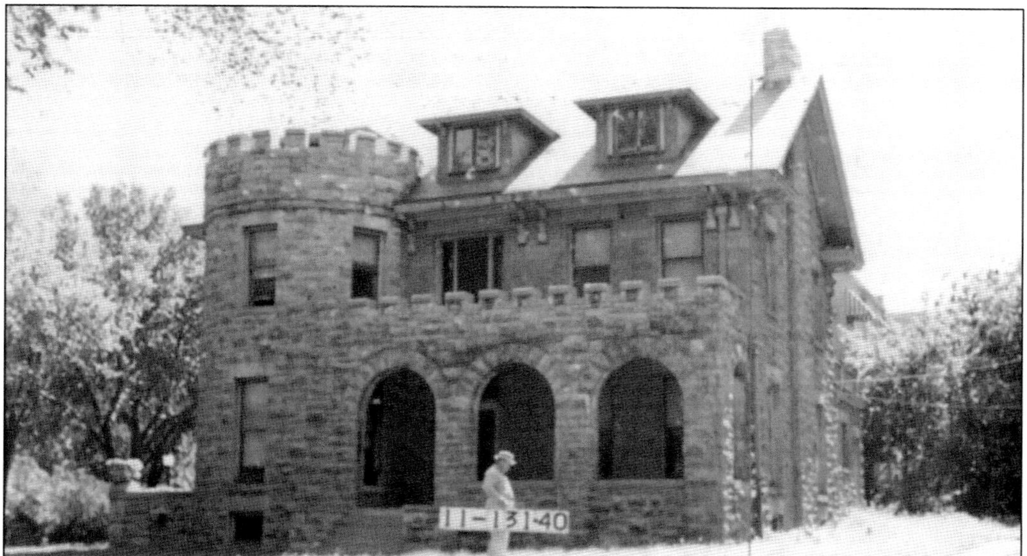

Valentine, 1940. After the turn of the century, Valentine filled with mostly three-story homes built for well-off owners. Builders made use of local limestone for entire houses or for the first stories of shirtwaist homes, a popular Kansas City style that features brick or limestone on the first floor and wood siding or stucco on the upper floors. Large stone front porches are also a signature of homes in Valentine and in other Midtown neighborhoods. (Courtesy of MVSC-KCPL.)

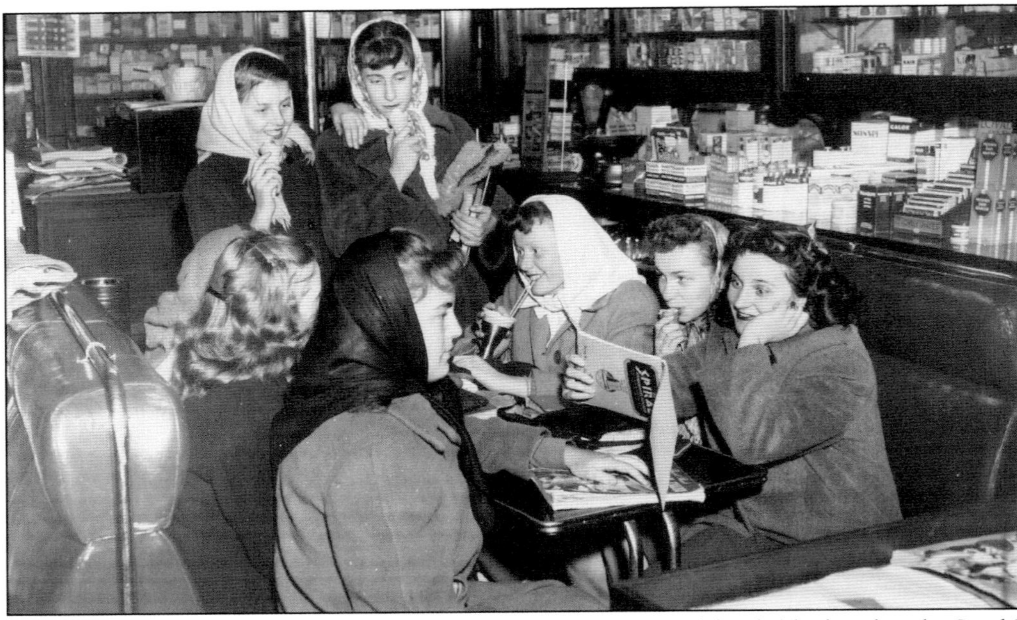

Stack's Drugstore, 1940s. The Byrne girls from Coleman Highlands liked to drop by Stack's Pharmacy at 3301 Summit Street after school in the 1940s. Broadway Boulevard also had an A&P grocery store, gas stations, and even an ice-cream shop during that decade. (Courtesy of Kerry Browne.)

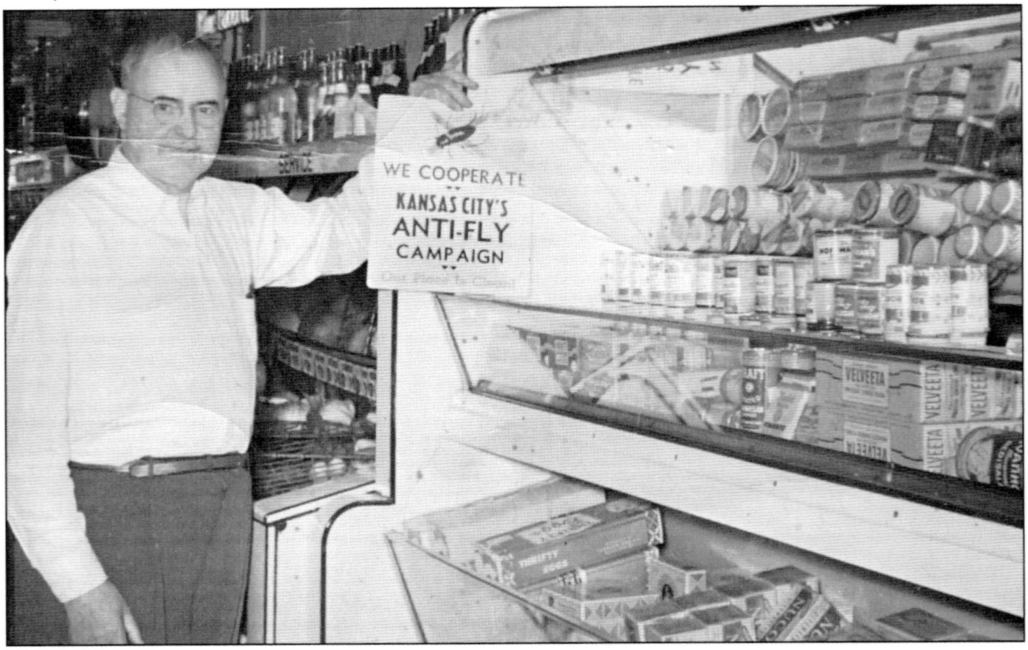

Browne's Deli, 1940s. Ed and Mary Flavin, immigrants from Ireland, opened Browne's Deli at Twenty-seventh and Jefferson Streets in 1887 and moved it to its present location at Thirty-third Street and Pennsylvania Avenue in 1901. The deli has been run by the family ever since. The store participated in the anti-fly campaign, a public health effort to clean up trash to get rid of the pesky insects in the 1940s. Like many Midtown businesses in the late 1800s, the shop was in the front of the family's home. (Courtesy of Kerry Browne.)

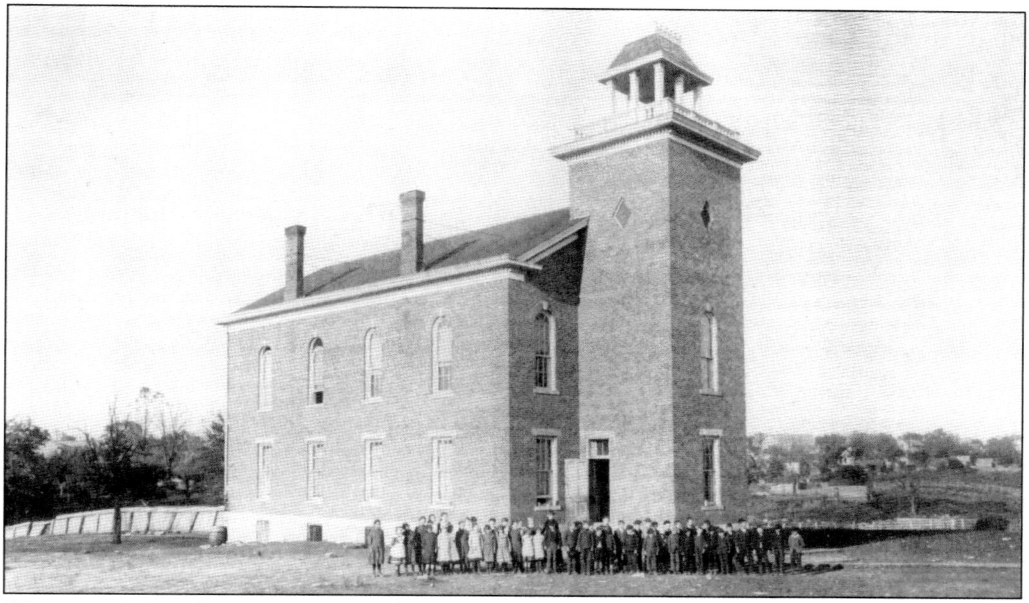

Westport Main School. Most south side children attended Westport schools before Westport was annexed to Kansas City. The first of the Westport schools was the Westport Main School, on the site of what later would be the Allen School. When Kansas City expanded to take in Westport, the Kansas City School District took over the south side schools as well. The Westport Main School burned down in 1895. (Courtesy of MVSC-KCPL.)

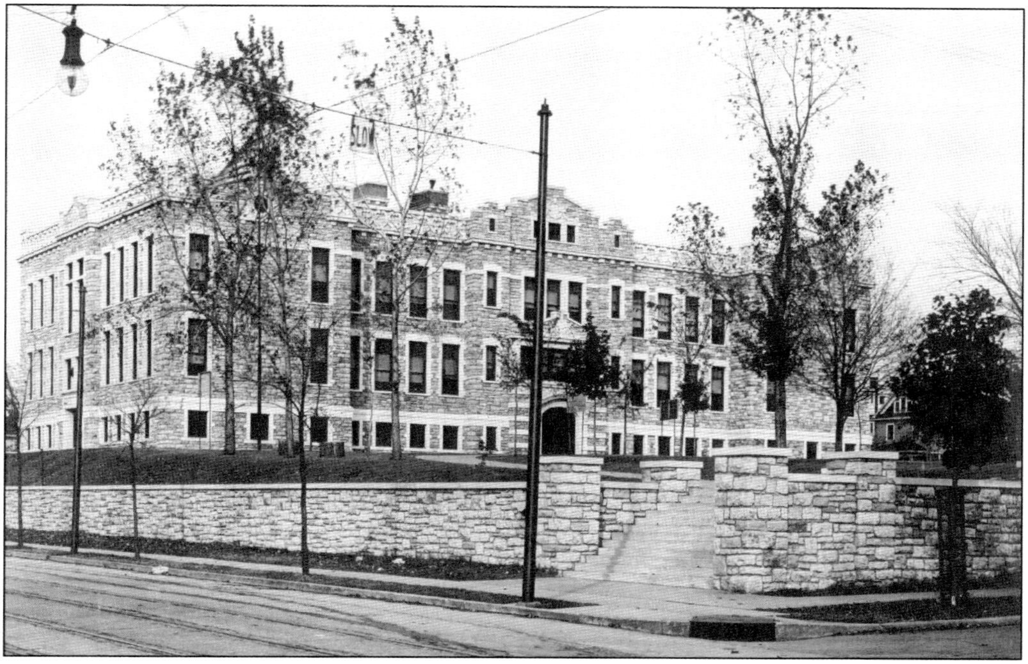

Norman School. By the time it built the Norman School at 3514 Jefferson Street in 1906, the Kansas City School District was struggling to keep up with a growing student population as the city expanded. The district had constructed or annexed about 50 buildings by the time construction of the first phase of the Norman School began. A second phase of construction continued in 1911. (Courtesy of MVSC-KCPL.)

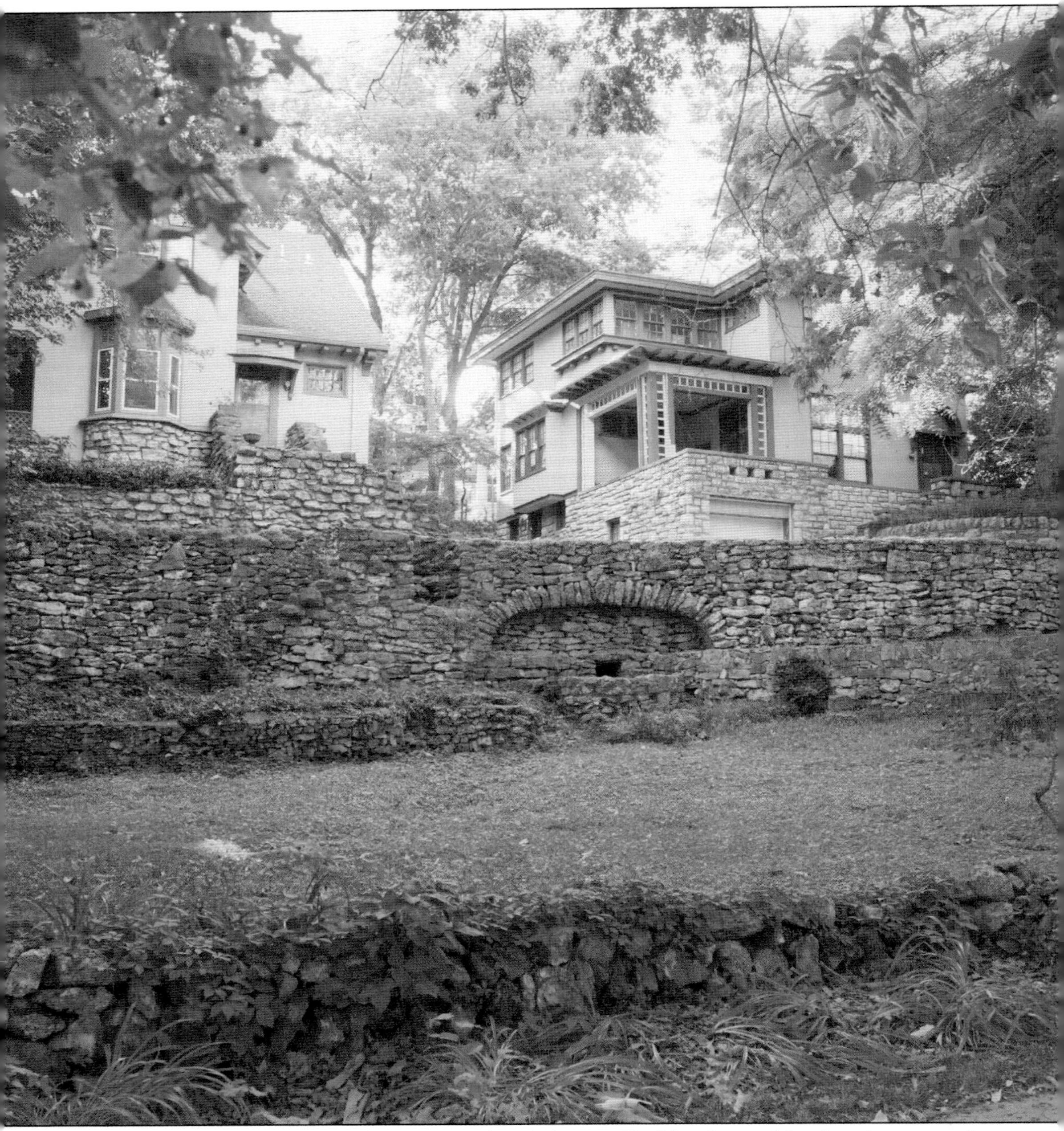

COLEMAN HIGHLANDS. What is now the Coleman Highlands neighborhood remained an undeveloped farm as other parts of Kansas City were built up until the 80-acre parcel was subdivided in 1907. The area extends to limestone bluffs on the north, south, and west. Early developers sang the praises of the hilltop development, claiming "a trip to this beautiful residential district is like a trip to a park." The sweeping curves of Karnes Boulevard today look much like they did when the Coleman Highlands neighborhood was founded. Karnes Boulevard was added to the parks-and-boulevard system in 1905, setting the stage for increased development of the neighborhood. Since it was first developed, a ravine in Coleman Highlands has been filled in and Coleman Road has been straightened, but most of the neighborhood retains its early-20th-century flavor. (Author's collection.)

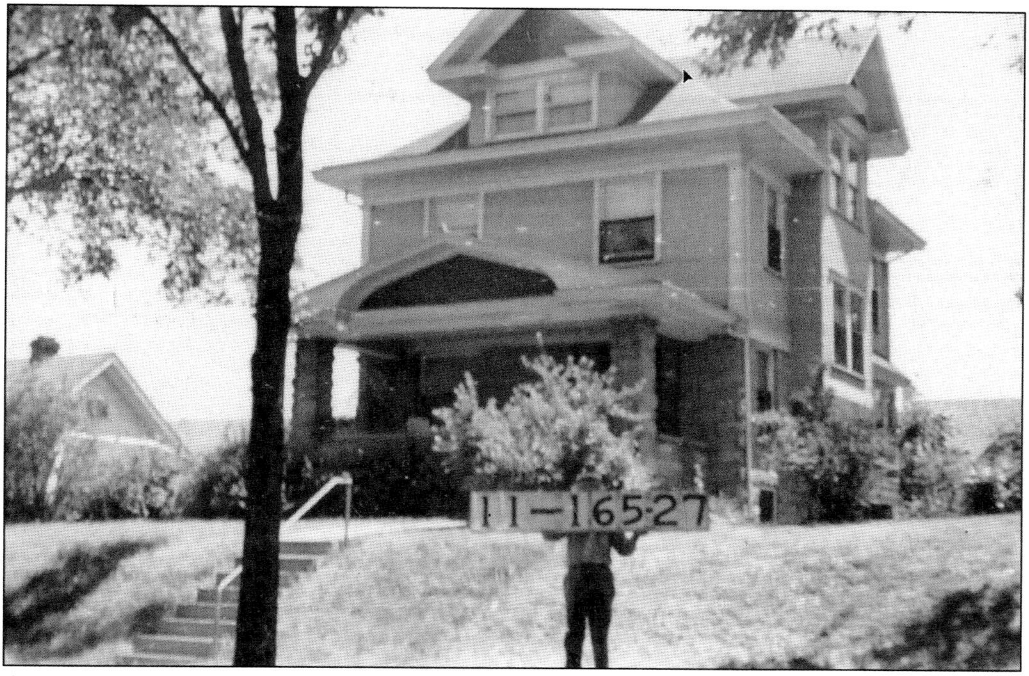

Coleman Highlands Neighborhood, 1940. Like the houses in neighborhoods around it, Coleman's homes benefited from the ample use of native limestone. Streets curving down to Roanoke Park are reinforced with stone walls, and first floors, or in some cases entire homes, were built from stone quarried from Roanoke Park. Coleman was another neighborhood restricted to single-family homes. When these photographs were taken in the 1940s, homes in most other Midtown neighborhoods were being subdivided during a severe housing shortage. However, Coleman remained a single-family neighborhood, and its homes were never subdivided. (Both, courtesy of MVSC-KCPL.)

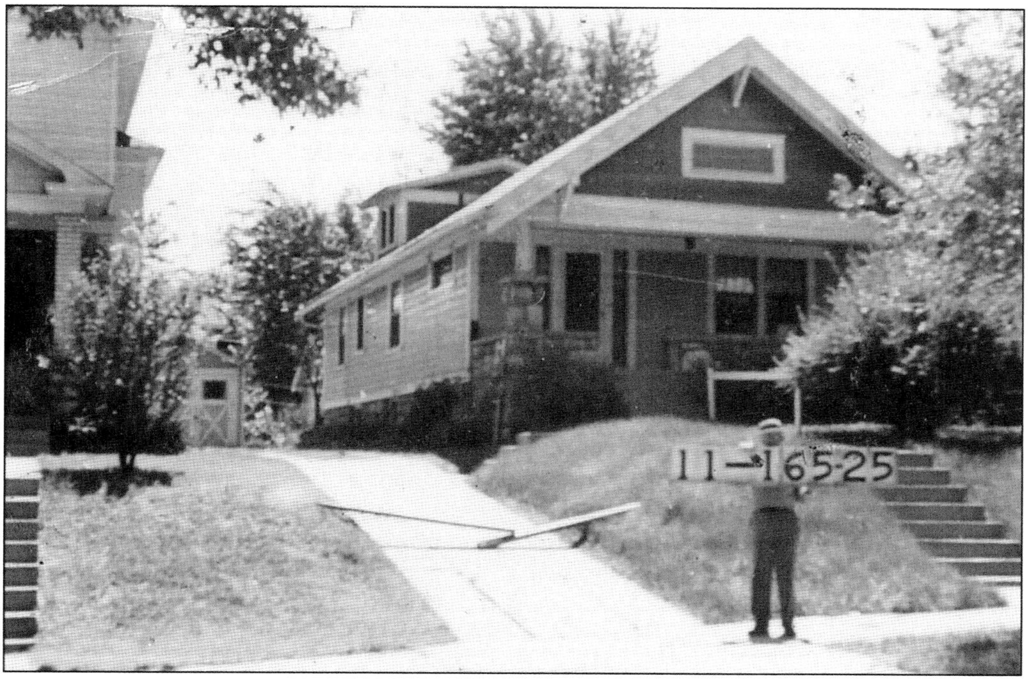

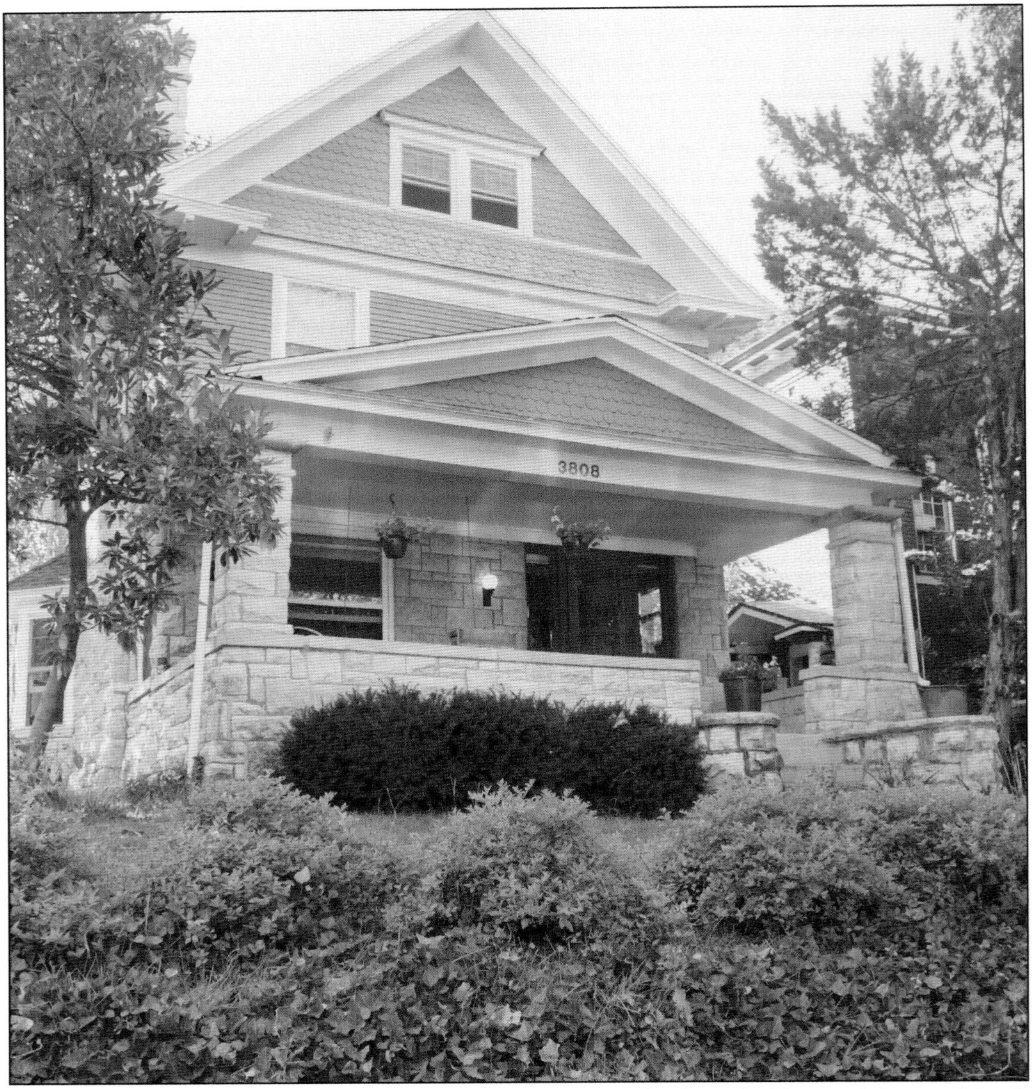

VOLKER. The current Volker neighborhood grew out of the large holdings of George Vogel. When Vogel died in 1901, the *Kansas City Star* said he was the town's oldest resident, born in a log cabin at 4026 Pennsylvania Avenue. Until he retired, his homestead consisted of 43 acres around Westport. "The growth of the city encroached on the farm until it dwindled to a few acres. Mr. Vogel saw wide stretches of his land transformed into paved streets lined with houses. He steadfastly refused to sell any land from the big lot which surrounds the house he built more than thirty years ago at 1606 West Forty-third Street [on Westport Road between Genessee and Wyoming Streets]," the *Star* said. Another early Volker landowner was Peter Muehlbach, who had a vineyard and wine garden near Thirty-ninth Street and State Line Road. But streetcars brought development to Volker, as it did to other parts of Midtown. By 1890, the Mellier Place streetcar line was running, and it led to a rush of development beginning with Mellier Place, a new subdivision at the end of the streetcar line around Thirty-ninth Street and State Line Road. (Author's collection.)

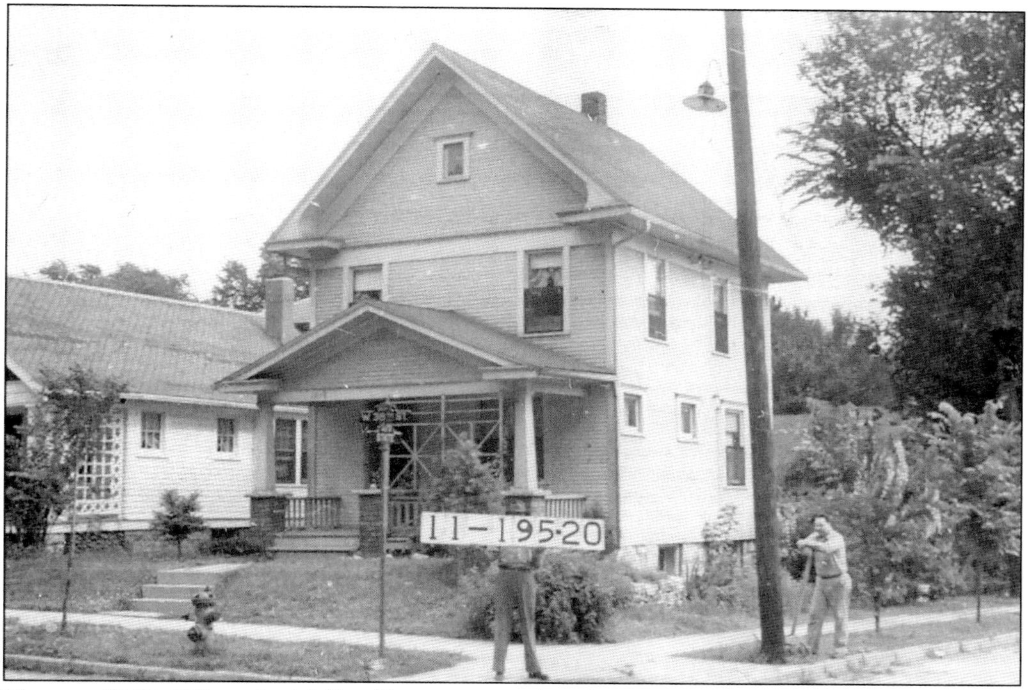

VOLKER, 1940. When the Mellier Place streetcar line began running in 1890, it offered would-be homeowners a direct route to affordable homes in the suburbs. Along State Line Road from Thirty-sixth to Forty-third Streets, developer William Mellier promised buyers a comfortable house for less than the $35 a month it then cost them to rent. On one day in 1895, hundreds of buyers rode the streetcar to the new suburb for an auction of lots. Families and speculators paid $6 to $9 a foot for the lots. By the time these 1940 tax photographs were taken, Volker was a thriving neighborhood. (Both, courtesy of MVSC-KCPL.)

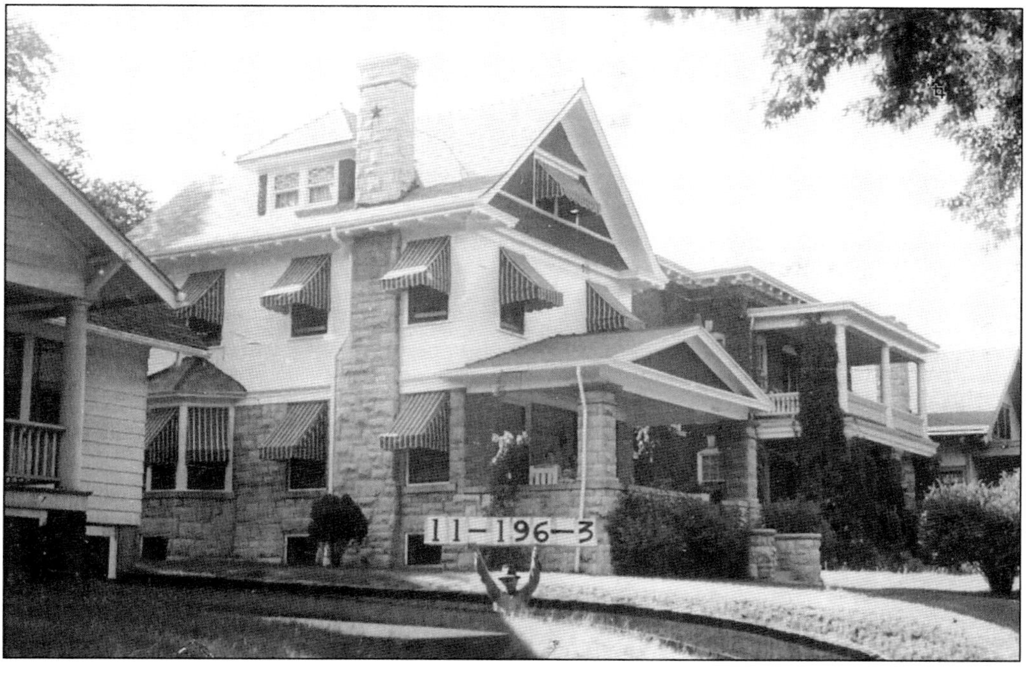

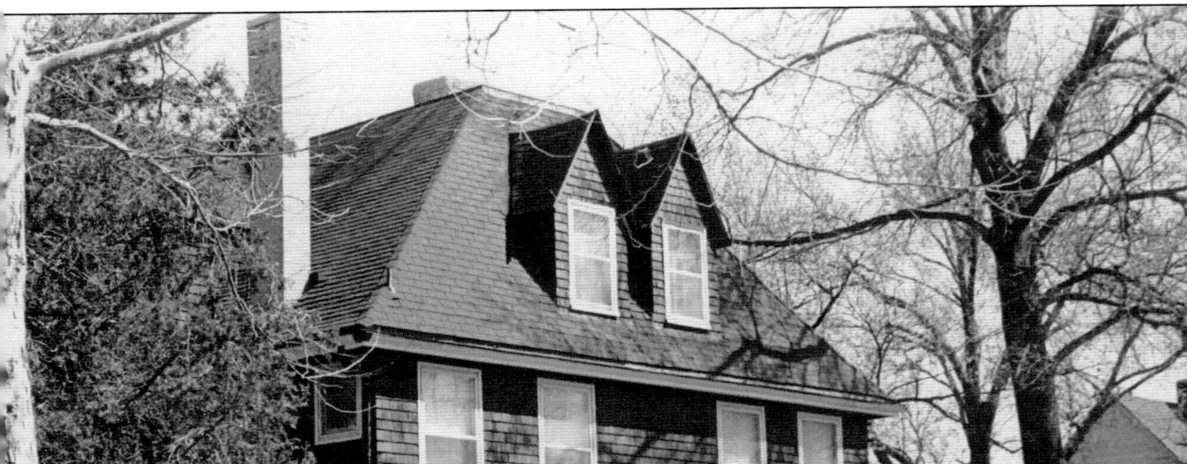

Roselawn. Volker is named after beloved Kansas City philanthropist William Volker, whose home, Roselawn, still stands at 3717 Bell Street. Volker started a business that manufactured window shades and many other household items. He became a millionaire in 1906 and gave one-third of his income for charitable purposes. The chamber of commerce named him "The First Citizen of Kansas City" in 1943. He bought his house at 3717 Bell Street in 1889 in the new Mellier Place subdivision. The philanthropist lived there with his parents and sister and, later, his wife. His sister called the place Roselawn because of the many varieties of roses their father planted in the gardens, but Volker liked to refer to the estate as Peaceful Valley. He had a greenhouse built on the property and also a stone carriage house, as Volker preferred to use a horse and buggy or saddle horse even after automobiles became popular. (Courtesy of MVSC-KCPL.)

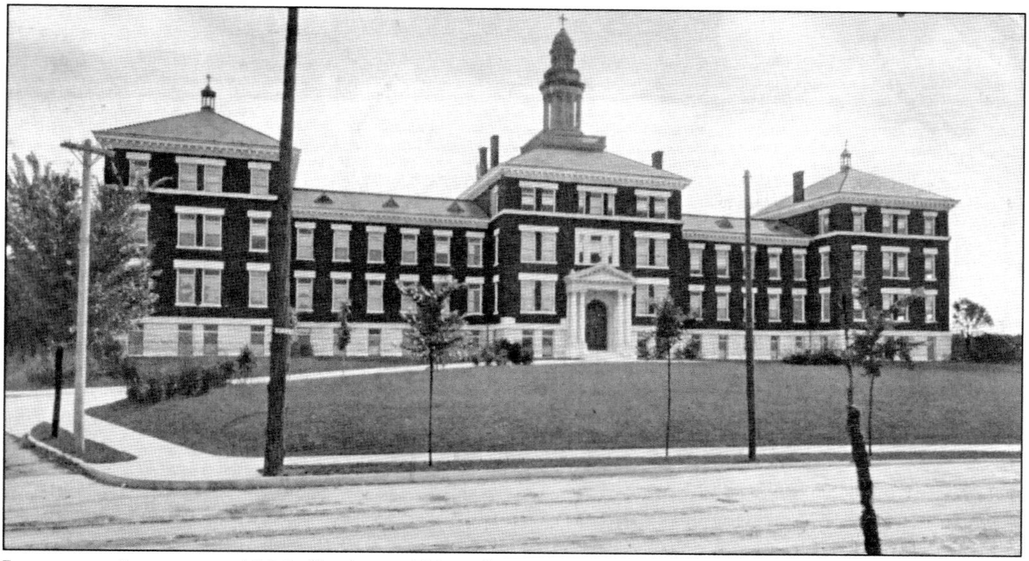

Loretto Academy, 1909. Built in 1904, the Loretto Academy at Thirty-ninth Street and Roanoke Road was a boarding and day school for girls. It was named after the Sisters of Loretto, a community of Catholic nuns founded in 1812 "to bring education to the poor children of the frontier." The school moved farther south in the 1960s, but the old building is still used today for special events. (Courtesy of *Midtown KC Post*.)

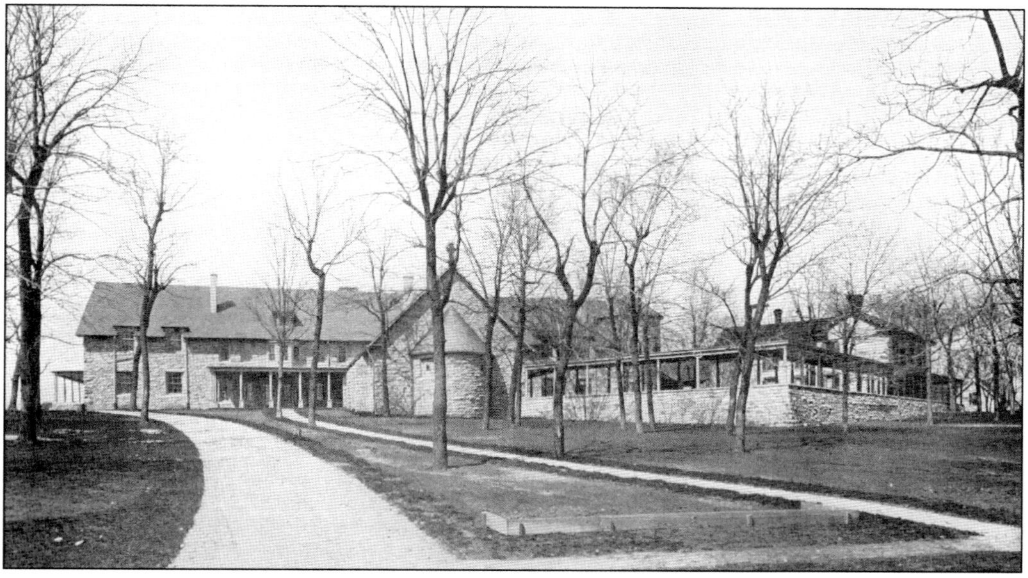

Orphan Boys Home. The Orphan Boys Home, which stood on the site of today's Old Westport Shopping Center, was run by local women and the Sisters of the Order of Vincent de St. Paul. They hoped to keep boys off the streets and help them learn a useful trade. The home, which stood until the 1960s, included dormitories for the boys, classrooms, reception rooms, and rooms for the sisters. (Courtesy of MVSC-KCPL.)

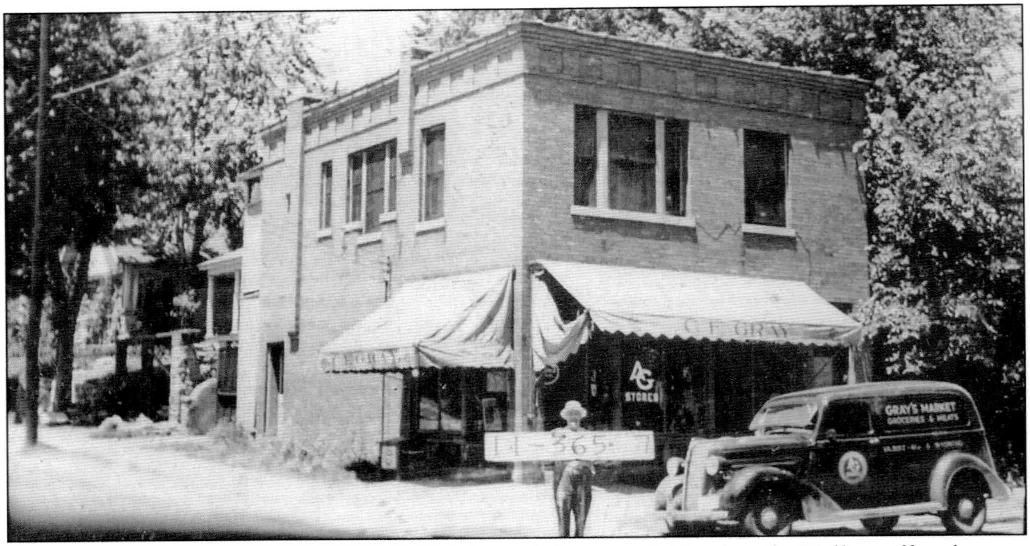

VOLKER BUSINESSES, 1940. As one of Midtown's larger neighborhoods, Volker offered many businesses within walking distances of its homes in the 1940s, when these photographs were taken. Gray's Market at Forty-first and Wyoming Streets (above) was just one of several neighborhood groceries. The Rainbow Grocery on Thirty-ninth Street made deliveries to surrounding homes. Another popular destination for neighborhood kids on bikes was Velvet Freeze Ice Cream at 1624 Westport Road. Residents remember that the Manor Bread Company still delivered by horse in Volker in the late 1940s (below). (Above, courtesy of MVSC-KCPL; below, courtesy of Wilborn and Associates.)

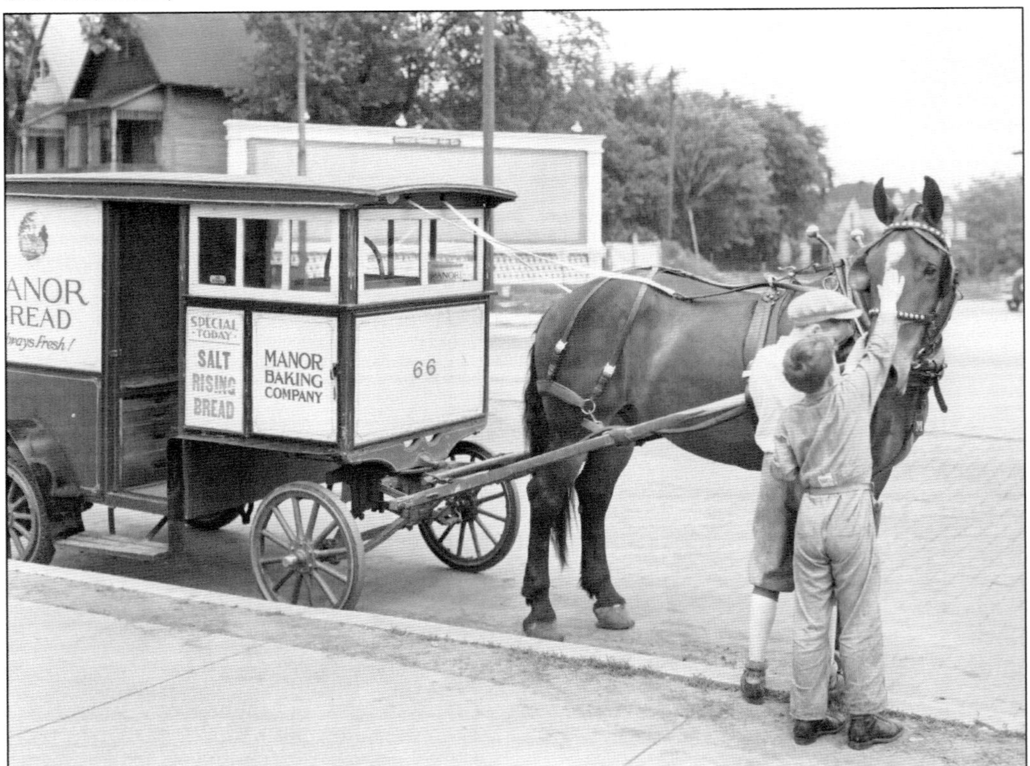

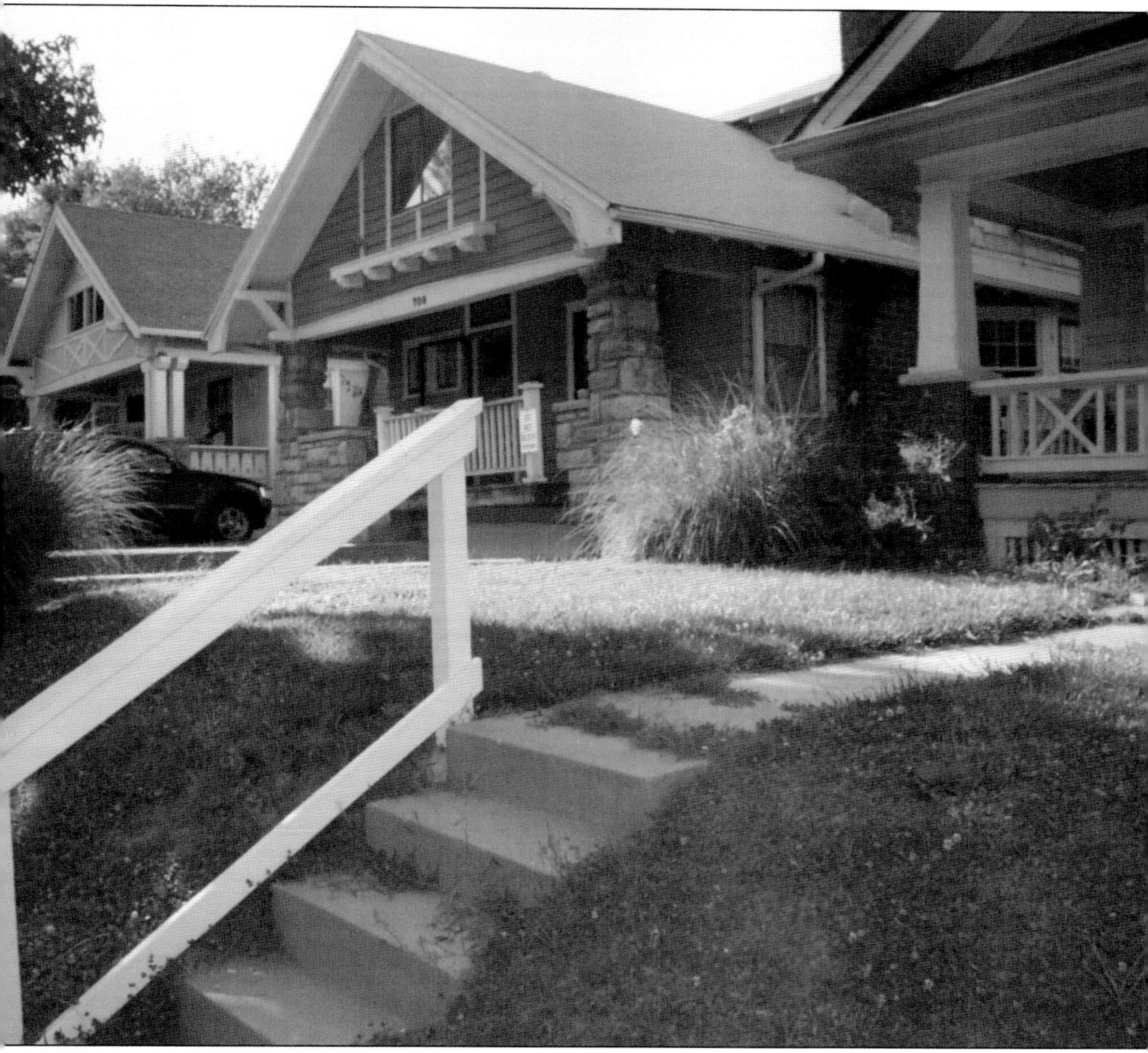

Plaza/Westport. Just south of Westport Road, the Plaza/Westport development began in 1887. Where farms once stood, developer S.H. Taylor advertised lots for sale in Bunker Hill. Taylor promised that his carriages were always ready to drive home buyers to see properties, where "you can make 100 percent of your investment inside of six months." The subdivision was attractive because schools, churches, and elegant residences were already in place in Volker, and the Westport Cable Line was under construction. Once complete, Taylor promised, it would cost only 5¢ to ride to work in the city business district. From the beginning, Plaza/Westport homes were intended for a working-class, immigrant population. Many of the original homes were later lost when St. Luke's Hospital was built in 1923 and expanded over the years. (Author's collection.)

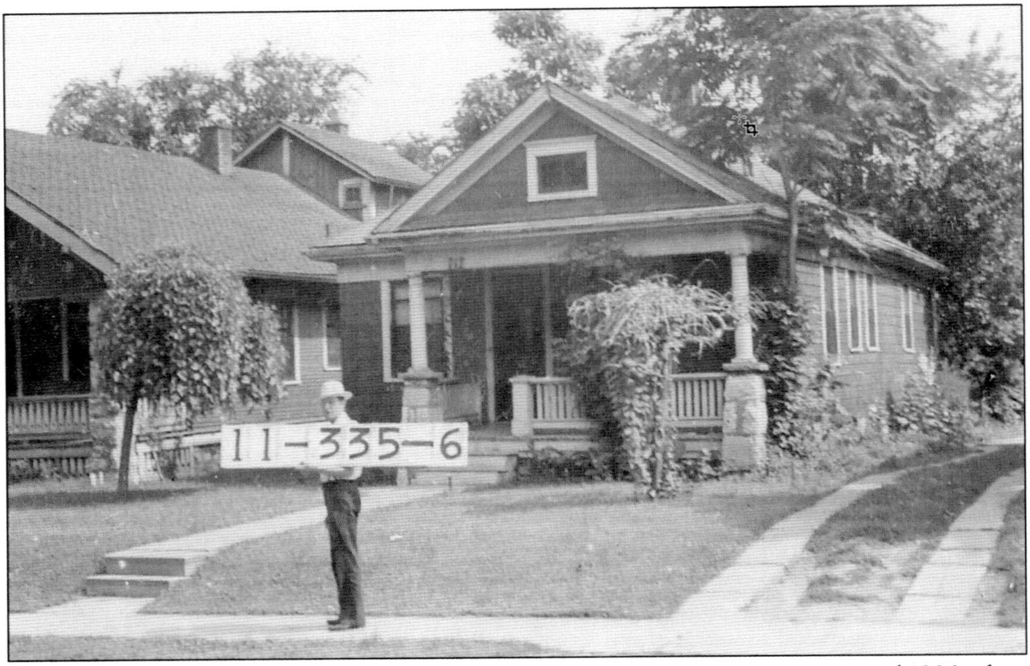

PLAZA/WESTPORT, 1940. A second wave of Plaza/Westport construction came around 1906, when Corbin Realty invited people to move in "where the bungalows grow." Corbin offered "thoroughly modern and up to date bungalow cottages and two-story houses" on 40-foot lots for $28 a month. Once again, proximity to streetcar lines was a selling point. Houses in Corbin's addition, although built to be affordable, featured many amenities homeowners still appreciate, such as oak floors, beamed ceilings, stone fireplaces, and bay windows with built-in window seats. Homes ranged in size from three to seven rooms. Corbin Park even had its own grocery store, the Corbin Park Cash Market, at 4303 Jefferson Street. (Both, courtesy of MVSC-KCPL.)

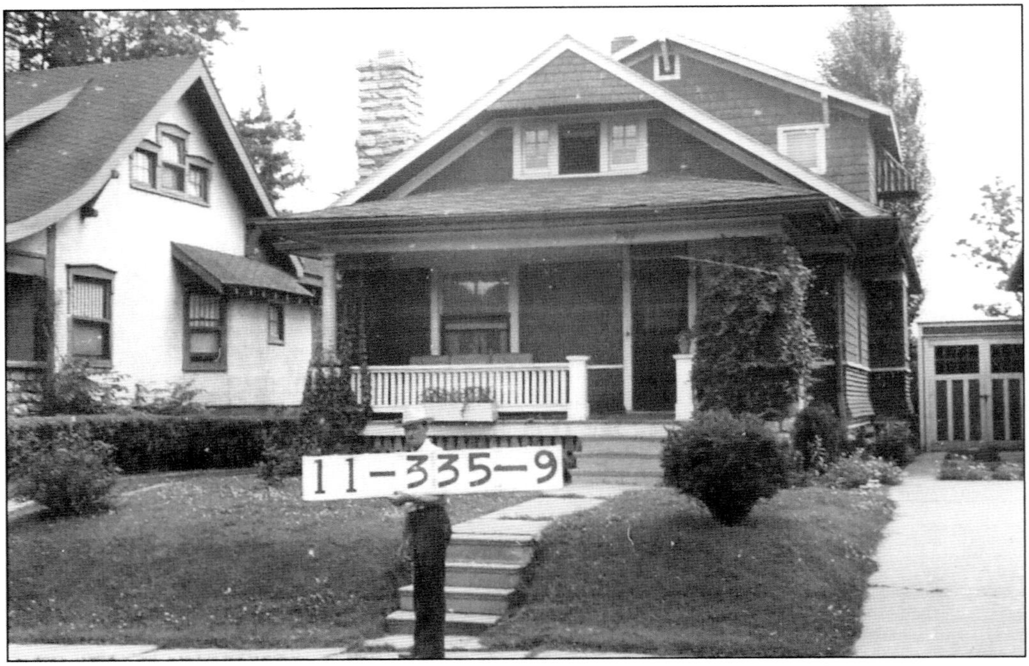

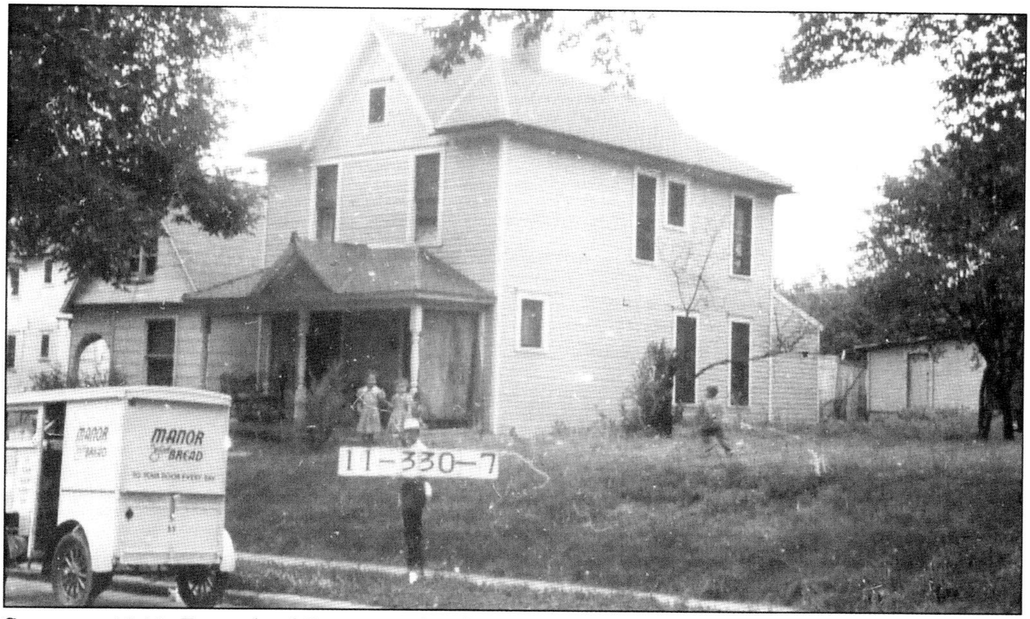

STEPTOE, 1940. Forty-third Street in Plaza/Westport was once known as Steptoe Street. Henry Clay Pate founded what was called Pate's Addition, which soon became a haven for slaves who had purchased their freedom. They bought land and built homes in Pate's Addition, and the area became known as Steptoe. Former residents who grew up in Steptoe described it as a small village. "Though there were segregationist attitudes, little overt racial tension was exhibited," Jackson County Historical Society archivist David Jackson wrote in 2006. "Longtime residents called their community 'a little island' and talked about having white, Jewish, German, Italian, Hispanic and Swedish people for neighbors." Only eight of the original Steptoe homes remain. (Both, courtesy of MVSC-KCPL.)

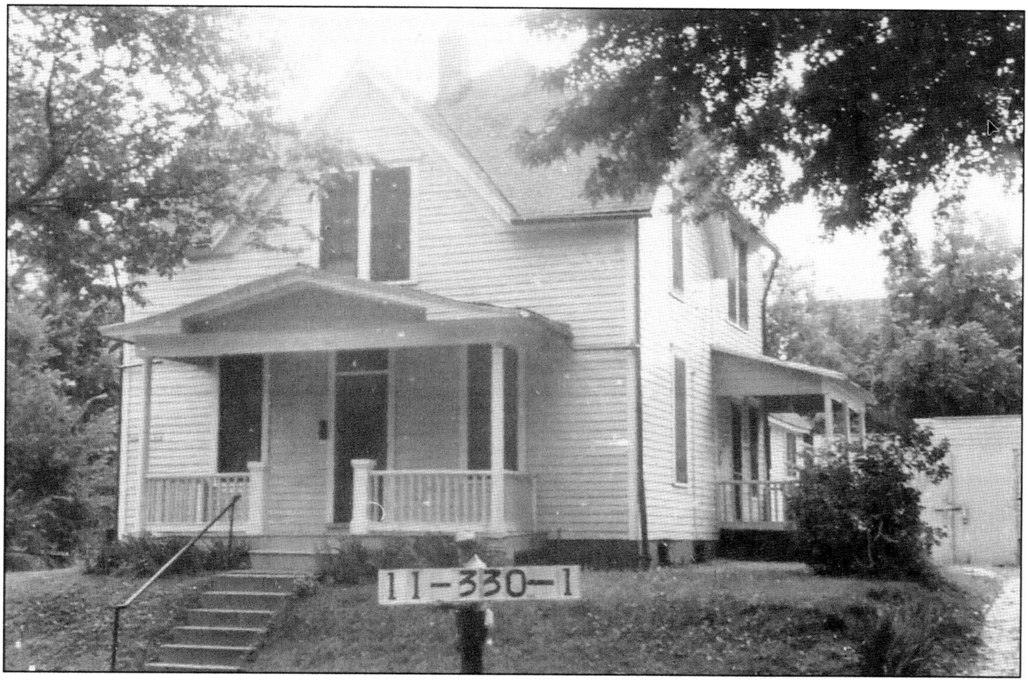

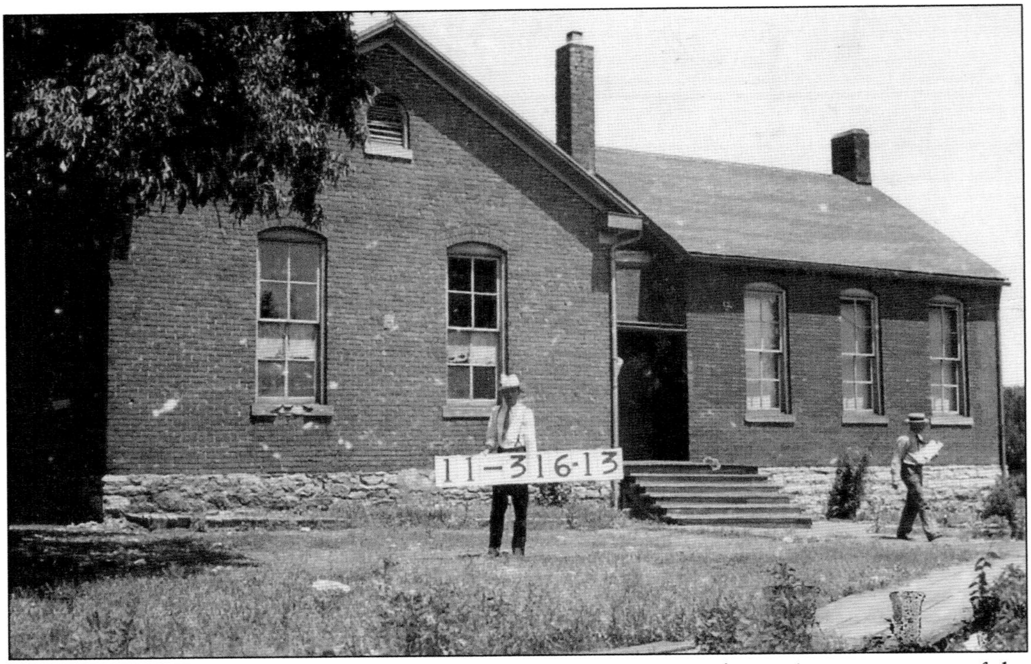

PENN SCHOOL, 1940. Steptoe was home to the oldest school for African Americans west of the Mississippi, the Penn School (pictured), which closed in 1957 and burned down in 1969. Steptoe also had two churches. The St. James Baptist Church still stands at the corner of Forty-third and Washington Streets. (Courtesy of MVSC-KCPL.)

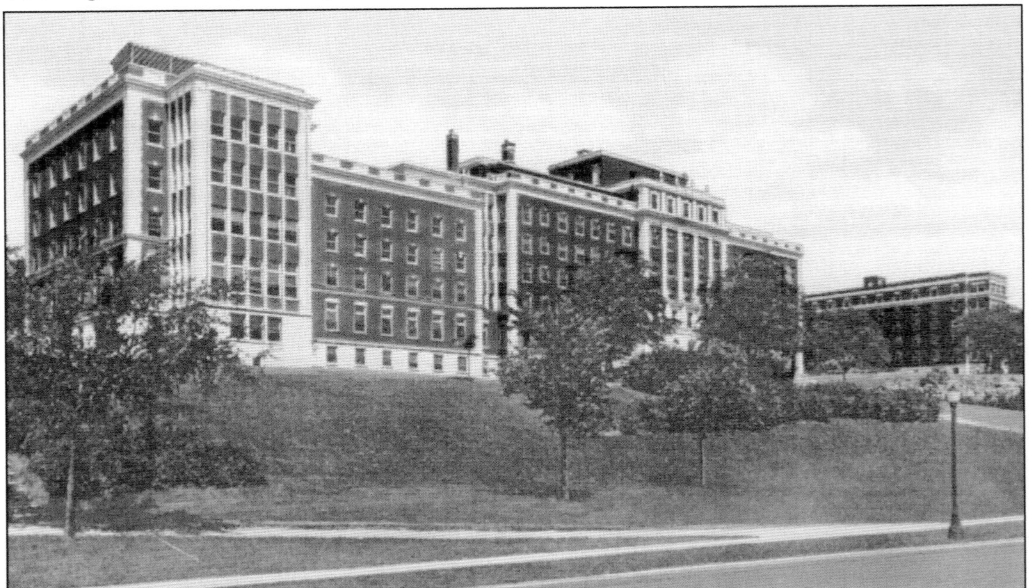

ST. LUKE'S HOSPITAL. This hospital, founded in 1882, moved to a four-acre tract at Forty-fourth Street and Wornall Road and opened its doors in 1923. Earlier, the hospital had been located downtown, but, like churches and schools, it followed residents as they moved south. In announcing the new site, a May 15, 1921, *Kansas City Star* article said the location between Mill Creek Boulevard and Wornall Road was chosen because it was in the heart of the new south side residential areas. (Courtesy of *Midtown KC Post*.)

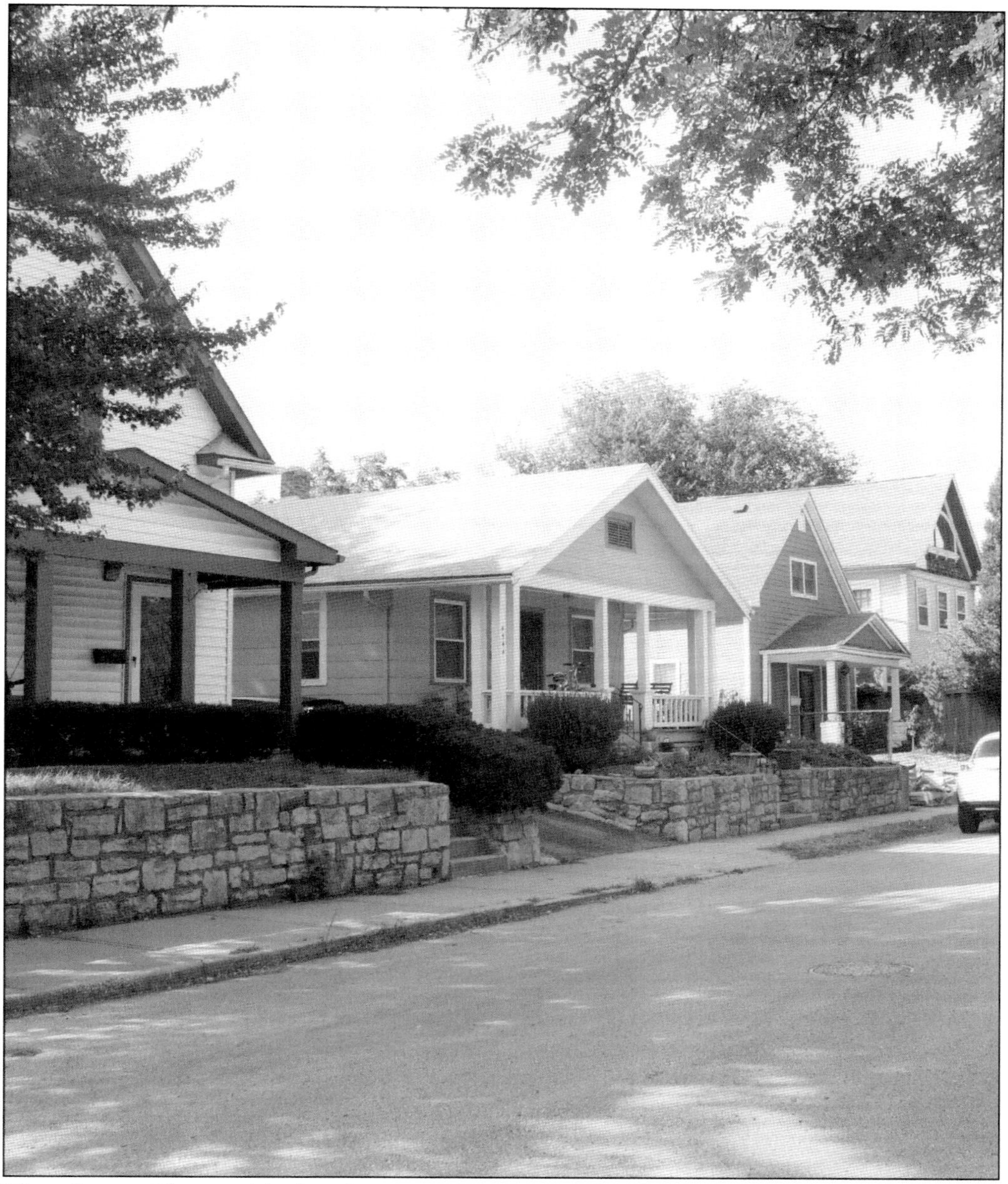

WEST PLAZA. This neighborhood was another section of Midtown generally built as a working-class area. There are still a few larger homes built by wealthy Westport businessmen at the end of the 1800s, but there are also a number of very small houses constructed on tiny lots for working-class people. According to Joe Montanari, a resident who has researched the history of the neighborhood, "Before World War I, there was no municipal gas line or water service, so most of the smaller houses were built on brick piers with a crawl space beneath and no basement. Three-room structures, they consisted of a living room, a kitchen with a wood burning stove in the middle, and a bedroom. Because there was no water service, there was no bathroom. The stove served the dual purpose of heating the house and cooking." By the 1920s, a streetcar line extended to Forty-fifth Street and State Line Road, where it turned around and went back downtown. (Author's collection.)

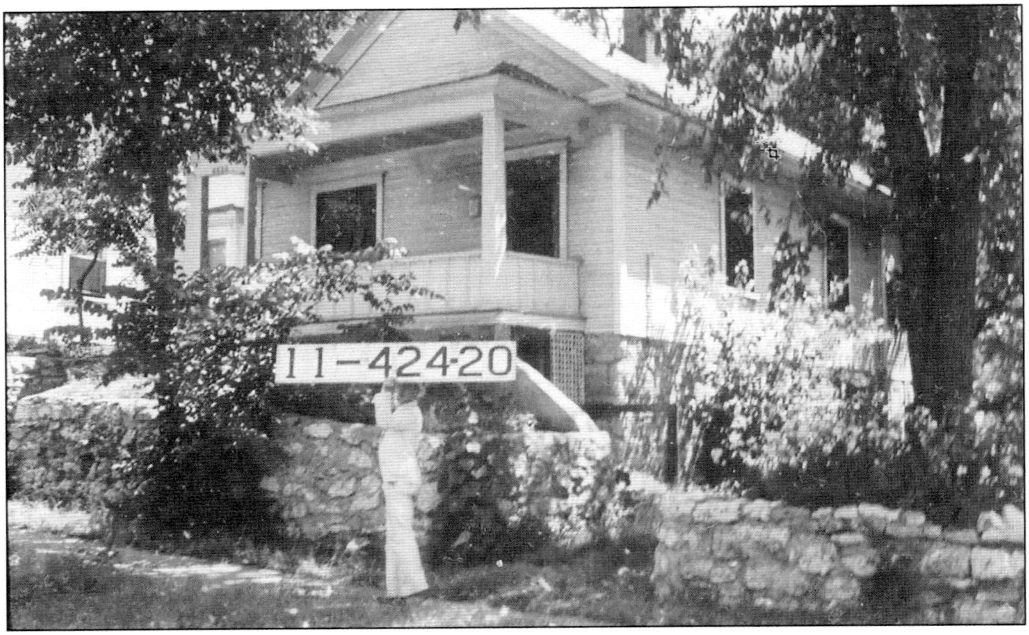

West Plaza, 1940. The West Plaza neighborhood is characterized by steep, narrow streets, some lined with stone walls. While stone walls were added as decorative touches in some parts of Midtown, they were often necessary in West Plaza. As water, sewer, and gas lines were installed, some of the steeper blocks, such as the 4600 blocks of Genessee and Bell Streets, were leveled out and then shored up by the stones. By the 1940s, when these tax photographs were taken, some of the smaller West Plaza homes had had upper stories added and all had modern utilities and indoor plumbing. (Both, courtesy of MVSC-KCPL.)

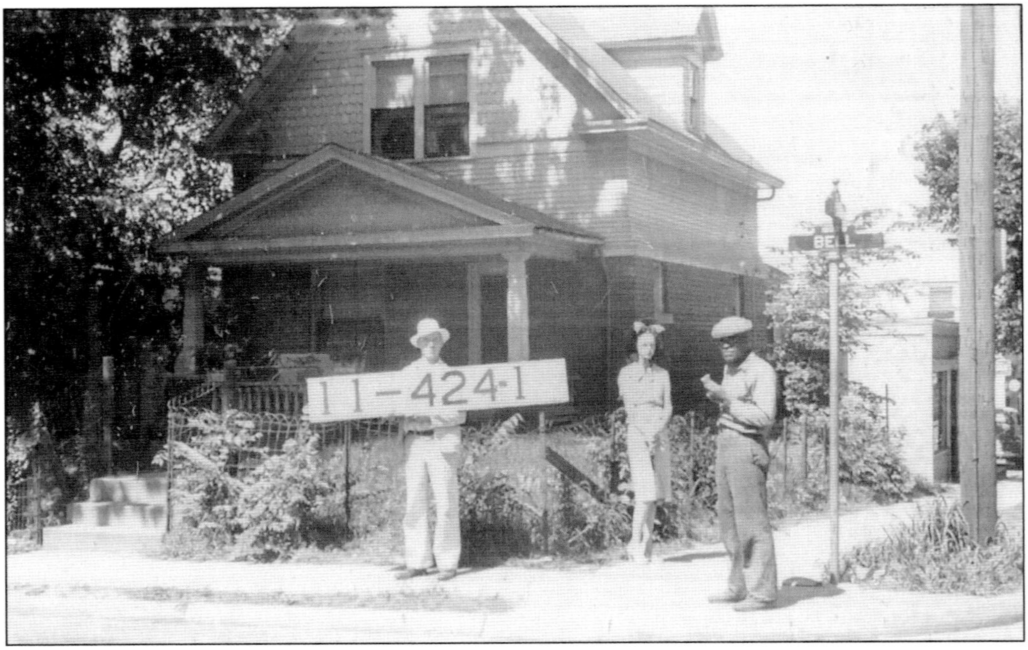

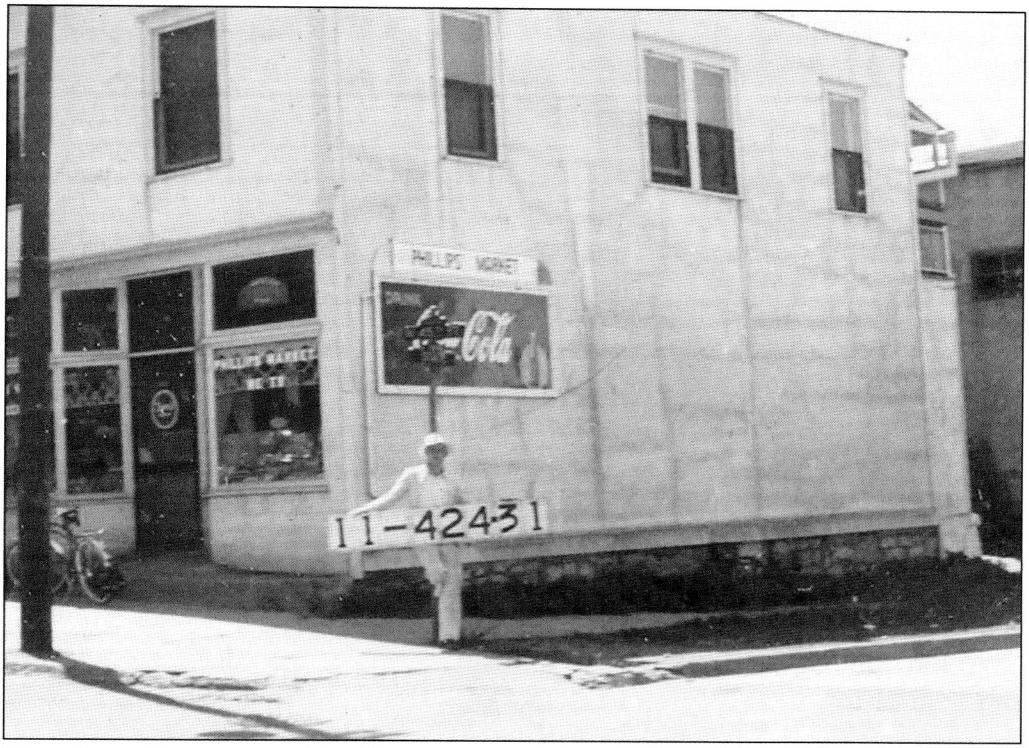

WEST PLAZA BUSINESSES, 1940. The area around Forty-fifth Street, today a popular antiques district, served as a neighborhood shopping area. It had a drugstore, a butcher, a bakery, and Phillip's Market (shown) at 1813 West Forty-fifth Street. (Courtesy of MVSC-KCPL.)

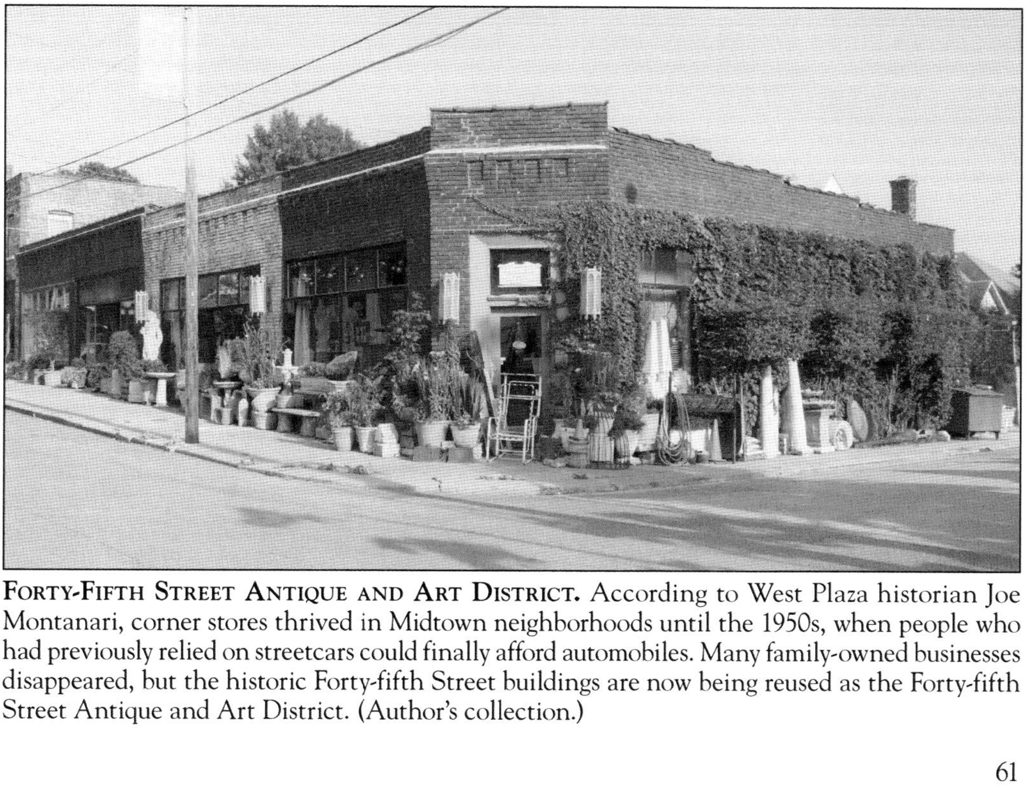

FORTY-FIFTH STREET ANTIQUE AND ART DISTRICT. According to West Plaza historian Joe Montanari, corner stores thrived in Midtown neighborhoods until the 1950s, when people who had previously relied on streetcars could finally afford automobiles. Many family-owned businesses disappeared, but the historic Forty-fifth Street buildings are now being reused as the Forty-fifth Street Antique and Art District. (Author's collection.)

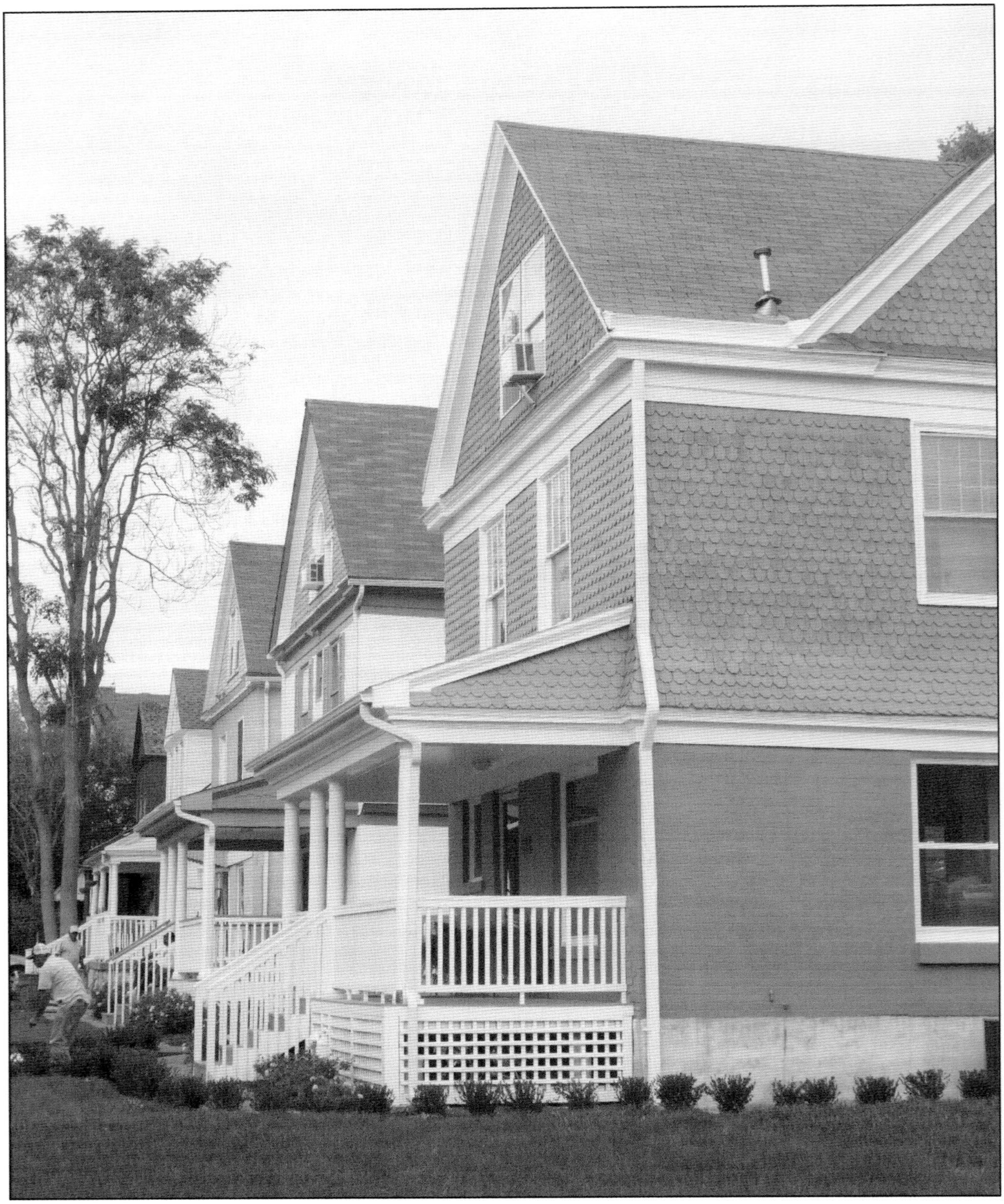

HEART OF WESTPORT. Visitors and residents of Kansas City know Westport as a major entertainment area, full of restaurants, watering holes, and shops. But Westport also has a thriving neighborhood tucked in between Broadway Boulevard and Main Street on either side of Westport Road. The Kearney-Harris Home once occupied the corner of Westport Road and Main Street, along with important institutions such as churches and the first library in Kansas City. As Westport developed, before it was annexed into Kansas City, Westport Road was its main street, and it has continued to be a major business area for local residents. Around the turn of the 20th century, blocks of small homes filled in the streets between Westport's major thoroughfares, creating what is today the Heart of Westport neighborhood. The neighborhood enjoys easy access to Main Street, Broadway Boulevard, Westport Road, and Thirty-ninth Street, making it one of the most walkable neighborhoods in the city. (Author's collection.)

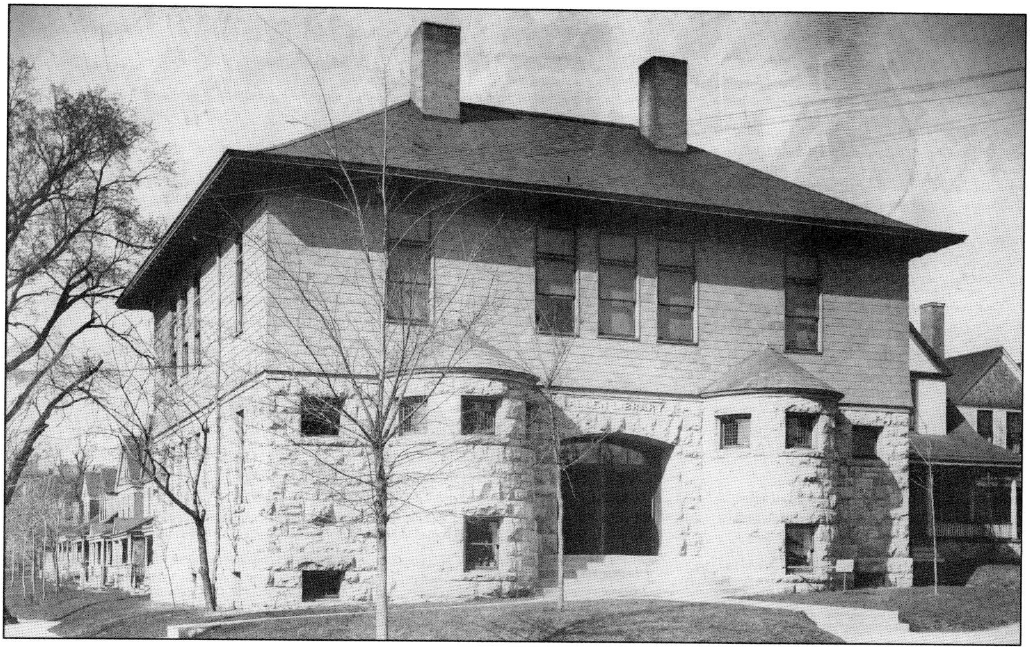

ALLEN LIBRARY. The Heart of Westport is home to the first branch of the Kansas City Public Library System. The Allen Library, built in 1898 by the Westport School Board before Westport was annexed by Kansas City, still bears the name of Arthur M. Allen, a school board member who was instrumental in its founding. Electric lights replaced interior gas lights in 1912. Behind the library in the above photograph, Heart of Westport homes stretch down Wyandotte Street north of Westport Road. Below, a 1940 tax photograph shows a Heart of Westport home. (Both, courtesy of MVSC-KCPL.)

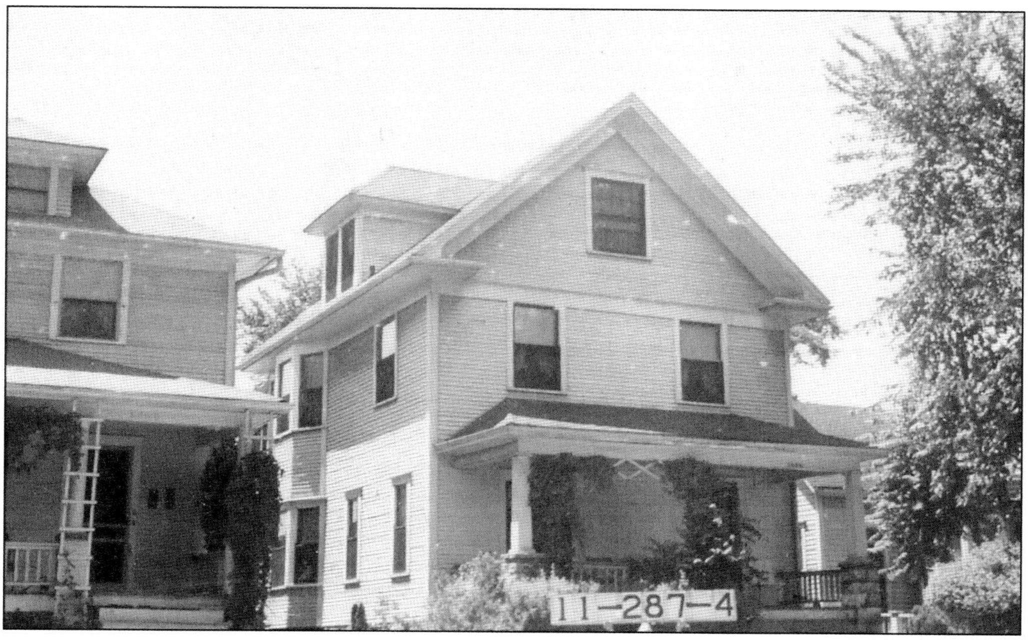

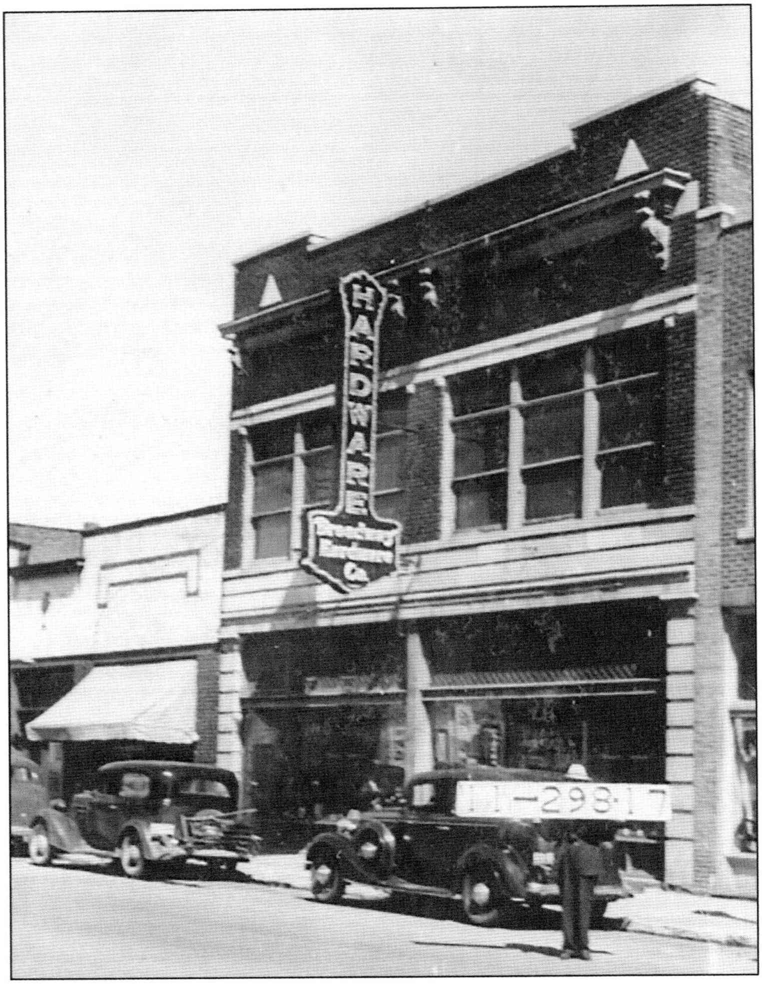

Heart of Westport Businesses, 1940. Westport Road remained an important shopping area for the Heart of Westport neighborhood in the 1940s. The street between Main Street and Broadway Boulevard housed several automobile-related businesses, garages, and gas stations. The Broadway Hardware Company (left) was at 311 Westport Road. The Westport Laundry Company (below) at 3954 Central Street offered hand shirt ironing. (Both, courtesy of MVSC-KCPL.)

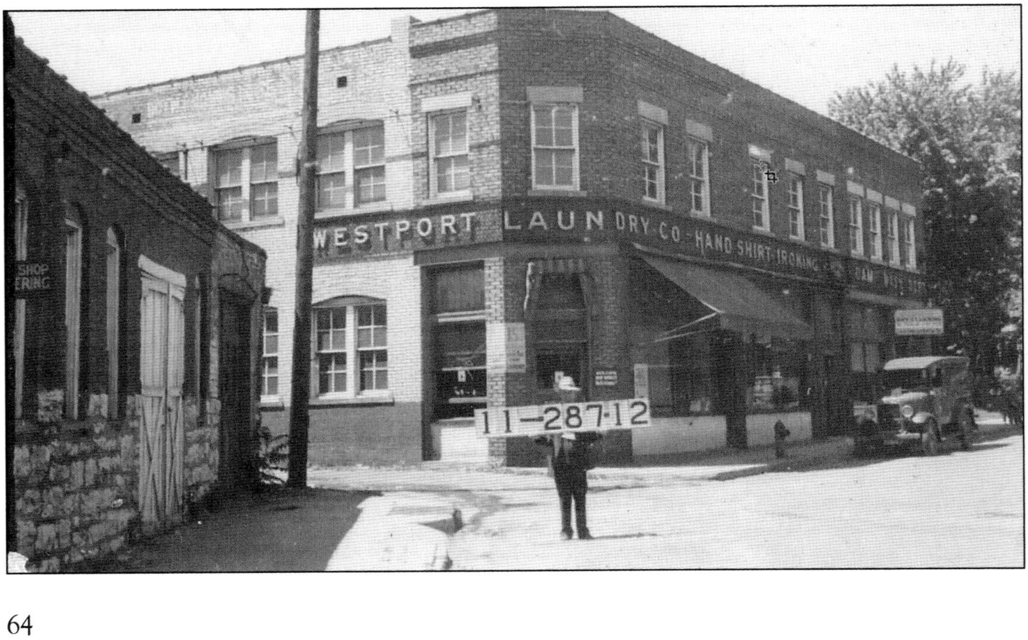

Four

Broadway Boulevard and Thirty-Ninth Street

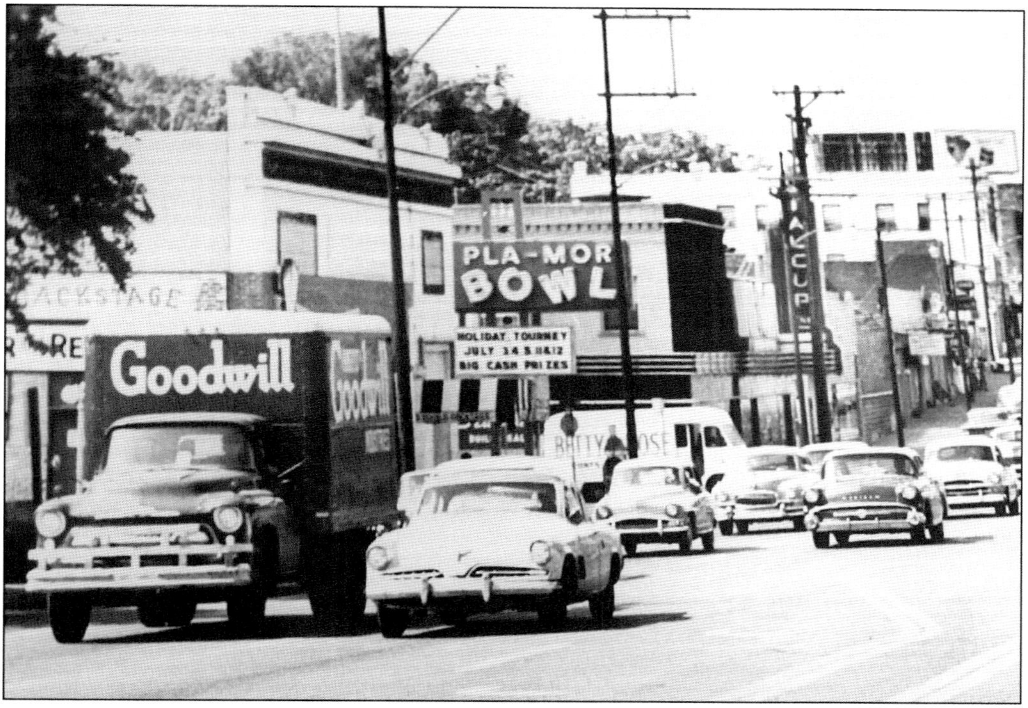

Broadway Boulevard, 1950s. Like other streets that became major commercial corridors, Broadway Boulevard started out residential. At the turn of the century, Broadway Boulevard was lined with large homes, but by the 1920s, the value of frontage along Broadway Boulevard had grown enough to encourage their replacement with businesses serving the south side. By the 1920s, Broadway Boulevard had become a major business corridor between the downtown Central Business District and the Midtown neighborhoods. It is also a major bus and automobile route, and its business owners today are working together today to improve the area. Thirty-ninth Street, with its more intimate streetscape, has been home to a wide range of neighborhood services. Currently, Thirty-ninth Street is a thriving entertainment district and home to restaurants and unique shops. (Courtesy of Wilburn and Associates.)

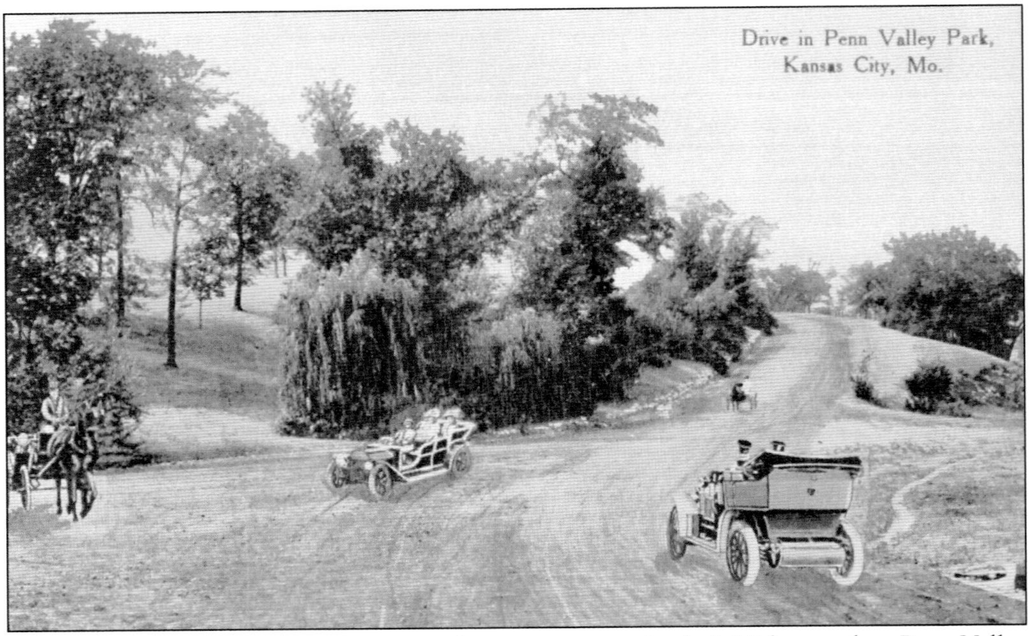

PENN VALLEY PARK. Big changes came to the western part of today's Midtown when Penn Valley Park was developed beginning in 1904. Before the area was a park, the Penn Valley ravine was "scarred by cheap houses and stores," according to William Wilson in *The City Beautiful Movement*. The new park replaced those blighted buildings and became a major focus of the evolving park-and-boulevard system that defined the growth of Kansas City. (Courtesy of *Midtown KC Post*.)

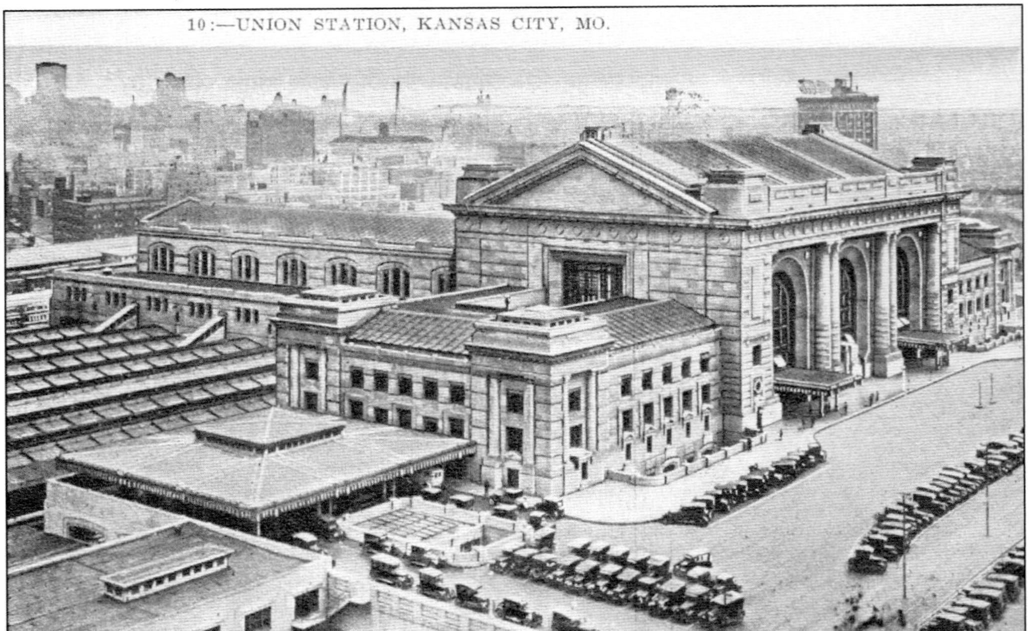

UNION STATION. The western side of Midtown got another boost in 1906, when voters approved the construction of a new Union Station at the intersection of Twenty-fourth and Main Streets. Before the new station was built, the area was a wasteland, but the facility offered the movement to the south a real shot in the arm. (Courtesy of *Midtown KC Post*.)

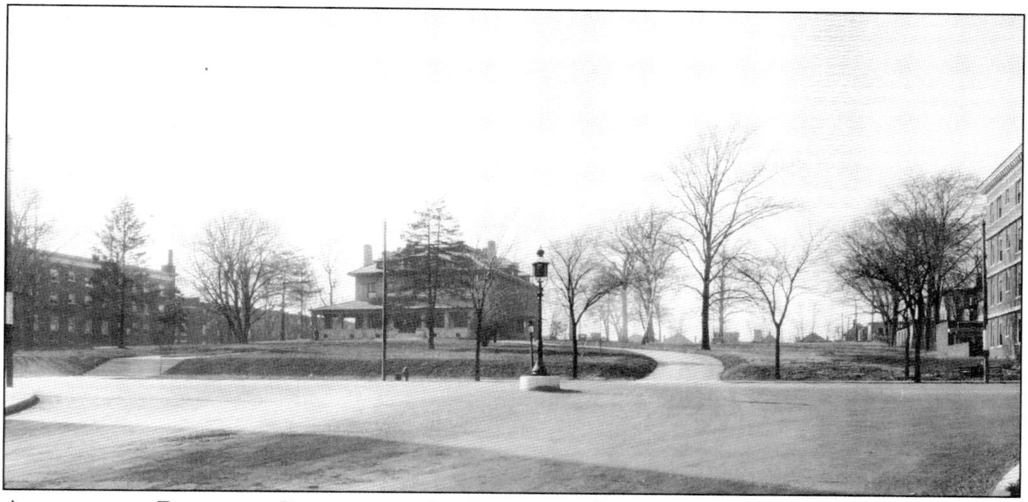

Armour and Broadway Boulevards. In the 1890s, when Thirty-first Street was the southern boundary of Kansas City, Broadway Boulevard was dotted with the estates of wealthy businessmen and prominent families. The A.B.H. McGee mansion stood at 3736 Broadway Boulevard until 1917. A large stone house built by George Jones (above) stood near Broadway and Armour Boulevards until 1922. That year, however, things were changing quickly on Broadway Boulevard. Reporting that the Kansas City Life Insurance Company was buying the old Jones estate for its new headquarters, the *Kansas City Star* said the company was persuaded by the "sunshine and open air" to leave downtown. It noted as well that Broadway Boulevard, along with other major streets, "has taken on a new importance as a suburban business thoroughfare." By the 1950s, the iconic stone lions proudly welcomed visitors to the Kansas City Life Insurance Company headquarters. (Above, courtesy of MVSC-KCPL; below, courtesy of Harold and Joie Tenenbaum.)

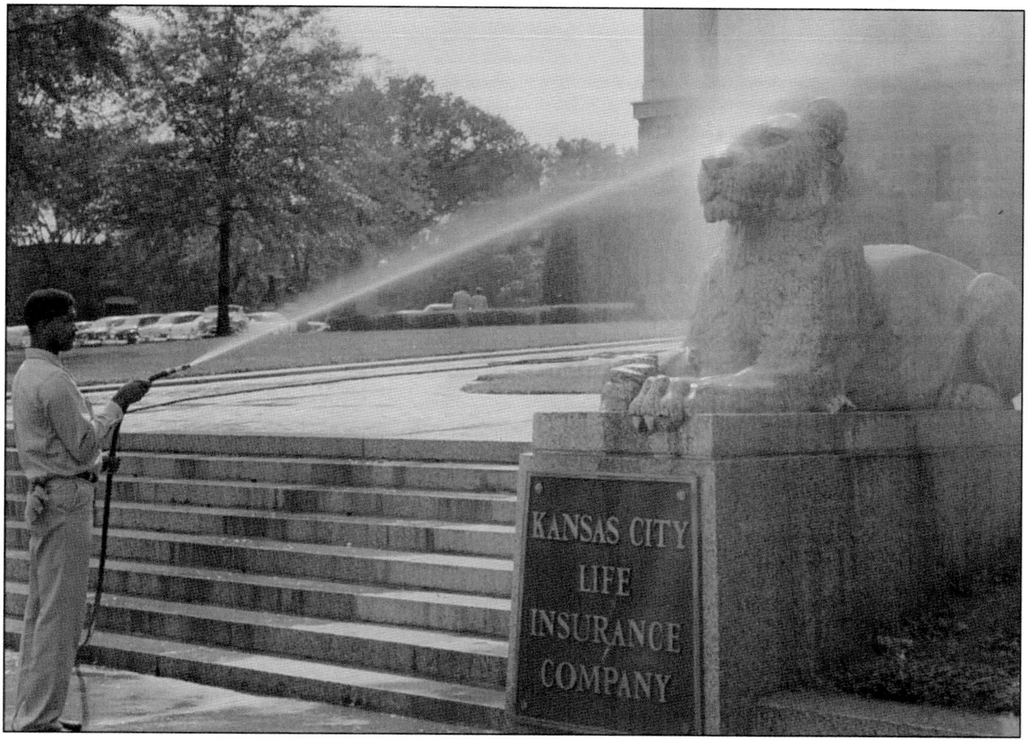

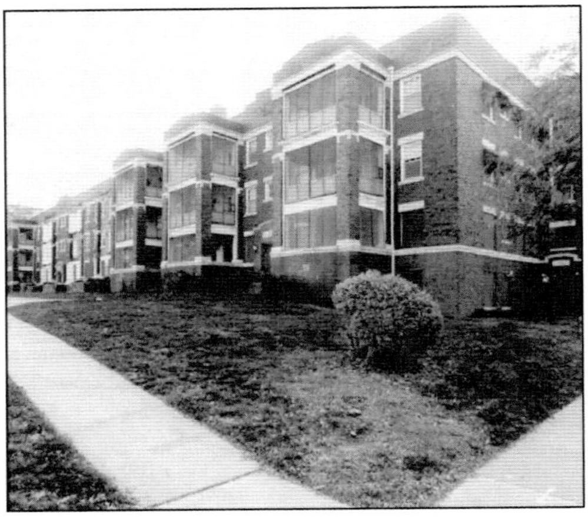

Knickerbocker Apartments. Broadway Boulevard also became home to luxury residential hotels, including the Knickerbocker, built between 1909 and 1910. The developers promised the "Uptown District" was surrounded by homes "of the better type" and close to cafés, a large theater, and first-class shops. The twin buildings on either side of Knickerbocker Place included 21 apartments, each featuring three bedrooms, two bathrooms, a dining room, and a living room with a fireplace and built-in bookshelves. One half of the Knickerbocker was razed in 1982. (Courtesy of MVSC-KCPL.)

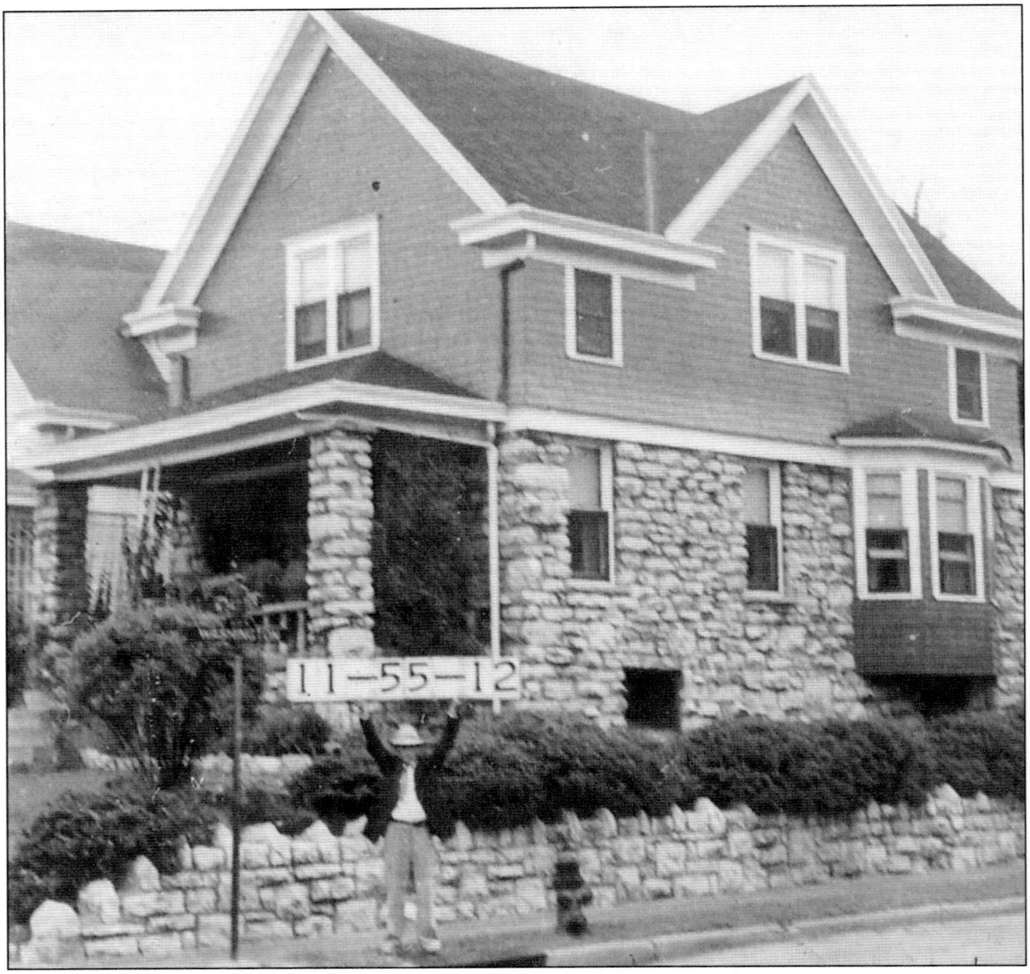

Lost Homes of Valentine. Over the years, the Valentine neighborhood lost many of its original homes as its area changed from residential to institutional use. Penn Valley Community College, built in the late 1960s, replaced some of the old homes. The Kansas City Life Insurance Company bought many Valentine homes in the 1970s and demolished some of them. (Courtesy of MVSC-KCPL.)

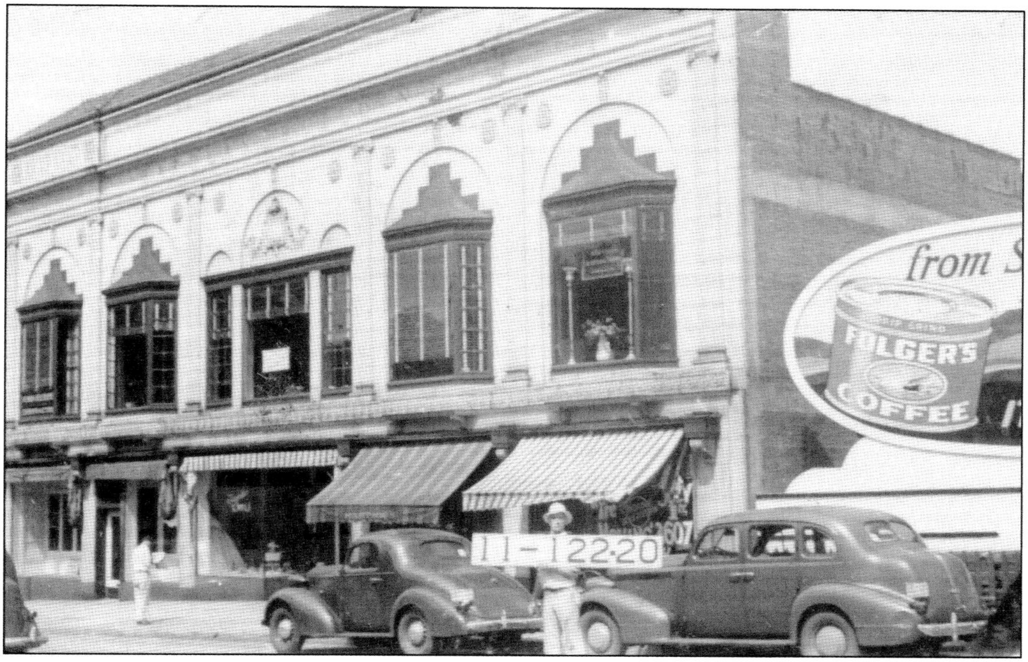

Congress Building Block, 1940. The 1920s and 1930s represented a major retail shift on Broadway Boulevard, as well as on Main Street and Troost Avenue. On the 3600 block of Broadway Boulevard, owners of retail businesses liked the large second-story windows that made great showcases as people passed by in their automobiles. The Garret Building (3601–3609 Broadway), the Betsy Ross Building (3611 Broadway), and the Barclay Building (3613–3625 Broadway) were all designed in the 1920s by prominent Kansas City architect Robert Gornall. (Courtesy of MVSC-KCPL.)

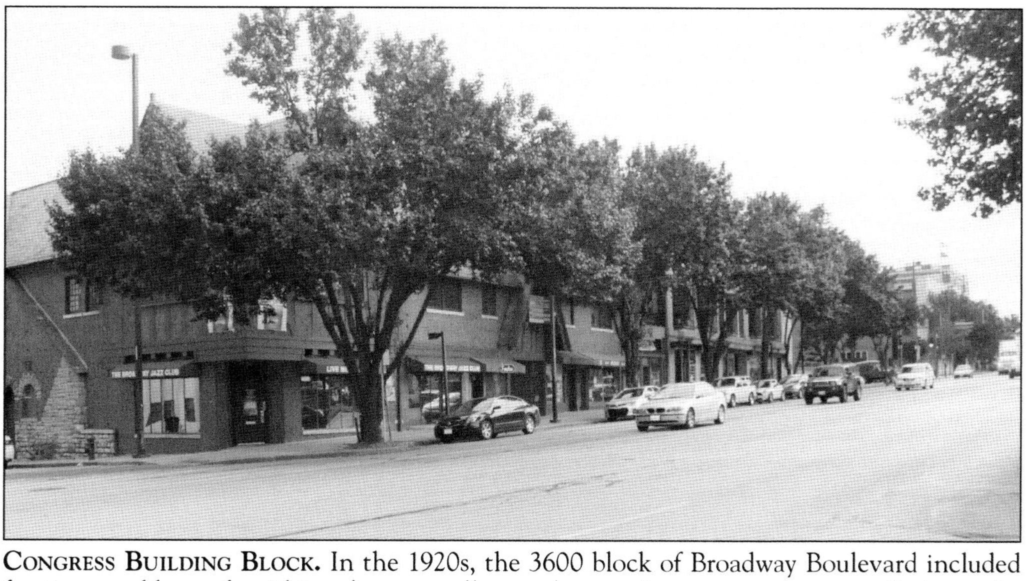

Congress Building Block. In the 1920s, the 3600 block of Broadway Boulevard included furniture and home-furnishing shops, a wallpaper shop, an insurance company, a florist, and a bank. Although they have been put to new uses, the buildings have not changed much since they were constructed. (Author's collection.)

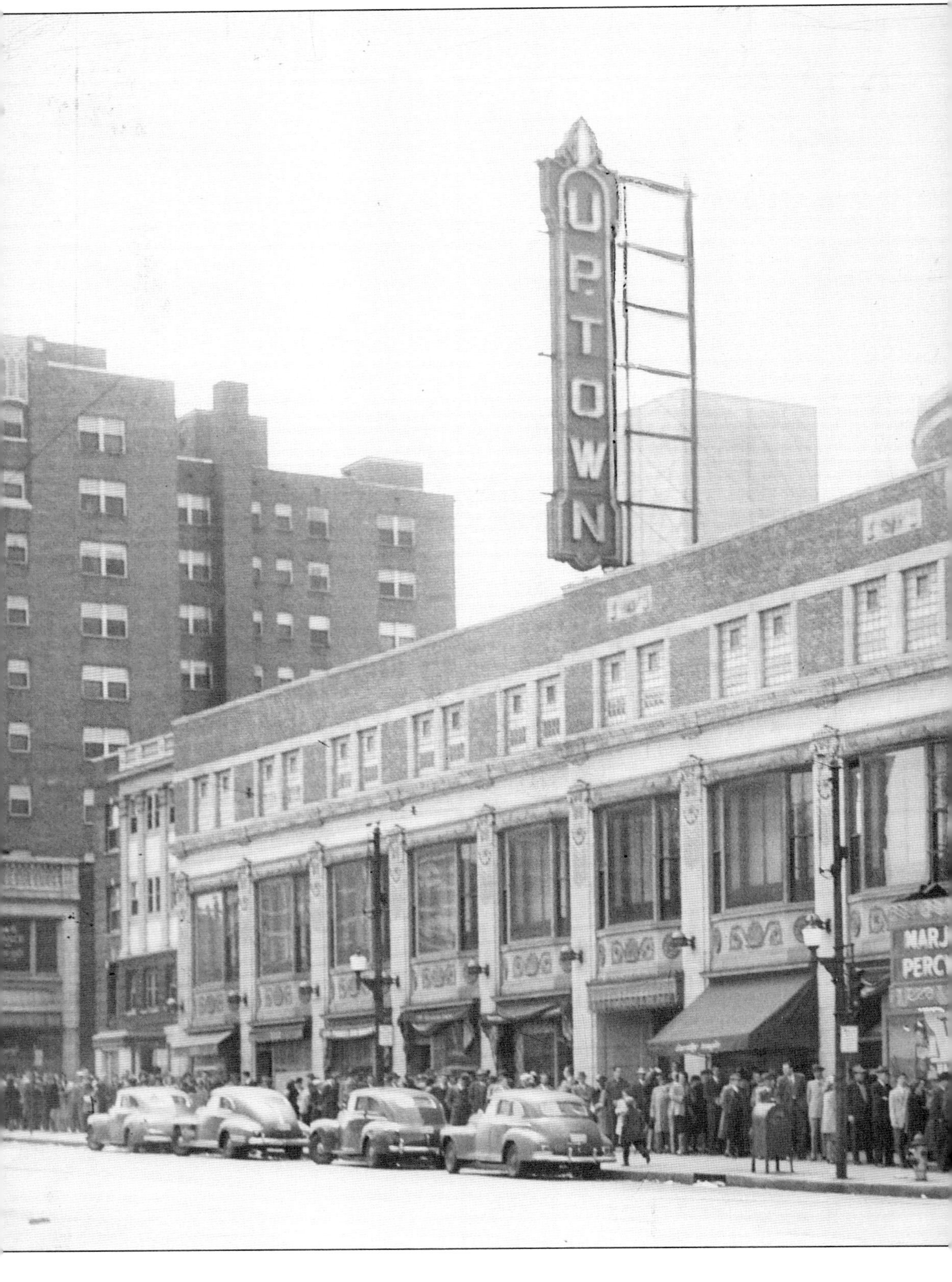
UPTOWN
MARJ
PERCY

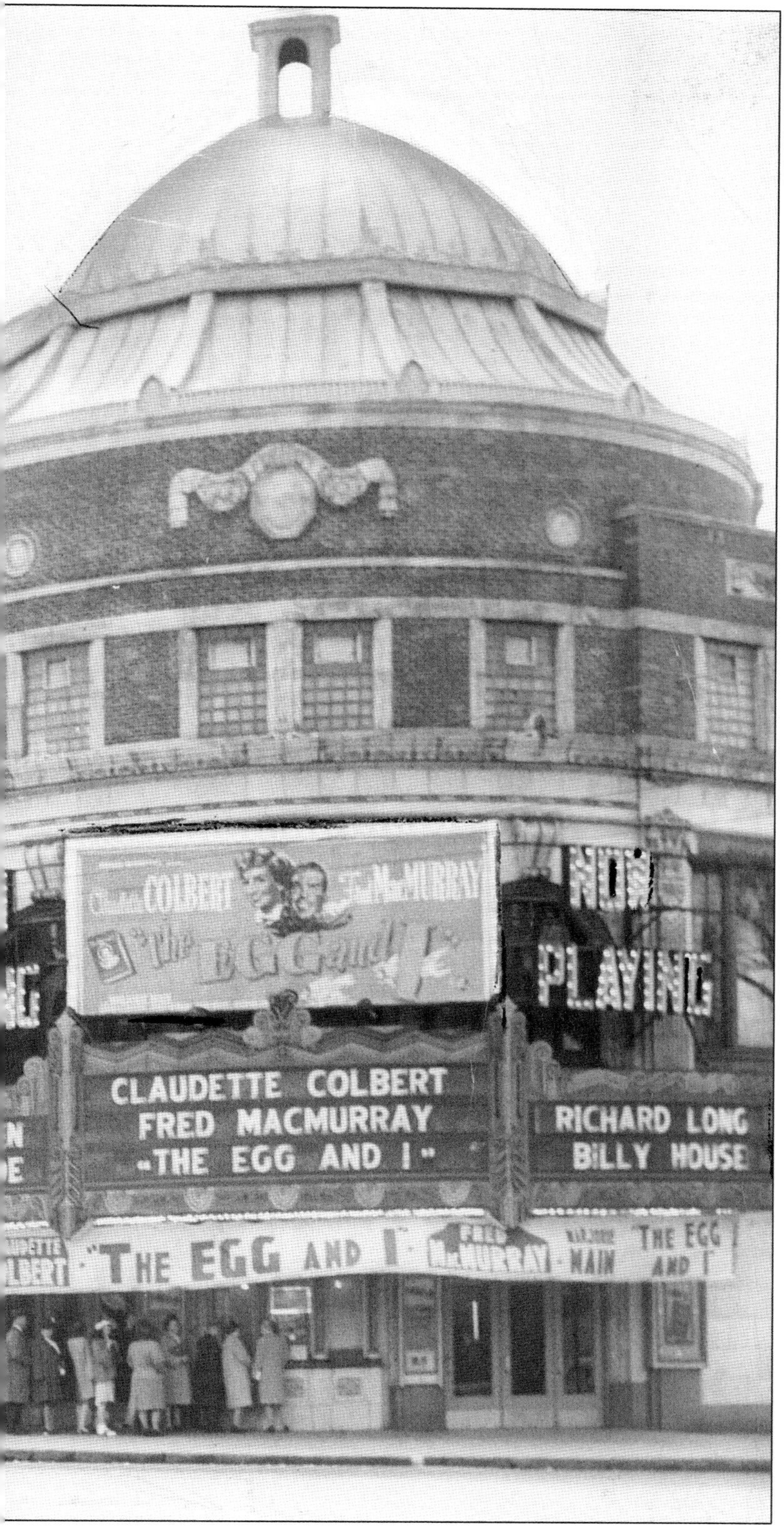

UPTOWN THEATER. This venue opened its doors at Thirty-sixth Street and Broadway Boulevard in 1928 to a full house of 2,300 patrons. The Uptown was an "atmospheric theater" created by designer John Eberson to make movie viewers feel like they were in a Mediterranean courtyard, "under a nighttime sky ceiling with twinkling stars, clouds, and mechanical flying birds," according to the Uptown's website. In 1939, the theater added a "FragraTone" experience, piping in aromas to match the entertainment. When patrons stopped relying so much on streetcars and began going to the theater in cars, the Uptown employed uniformed footmen to escort people across the street from the parking lot. Bob Hope, then an unknown performer, took the stage at the Uptown in 1928 and was followed by a host of stars, including Will Rogers, Claudette Colbert, and Shirley Temple. The theater closed in 1989, but it reopened in 1994 as a concert venue. (Courtesy of UMKC–LaBudde.)

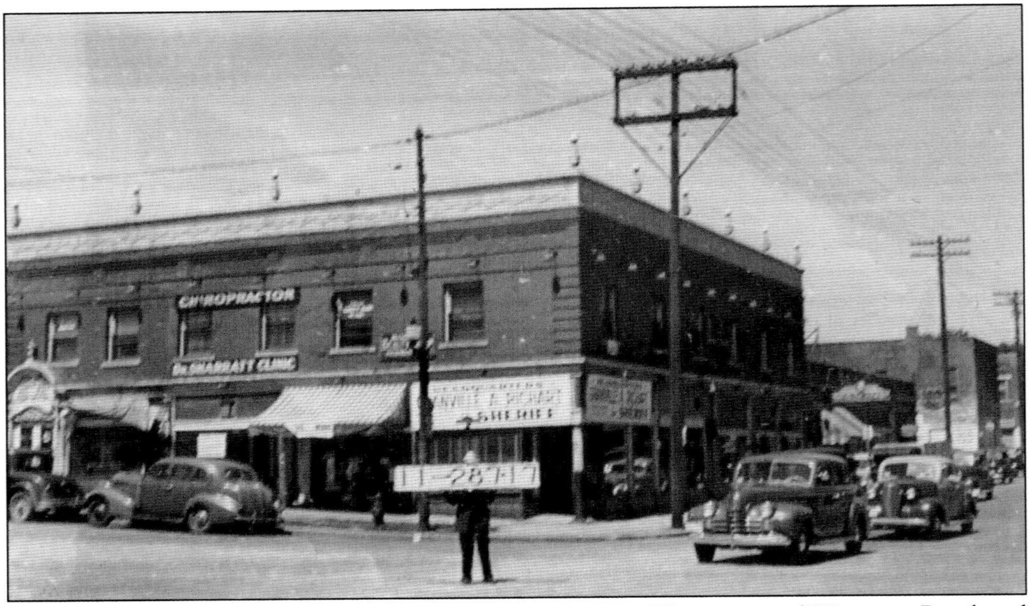

Broadway Boulevard Businesses in Westport, 1940. The corner of Westport Road and Broadway Boulevard is an important Midtown crossroads and has always attracted businesses, from the early days of Westport until today. The northeast corner (above) has been home to two different restaurants called simply The Corner, a tribute to the value of the intersection. The Westport Avenue Bank (below) stood on the southeast corner in 1940, and the building is a bank today as well. (Both, courtesy of MVSC-KCPL.)

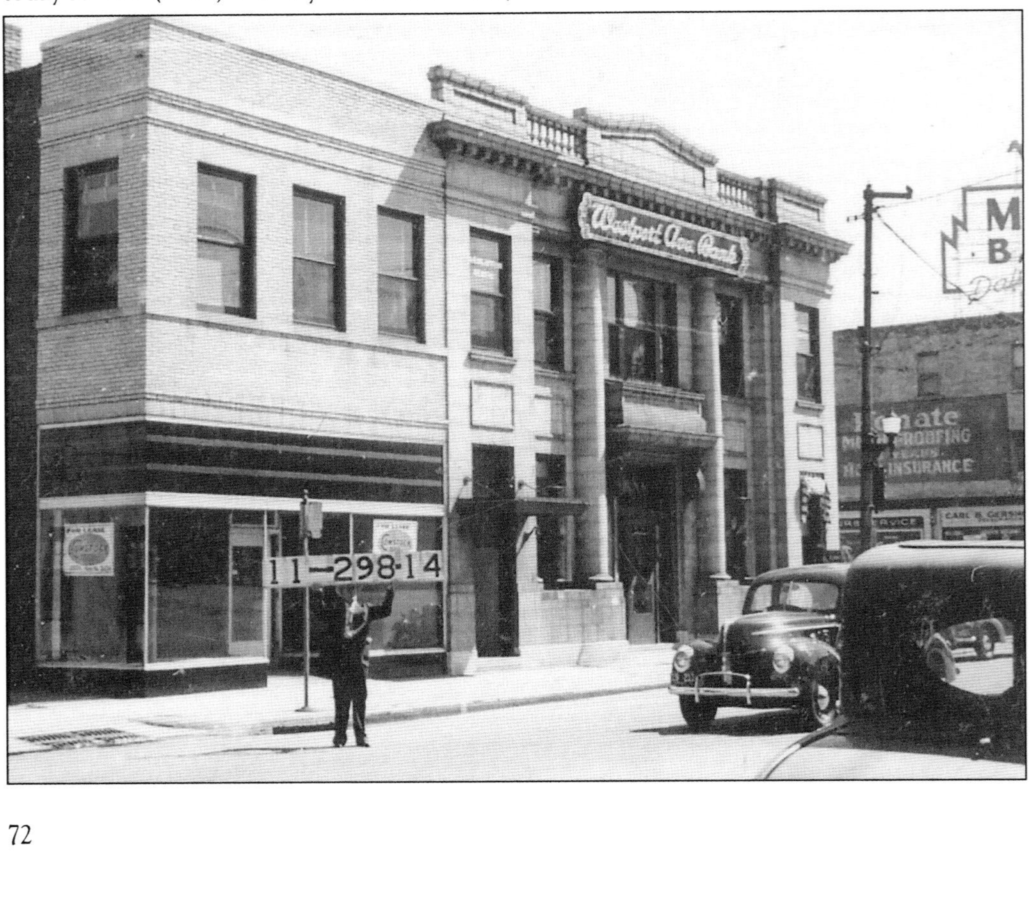

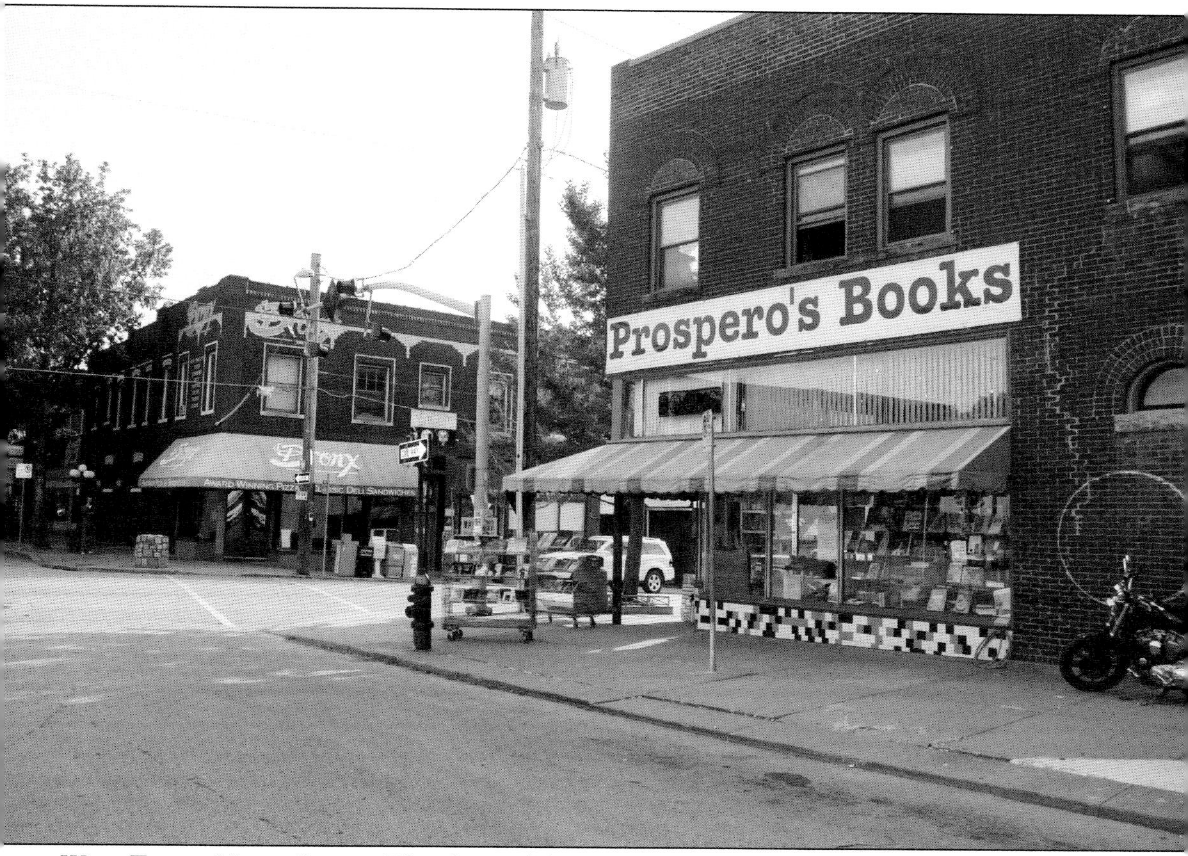

West Thirty-Ninth Street. This thoroughfare, especially the westernmost section near State Line Road, grew along with the developing Midtown neighborhoods around it to become a major local commercial center. From the turn of the century, the blocks of Thirty-ninth Street filled in with solid rows of small shops and storefronts. At the turn of the century and through the 1920s, residents could hop off the streetcar or the bus along Thirty-ninth Street and find just about anything they needed. In the 1940s, Volker residents had grocery stores, beauty shops and barbershops, and hardware stores in their neighborhood. The street also had a meat and sausage factory, a liquor store, and a produce stand. Today, the historic brick buildings along West Thirty-ninth Street have been put to modern use as bookstores, coffee shops, and restaurants, but the streetscape on some blocks remains much the same. (Author's collection.)

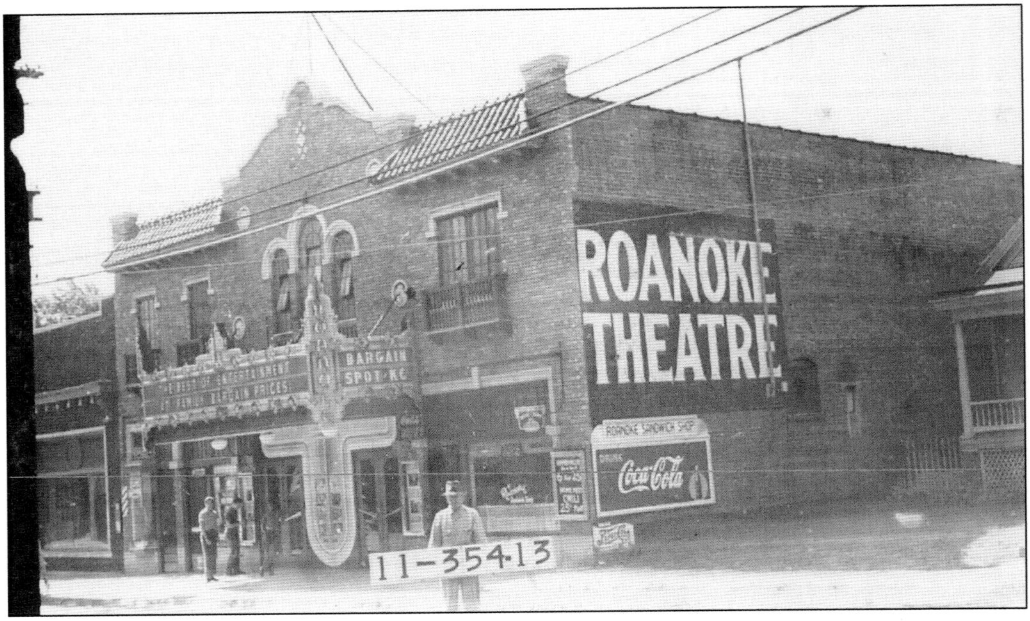

ROANOKE THEATER AND JOHNSON'S HARDWARE, 1940. The residential density around Thirty-ninth Street allowed the area to support a local movie theater, the Roanoke (above), which offered entertainment, as its marquee read, "at family bargain prices." Neighborhood theaters did not show first-run pictures, but they made up for it by changing movies several times a week so people could go back again and again. Next door to the theater was the Roanoke Sandwich Shop. At Thirty-ninth and Bell Streets, Johnson Hardware (below) stood beside the Rainbow Grocery Store, one of two markets on the block. (Both, courtesy of MVSC-KCPL.)

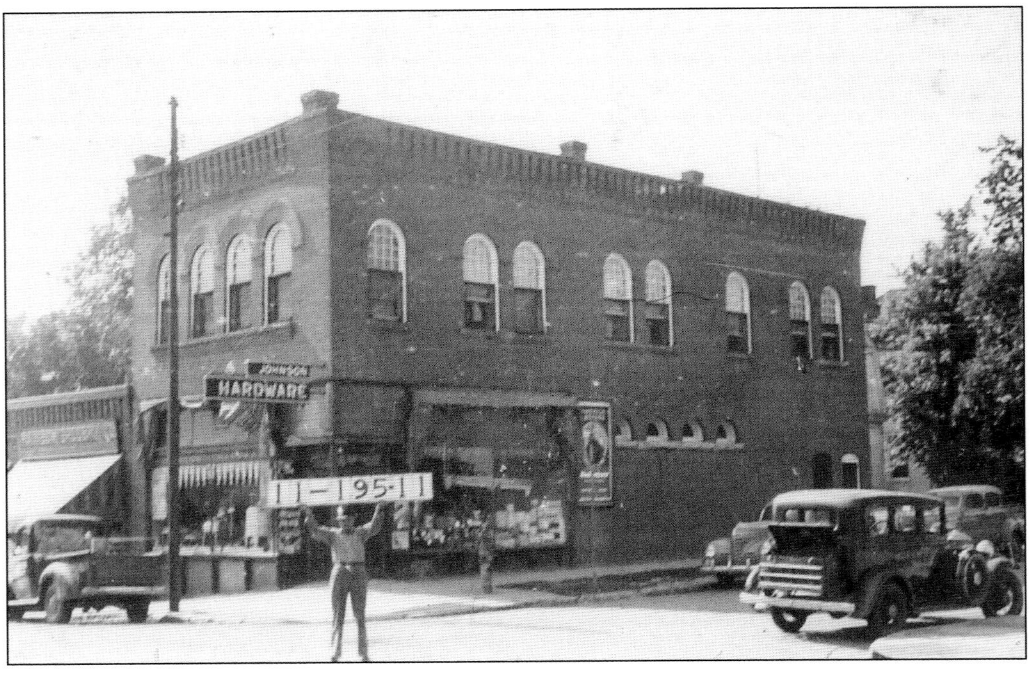

Five

Neighborhoods between Troost and the Paseo

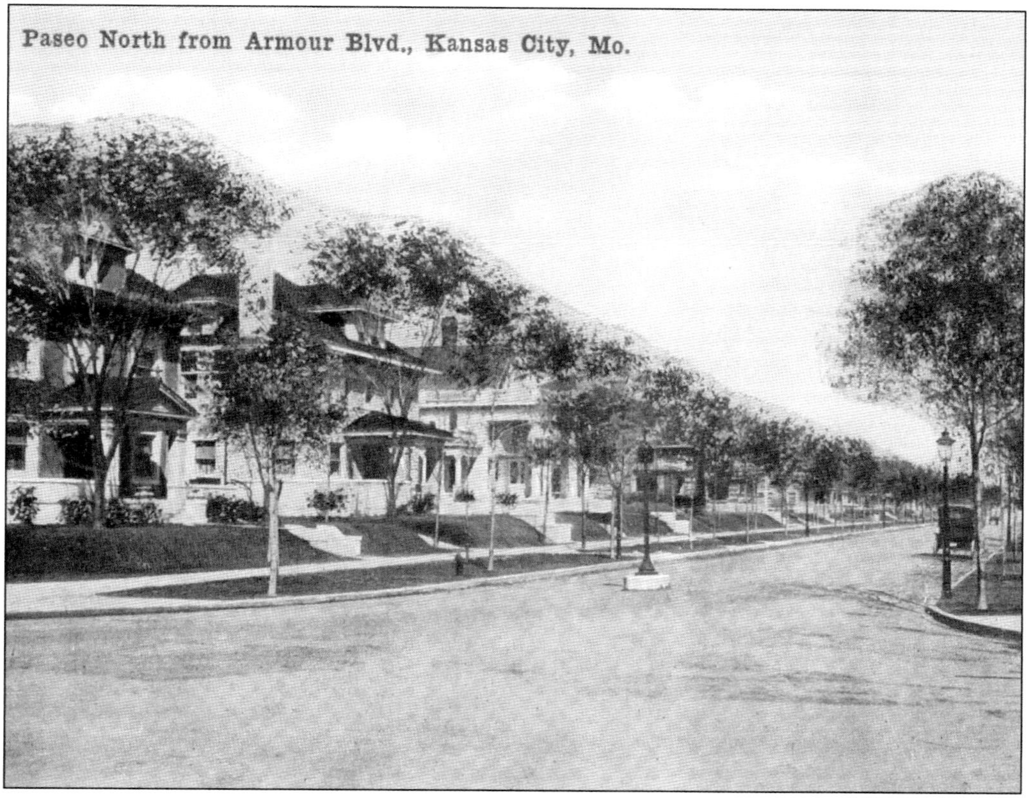

Paseo, 1910. The Midtown neighborhoods of Center City, Squier Park, and Manheim Park developed between two important streets: Troost Avenue, upon which ran the most active streetcar line in the city, and the Paseo, once the most spectacular of the boulevards in Kansas City's park-and-boulevard system. Both helped to shape these neighborhoods into a unique part of Midtown. (Author's collection.)

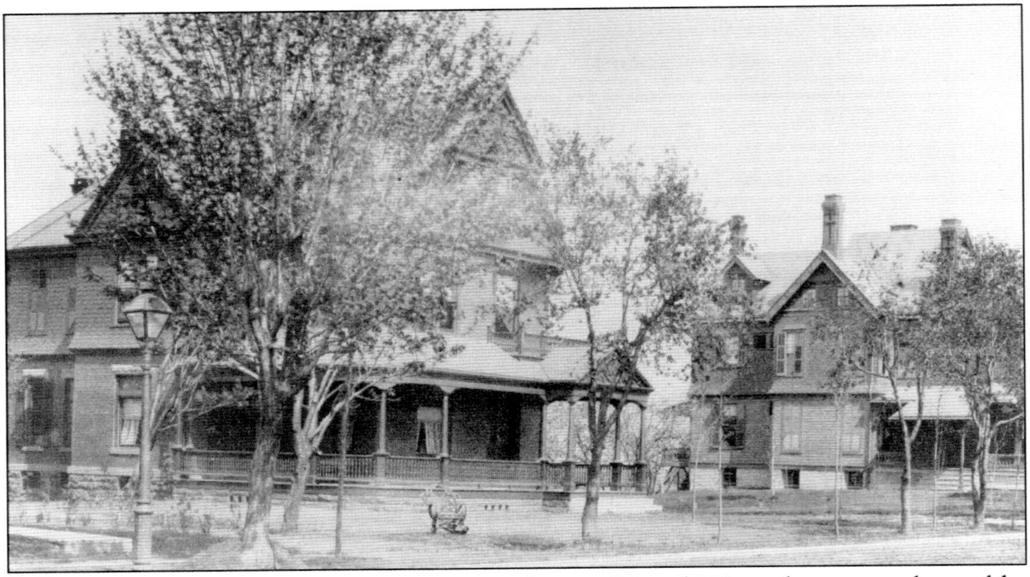

Troost Avenue Residences, 1880s. The first folks to call "south" Troost home were the wealthy businessmen who moved south in the 1880s. The area just south of Thirty-first Street and Troost Avenue was developed as a plantation by Rev. James Porter, a Methodist minister who owned 365 acres. Porter kept slaves who cared for his livestock and worked in his orchards. He died in 1851, but his land was not subdivided until 1880. Once Kansas City's richest men began to build in the area, it quickly filled with mansions. The residences of A.J. King and Henry Rickar, both in the real estate business, stood on the 3100 block by 1890 (above). The George Winter home at 3000 Troost Avenue (below) became the Horner Institute of Fine Arts in 1920. By 1938, however, it had been razed to make room for commerce. (Both, courtesy of MVSC-KCPL.)

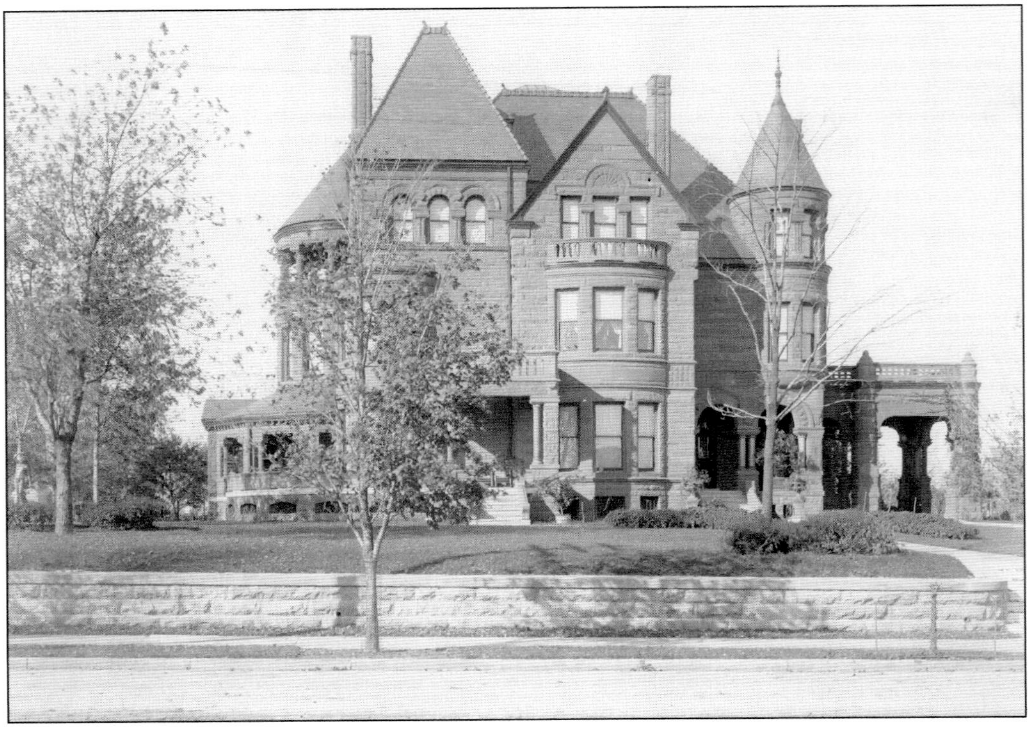

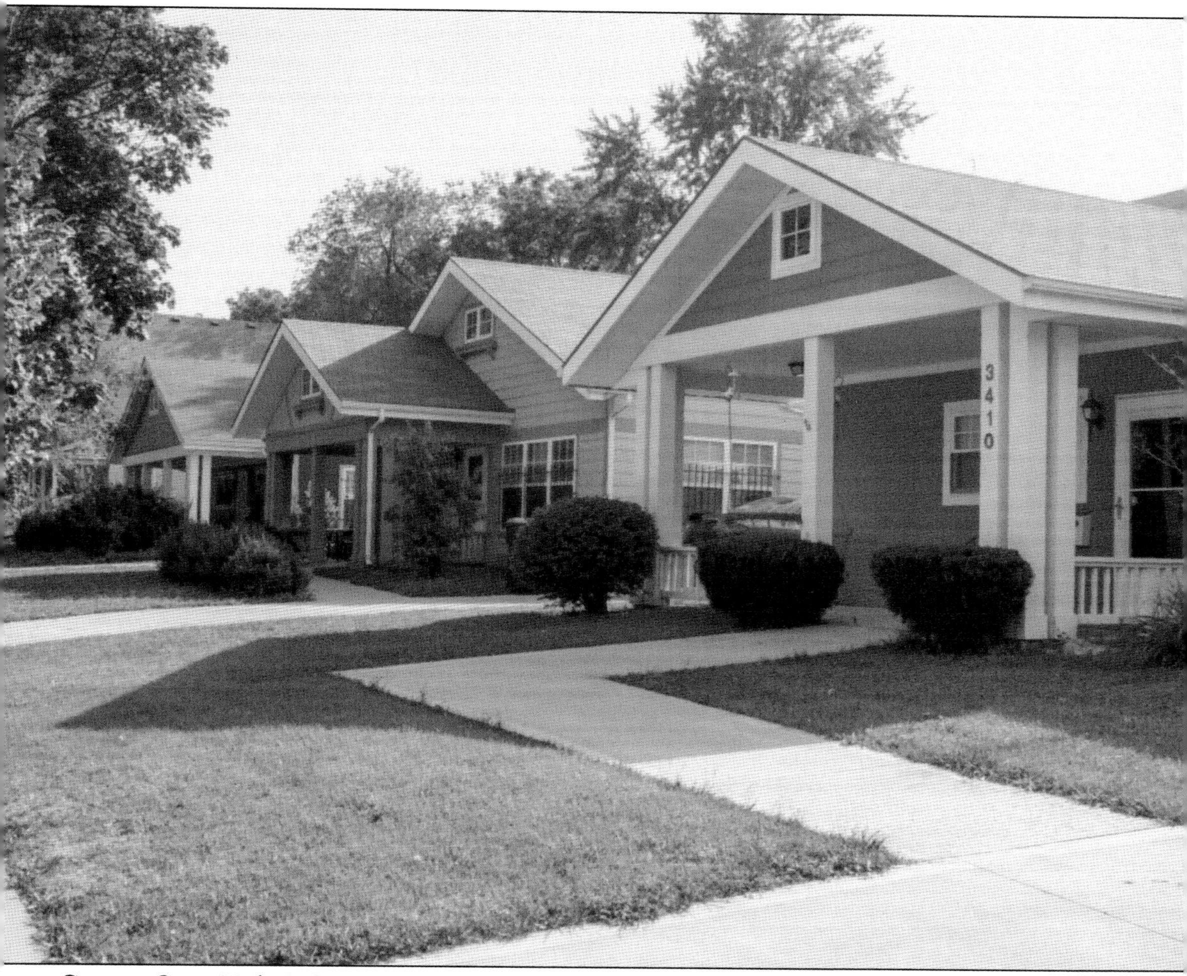

Center City. Today's Center City neighborhood is bounded by Troost Avenue and the Paseo and from Linwood Boulevard to Armour Boulevard. Although many of the large mansions that once stood in the area are long gone, the more humble homes of middle- and working-class folks who followed them to the area still exist. Center City stands in a strategic location that made it attractive in the early 20th century to several religious and civic organizations. These groups wanted to locate near their members as residents moved out of downtown. Although several of these organizations have moved on to other neighborhoods, they left behind temples and other buildings that are still part of the Center City landscape. Today's Center City has a neighborhood association, and its diverse residents are restoring single-family homes and reclaiming vacant lots. (Author's collection.)

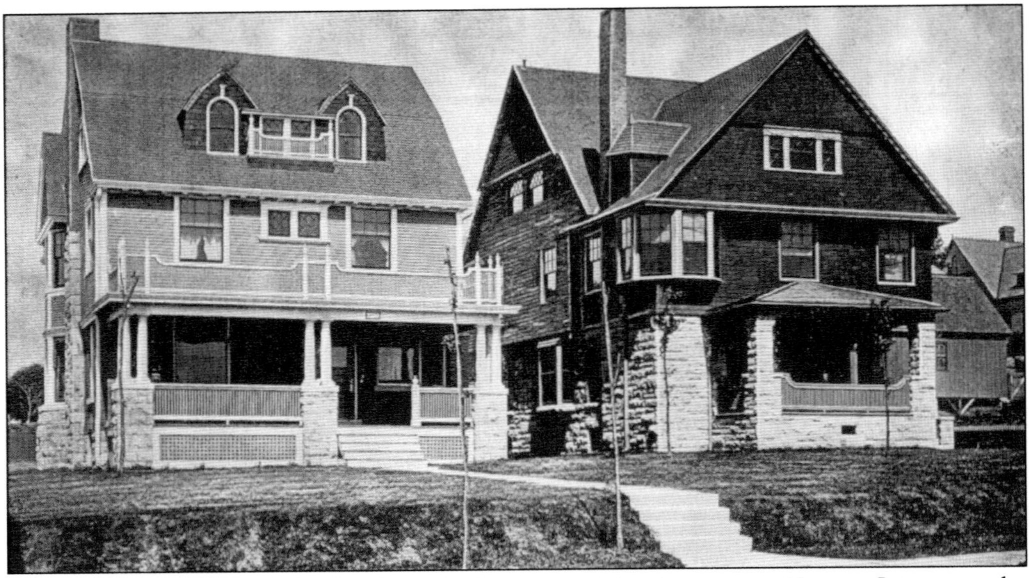

Center City, Early 1900s. In the typical pattern of development in Kansas City, once the upper crust staked out an area such as Thirty-first Street and Troost Avenue, the middle class followed. In the early 20th century, developers were building homes for these eager new residents, such as those shown above, built by the Cowherd Brother Company at Thirty-third Street and Troost Avenue. These houses are no longer standing. In 1900, a popular publication showcasing Kansas City homes included the O.D. Woodward residence (below) at 3324 Troost Avenue. (Both, courtesy of MVSC-KCPL.)

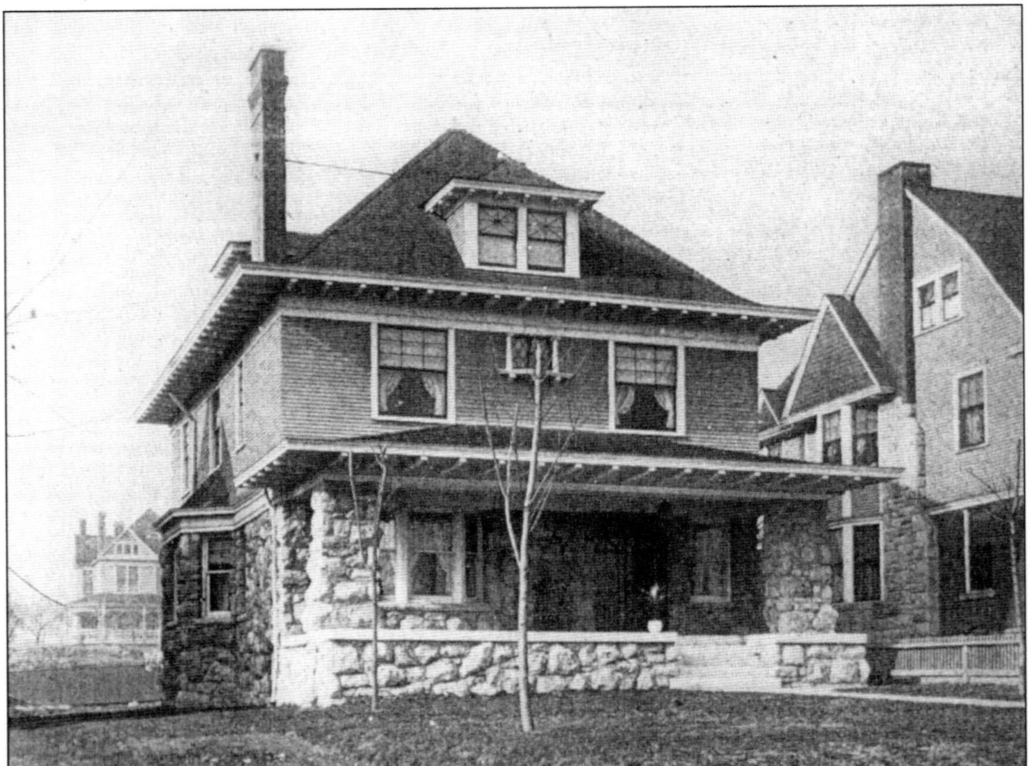

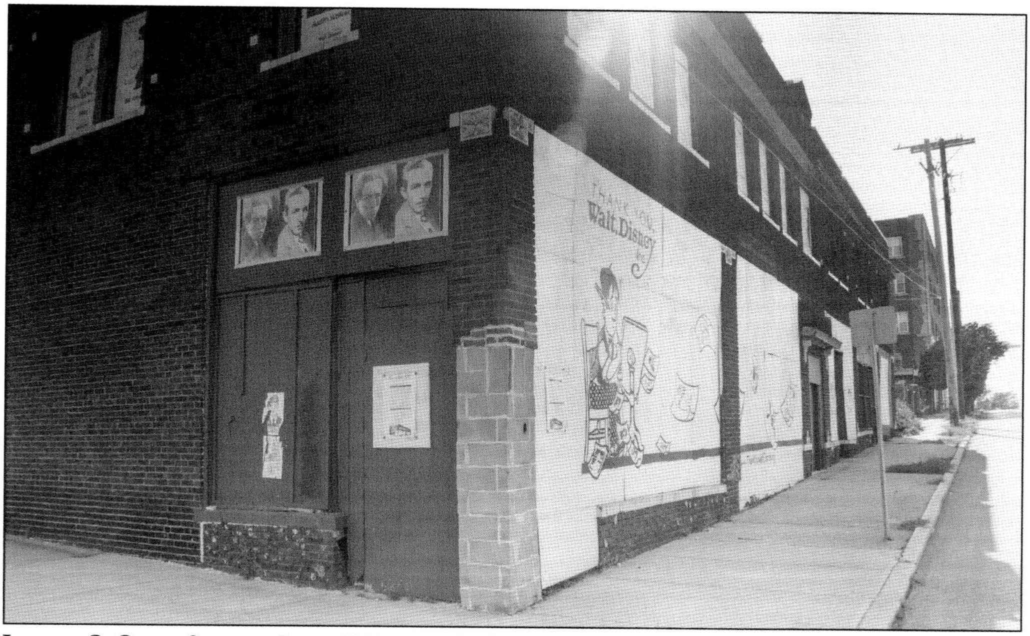

Laugh-O-Gram Studio. From 1921 to 1923, the Laugh-O-Gram Studio at Thirty-first Street and Forest Avenue housed the offices of Walt Disney's first animation company. Disney reportedly lived in his office and bathed at Union Station. Disney later said that a tame mouse at Laugh-O-Gram gave him the idea for Mickey Mouse. (Author's collection.)

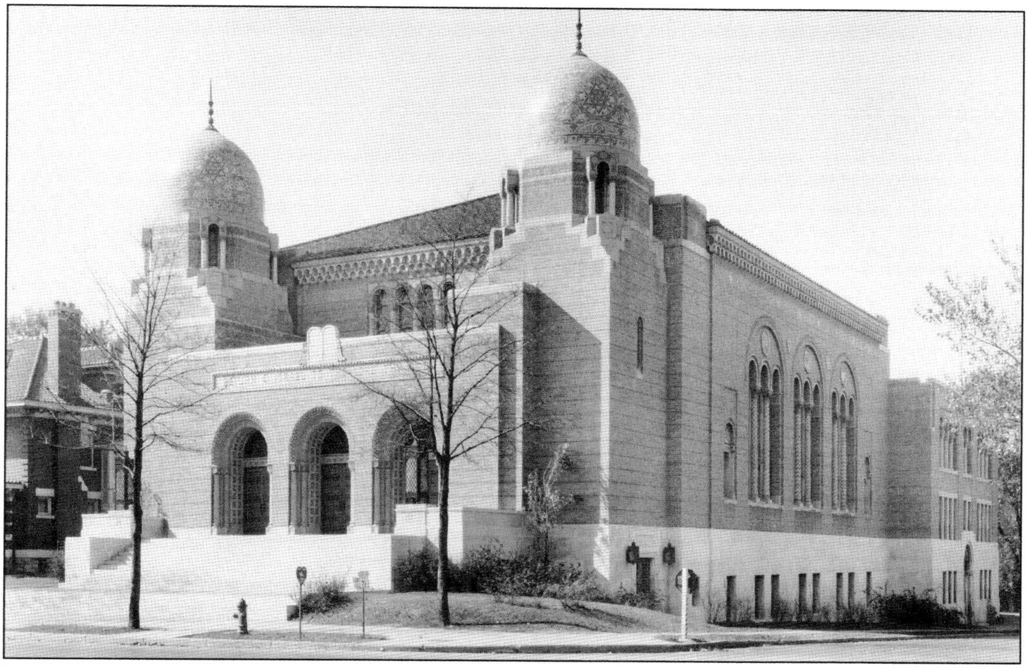

Beth Shalom Building. As Jews immigrated to Kansas City in the early 1900s, many settled in and around the Center City area. Jewish synagogues and social services followed. In the 1920s, Beth Shalom, in the 3400 block of the Paseo, had a 1,500-member congregation. Another temple, B'nai Jehudah, was located on the southeast corner of Linwood Boulevard and Flora Avenue. (Courtesy of *Midtown KC Post.*)

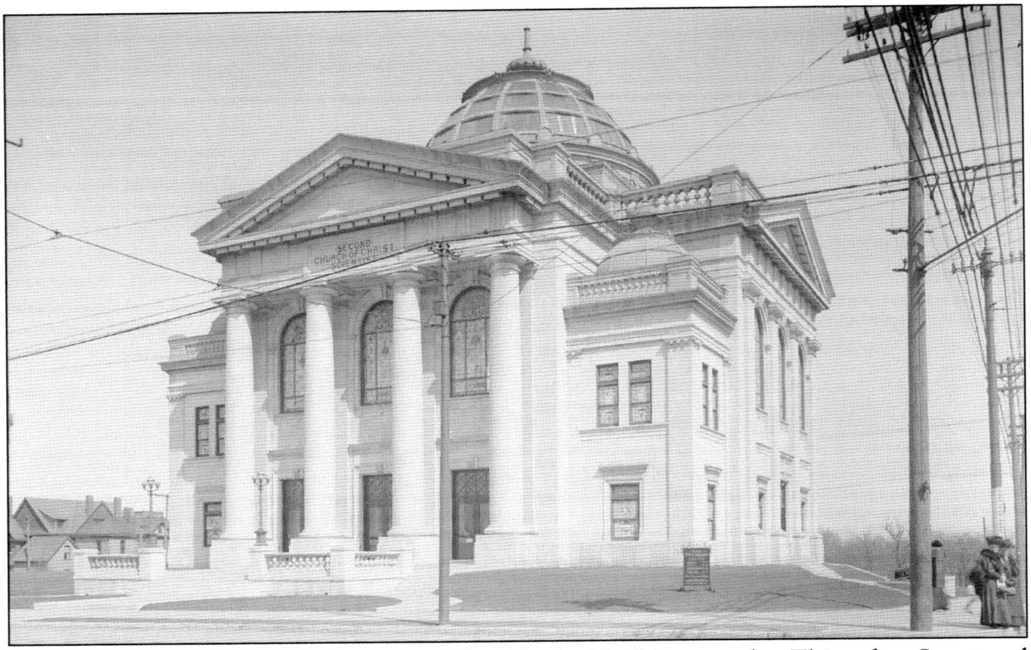

Second Church of Christ, Scientist. This Classical building stood at Thirty-first Street and Troost Avenue. The Christian Science movement had grown from 100 churches in 1894 to nearly 1,000 in 1904. The church featured colored art glass illuminated by electric lights. It was built in 1902 and was demolished in 1955. (Courtesy of the Library of Congress.)

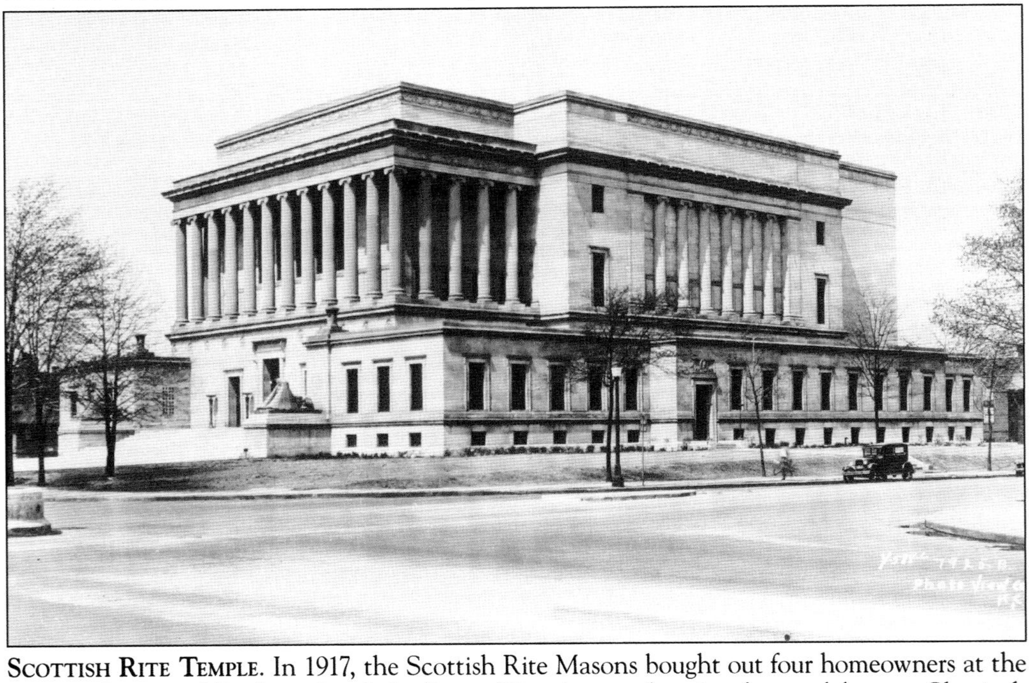

Scottish Rite Temple. In 1917, the Scottish Rite Masons bought out four homeowners at the corner of Linwood Boulevard and the Paseo. They began planning for an elaborate, Classical-themed temple, which was built at 1330 East Linwood Boulevard between 1928 and 1930. The front of the building is dominated by two large sphinxes. The building also has a marble foyer and elaborate ceilings. (Courtesy of MVSC-KCPL.)

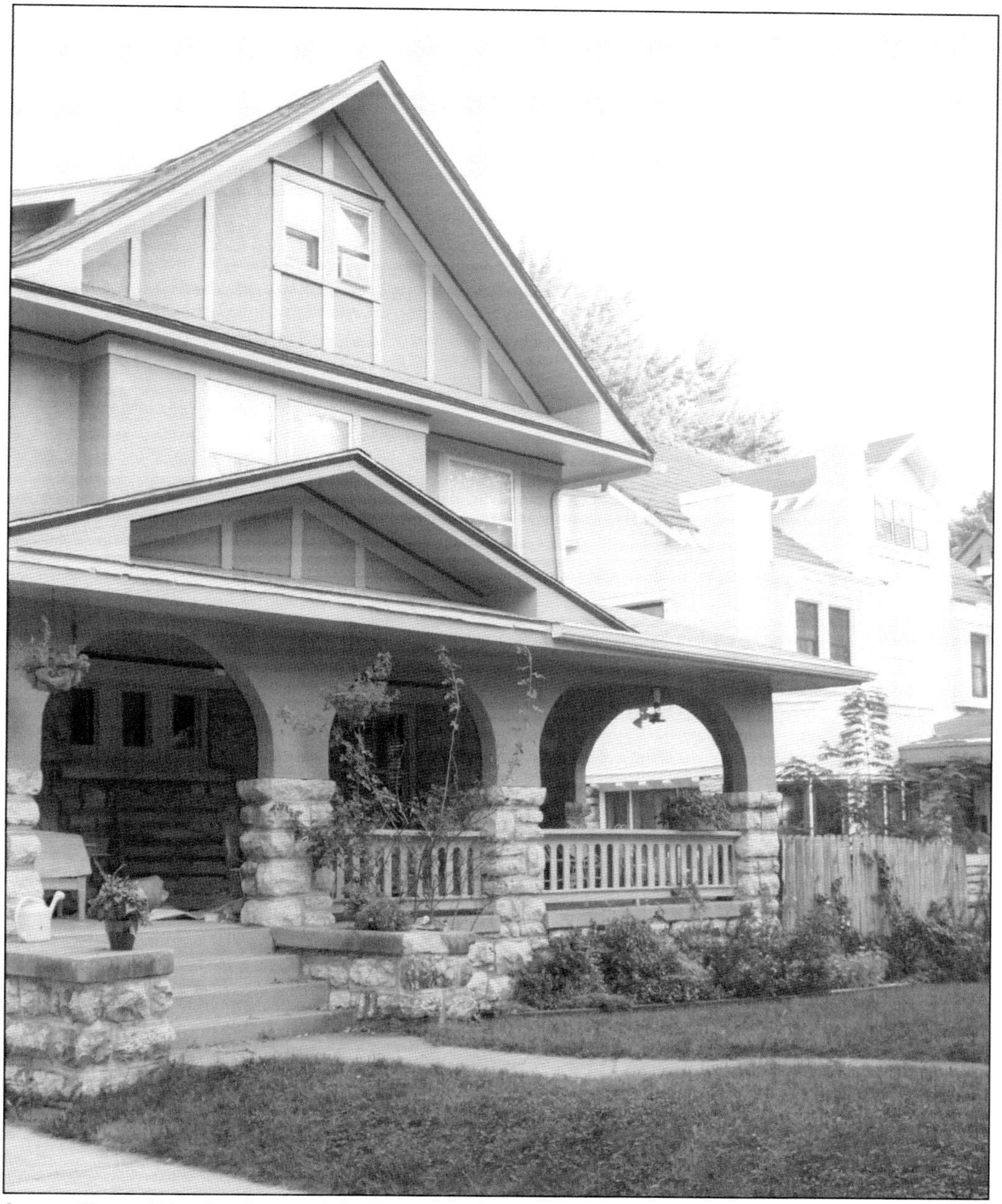

Squier Park. The developer of the Squier Park neighborhood thought upper-class people would like to live in a country manor within commuting distance of the city. That is the environment Robert Jones hoped to create as he laid out Squier Park. The land, a large tract between Thirty-sixth and Forty-first Streets, from Troost Avenue to the Paseo, had been the estate of J.J. Squier, a cattleman. His 160 acres were well known to Kansas Citians in the late 1800s; they liked to take weekend drives to visit the deer park at Squier Manor. But when Jones got the chance to design a vision, he rejected the conventional wisdom that said suburbs should be laid out on a grid. In 1909, the *Kansas City Star* called Jones "the man who dared to make a crooked road." He said he laid out the roads along the natural contours of the property, which left the best building sites for homes. (Author's collection.)

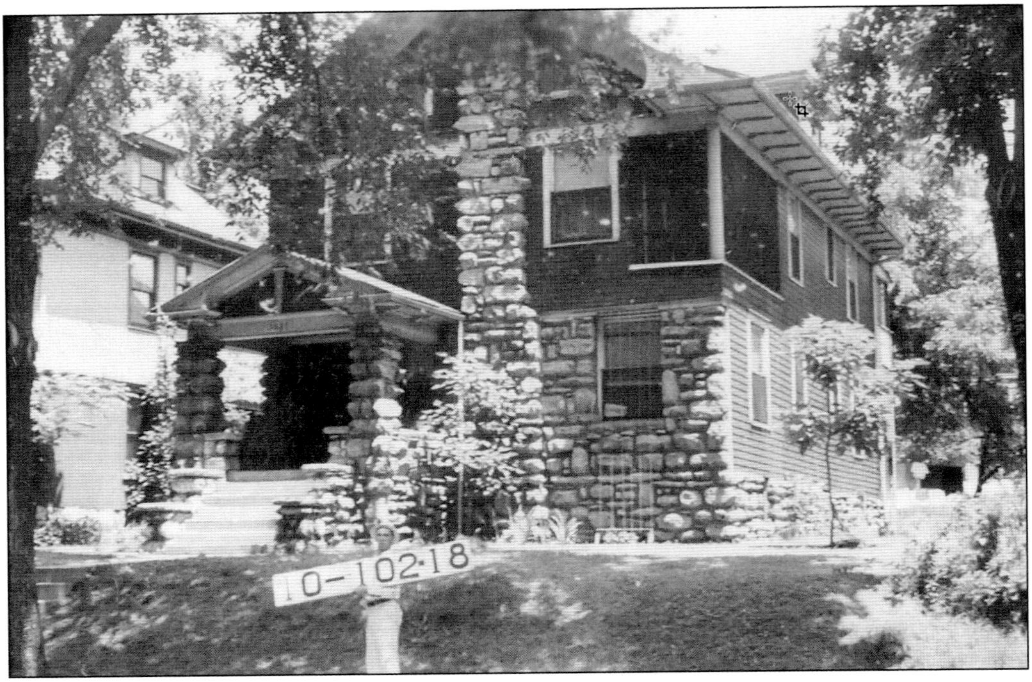

Squier Park, 1940. "I will make a crooked road. I will not build two houses alike. And my houses will not have a chance of putting their front porch legs on the sidewalk," Robert Jones told the *Kansas City Star.* He situated the houses in Squier Park as far back from the street as possible, in order to allow for a big front garden. Jones said that, although he wanted each house to be different, they should all be simple and livable rather than ostentatious. Most homes in Squier Park, such as the one seen below in 1940, were frame construction and were built between 1900 and 1915. (Both, courtesy of MVSC-KCPL.)

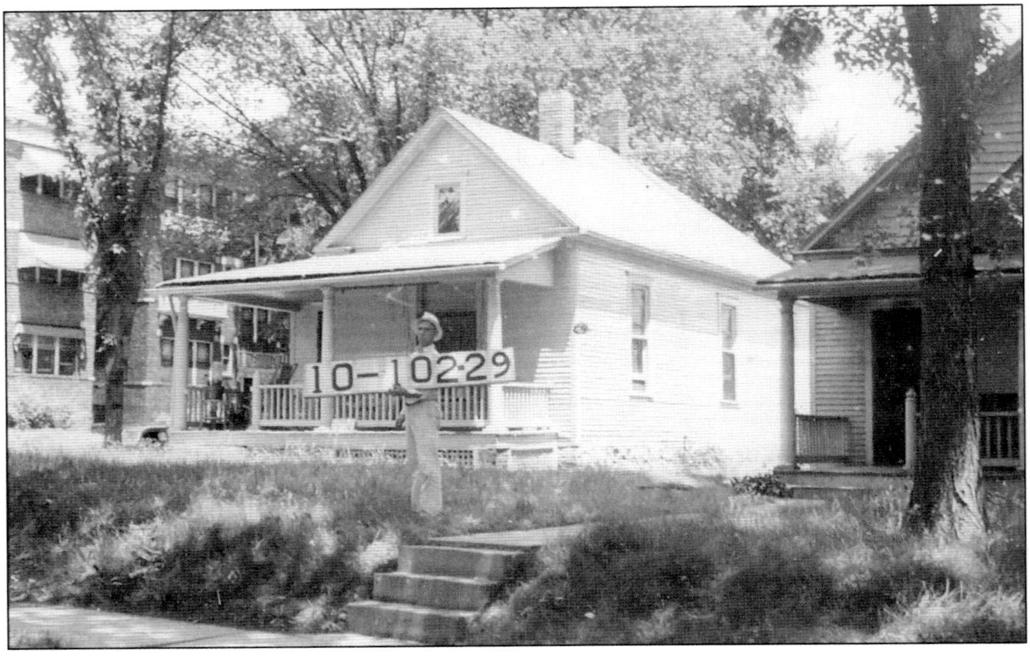

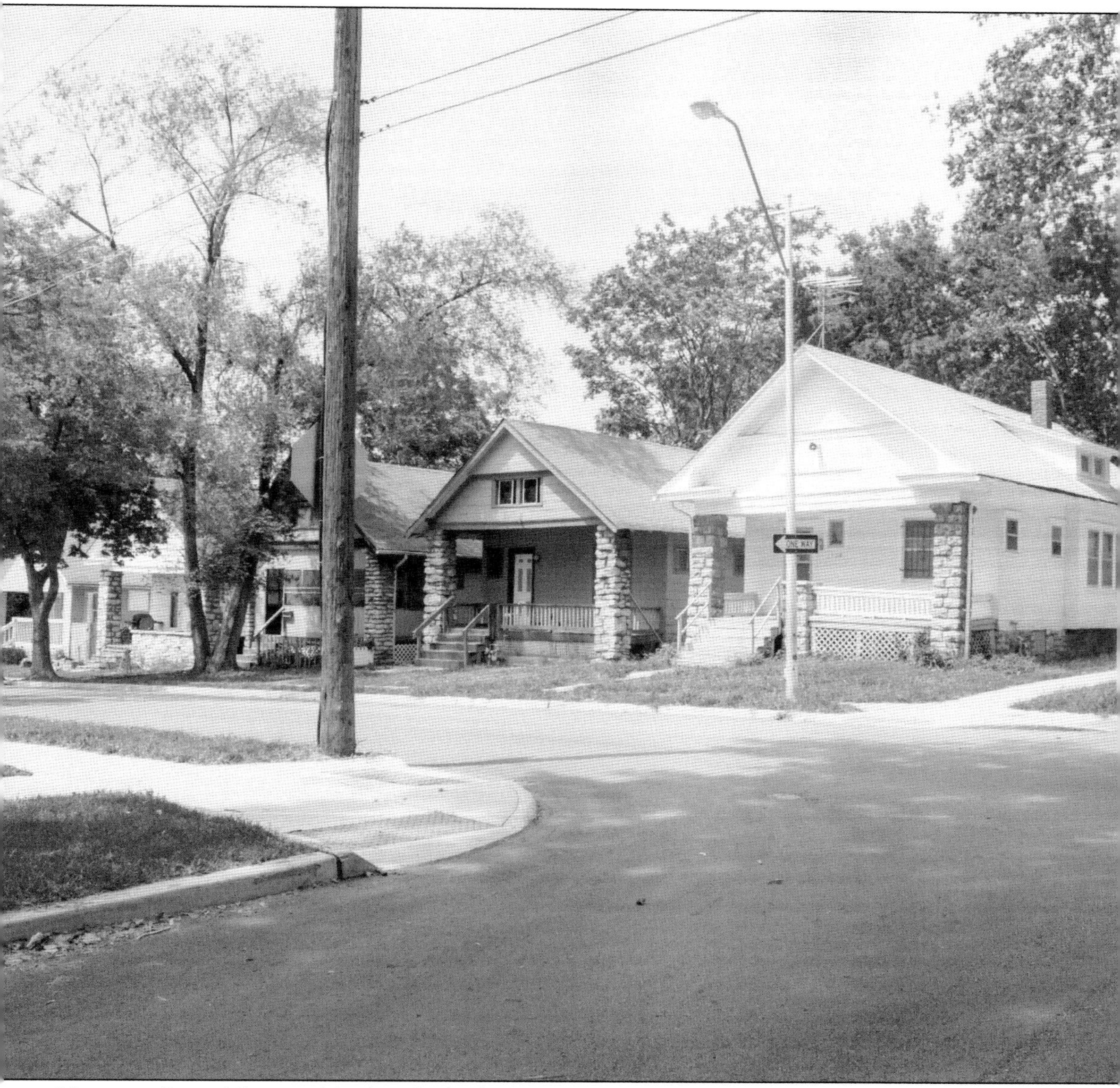

MANHEIM PARK. This neighborhood is built along a hilly section of land between Troost Avenue and the Paseo. It was developed because of its easy access to the popular Troost Avenue cable line. In 1887, George B. Wightman and Company advertised lots for sale on "Booming Troost Avenue," promising "The Cable Line will be running this summer and all eyes will be turned to Troost Avenue—80 feet wide and paved to Brush Creek." The company predicted prices would soon double in the subdivisions being built south of Thirty-first Street. Nearby suburbs were filling in with homes and small apartments. Potential homeowners regularly traveled through Manheim Park on their way to the popular Electric Park, and Troost Avenue offered residents access to a wide variety of shops and services. Manheim Park also had two schools, the St. James Catholic School, built at Fortieth Street and Tracy Avenue in 1907, and Bancroft, a public school that opened in 1904. (Author's collection.)

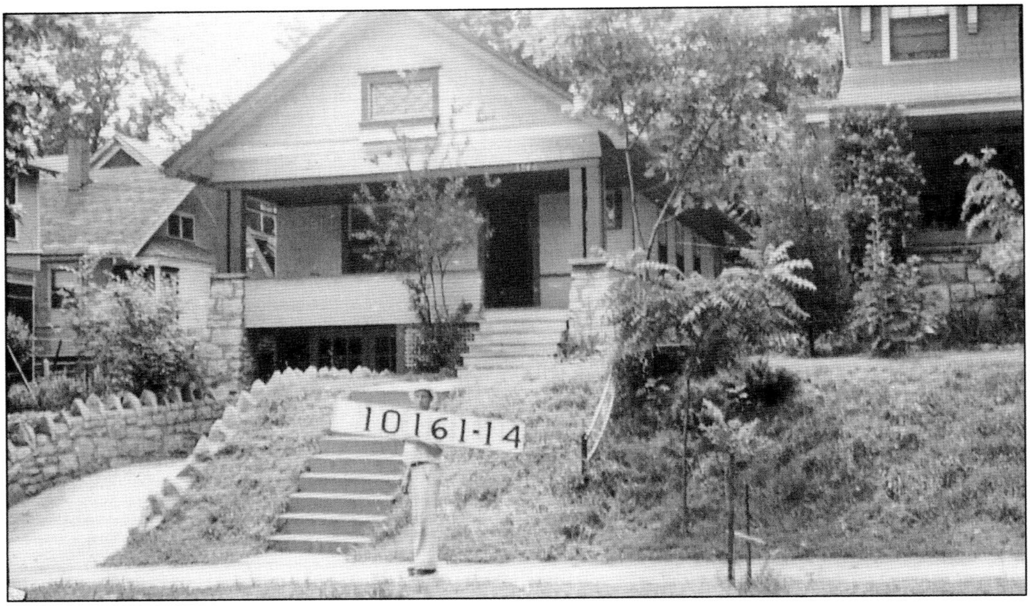

Manheim Park, 1940s. The southern areas between Troost Avenue and the Paseo filled from the 1880s through the 1920s with rows of small homes and apartments. Unlike the mansions that had once stood farther north along Troost Avenue, the neighborhood was built for middle-class or working-class folks who wanted to own a home along a streetcar line. The majority of its homes were frame construction. Many homes featured stone foundations or porches, and stone walls held up the steeper slopes. Manheim also has smaller apartment buildings that were intermingled with its homes after the turn of the 20th century. (Both, courtesy of MVSC-KCPL.)

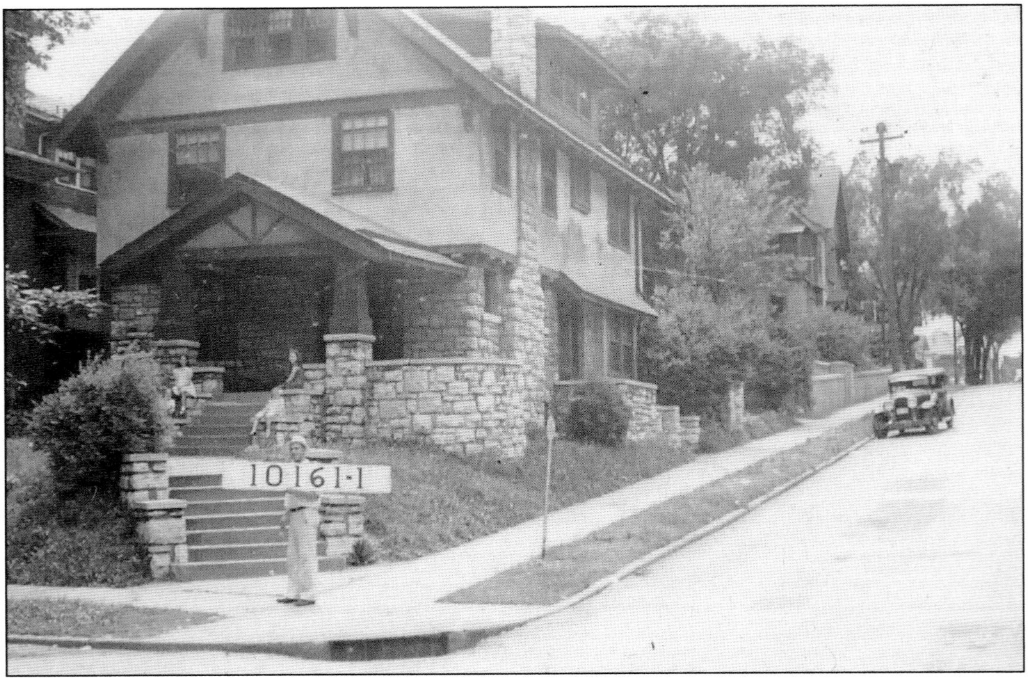

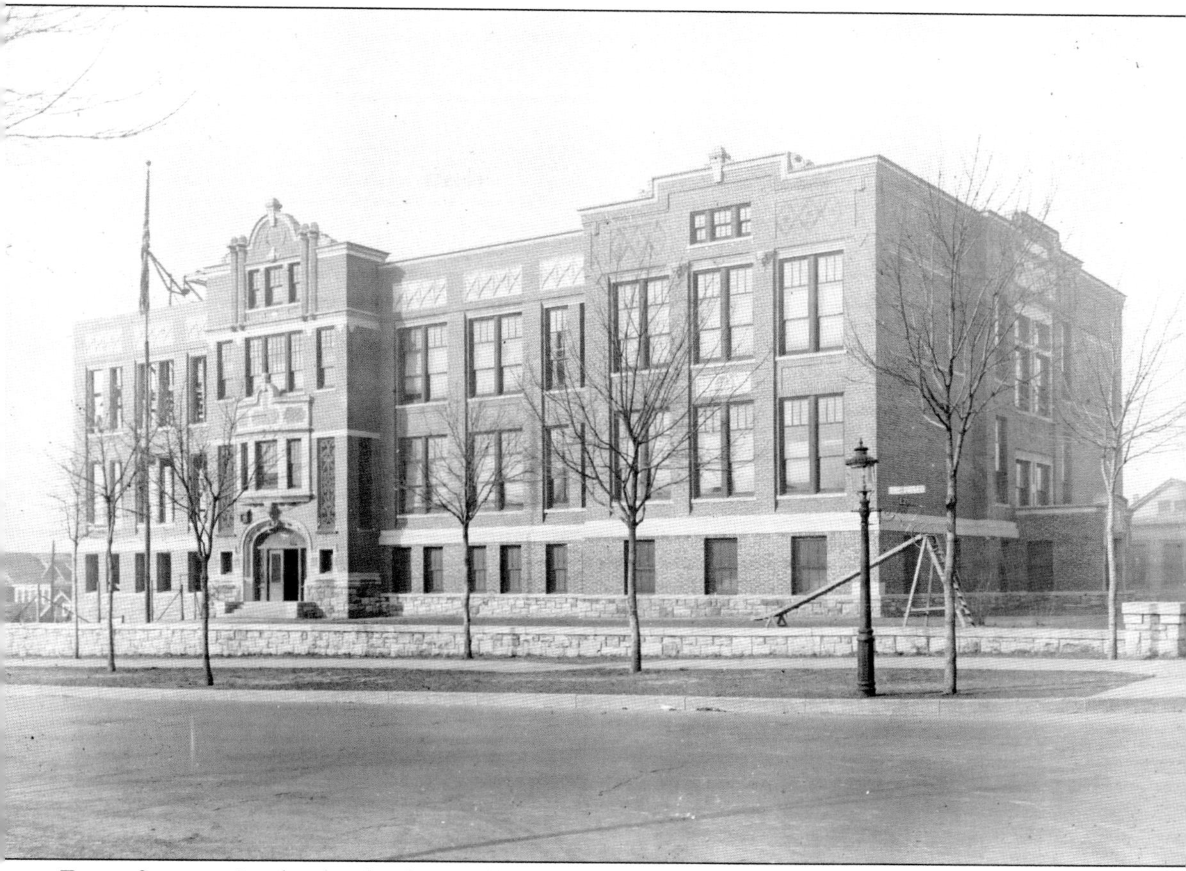

FAXON SCHOOL. South side schools were filled to capacity in 1906, and the school board considered where to build a new school in the area. Some favored the corner of Armour Boulevard and the Paseo, while others said it would take 25 years before there would be enough residential development south of Thirty-seventh Street to justify the location. The district chose an apple orchard at Thirty-seventh Street and the Paseo. Faxon School was completed in 1911. (Courtesy of MVSC-KCPL.)

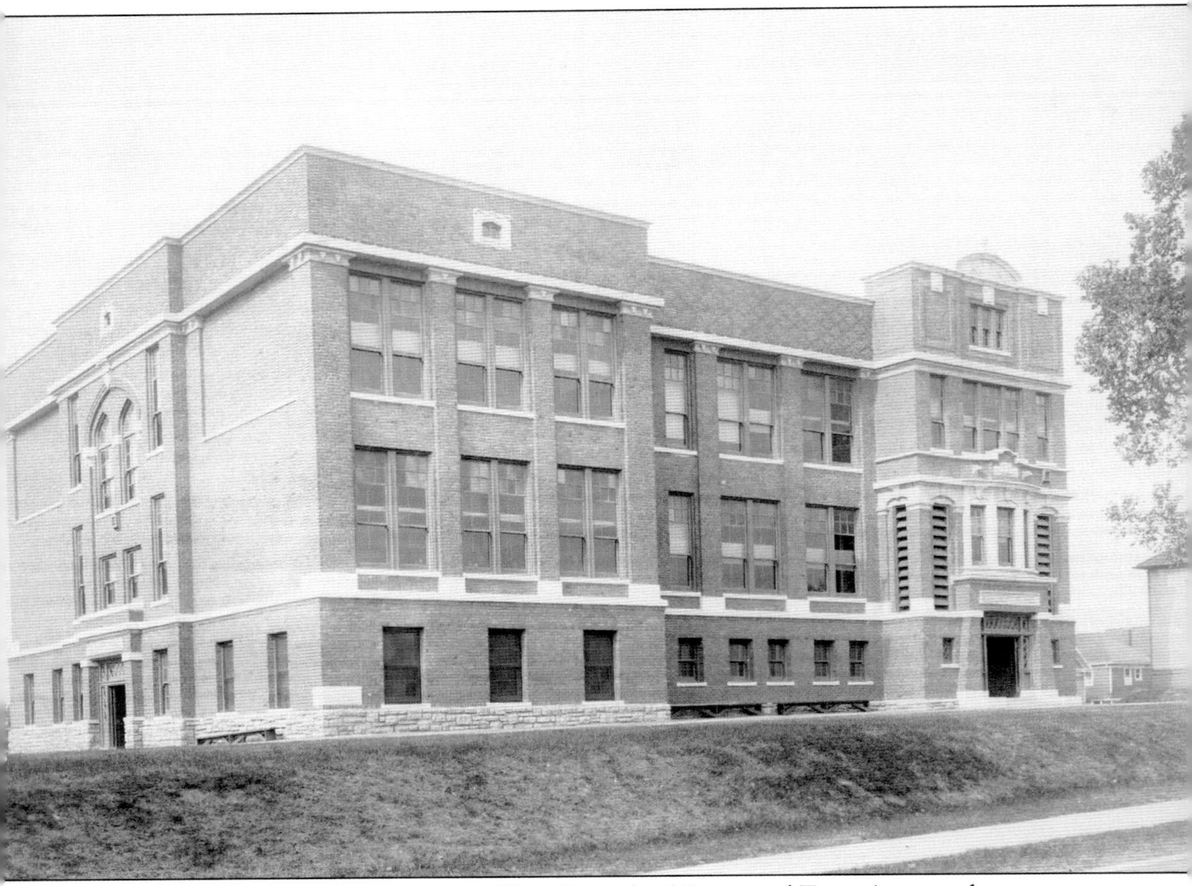

Bancroft School. At the corner of East Forty-third Street and Tracy Avenue, three two-room frame buildings opened in 1904 and 1907 as the Bancroft School. A fourth building was moved there in 1908 to meet the increased demand for seats. In 1908, the school district opened a 21-classroom building (pictured); it added an addition in 1922 that included an auditorium, a gymnasium, and additional classrooms. (Courtesy of MVSC-KCPL.)

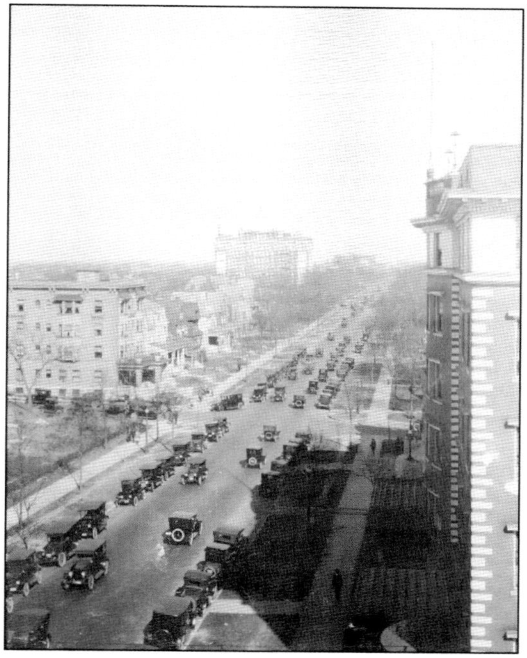

LINWOOD BOULEVARD, 1920s. Linwood Boulevard, a major east-west artery across Midtown, passes through neighborhoods from Broadway Boulevard to the Paseo and continues to the east. Linwood Boulevard was once a 40-foot-wide boulevard lined with three rows of trees. The western end, from Main Street to Troost Avenue, has lost most of the trees and grass strips that were part of its original design, and the street has become commercial over the decades. Linwood Boulevard attracted a number of social and civic organizations and was known as the "Boulevard of Churches," according to park department history. This photograph shows Linwood Boulevard as a major thoroughfare carrying heavy traffic. The large building at right is the St. Regis Hotel at Linwood Boulevard and the Paseo. (Courtesy of MVSC-KCPL.)

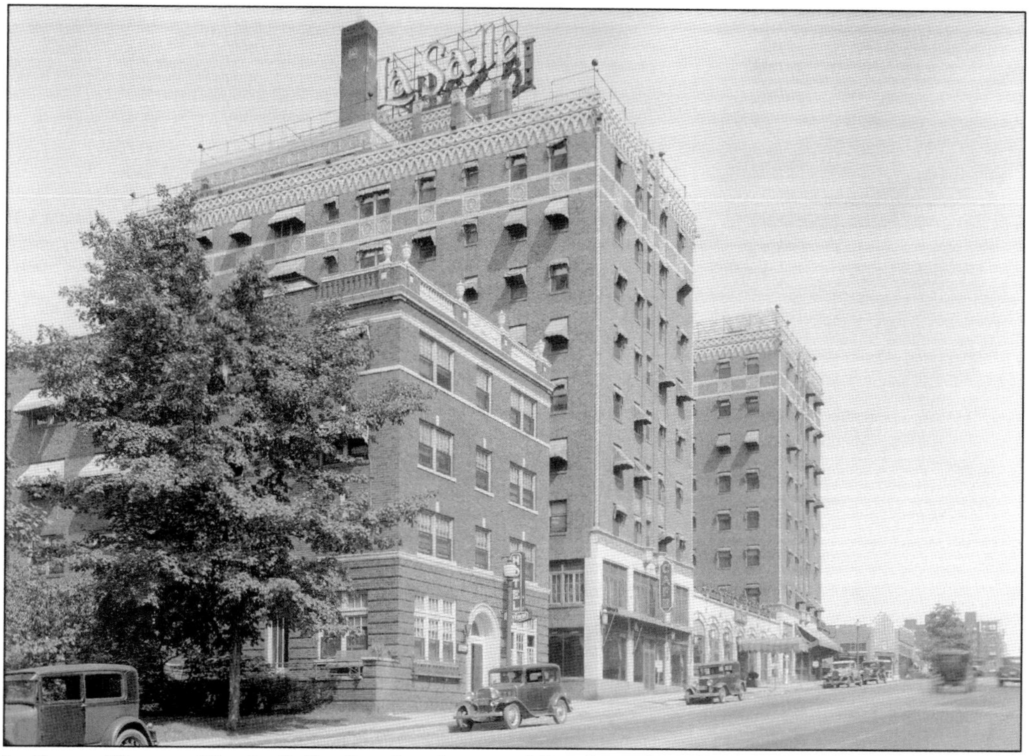

LASALLE HOTEL. The LaSalle Hotel at Linwood Boulevard and Harrison Street was an elite address, home to doctors, lawyers, and business executives. In the 1940s, the LaSalle's Crown Room was a popular nightspot featuring crowd-pleasing bands. It also had novelty nights, when guests could participate in the entertainment and win prizes for their display of talent. (Courtesy of MVSC-KCPL.)

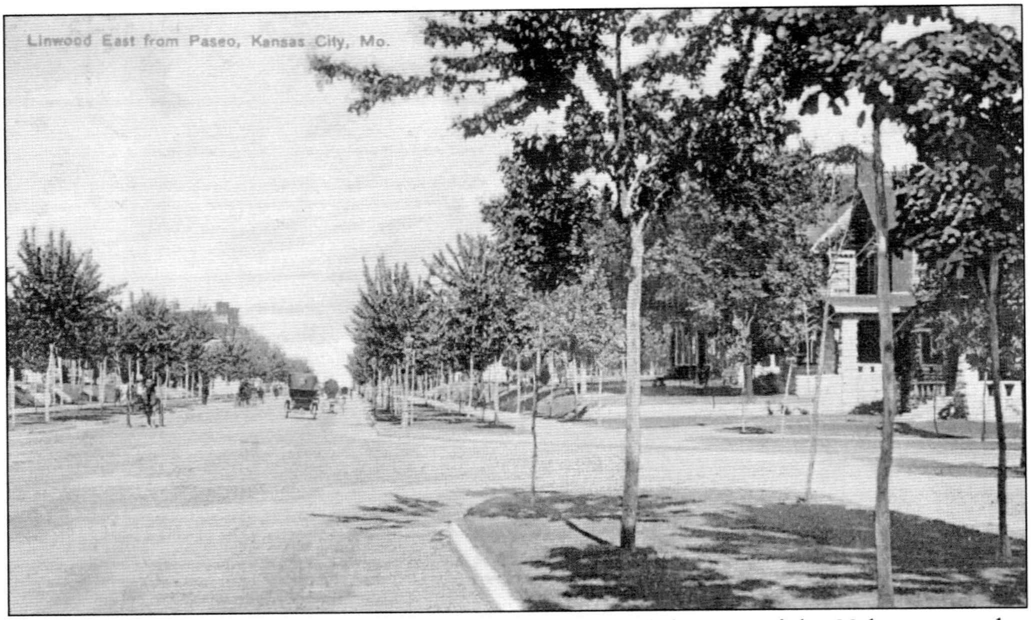

LINWOOD BOULEVARD. Looking east from the Paseo around the turn of the 20th century, this postcard shows the pride Kansas City took in Linwood Boulevard, one of the major boulevards in its growing park-and-boulevard system. (Courtesy of *Midtown KC Post.*)

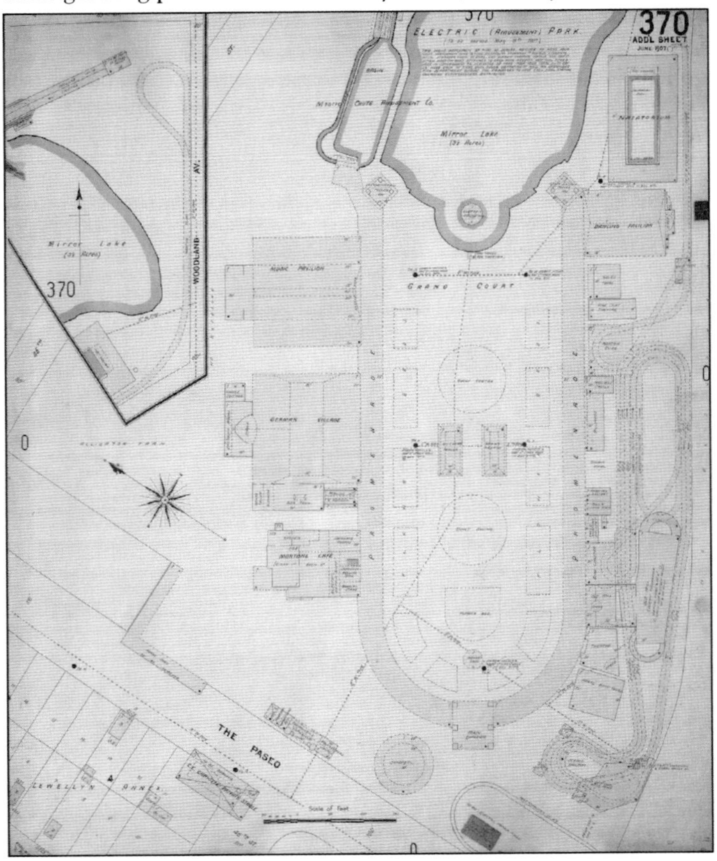

ELECTRIC PARK MAP. One way potential Troost homeowners first spied these neighborhoods was on the streetcar ride to Electric Park, shown in this insurance map from 1907. John Phillip Sousa said the band shell was unequalled in the world. Music wafted out into the park where swimmers frolicked. The highlight of the park, many thought, was the night spectacle of "living statuary rising from the center of the lake." (Courtesy of MVSC-KCPL.)

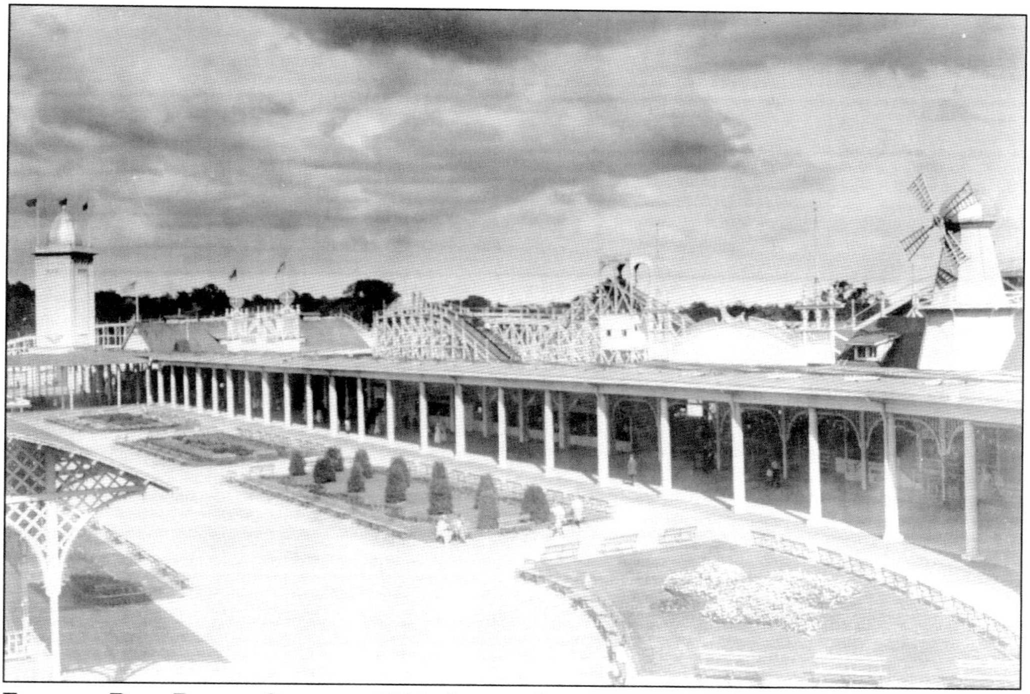

ELECTRIC PARK ROLLER COASTER, 1910. Among the attractions at Electric Park were a bathing beach and a natatorium, an indoor swimming pool. The roller coaster was another popular amusement at what was called Kansas City's Coney Island. (Courtesy of MVSC-KCPL.)

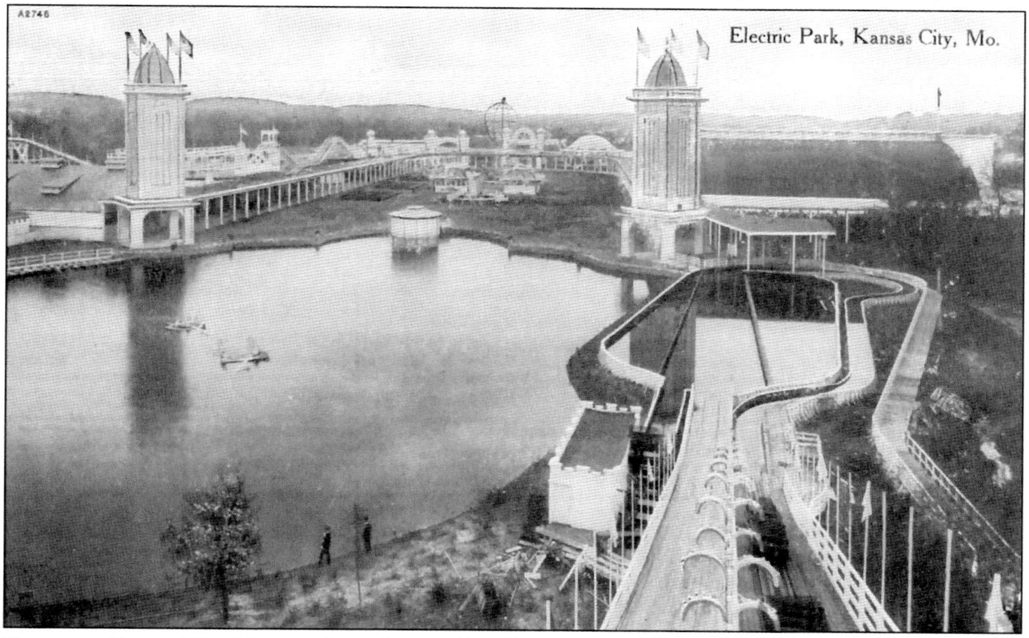

ELECTRIC PARK. The Metropolitan Street Car Company ran special open-air streetcars to carry people to Electric Park in the summer. For just a nickel, cars brought visitors to the park every five minutes. There was even a special streetcar entrance. Much of the park burned down in 1925 and was not rebuilt. In 1948, the Village Green Apartments were built on the site. (Courtesy of *Midtown KC Post.*)

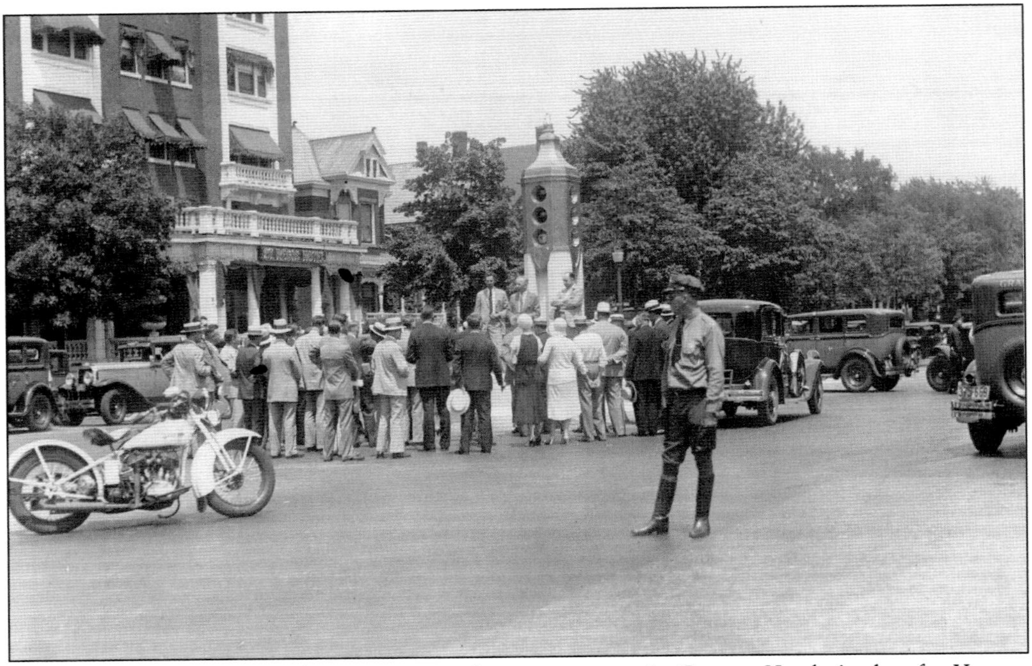

Paseo Stoplight, 1932. The Paseo was a key component in George Kessler's plan for Kansas City's park-and-boulevard system. He intended it to be a blend of a boulevard and a park. Its unique stoplights were installed in 1932, and crowds turned out for the dedication. (Courtesy of MVSC-KCPL.)

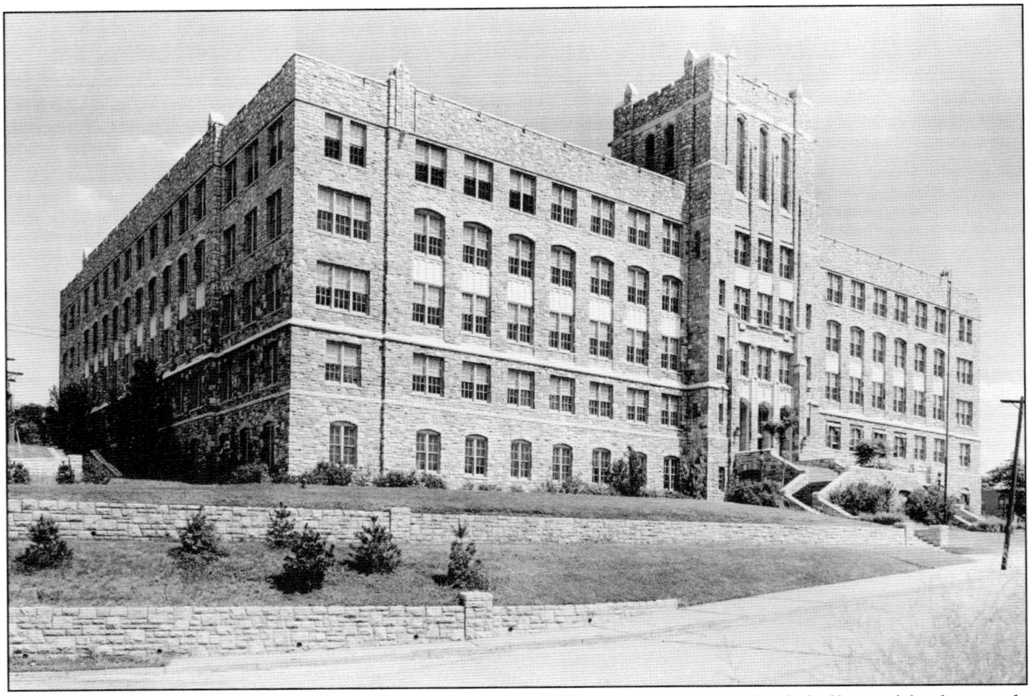

Paseo High School. When this school opened in 1926, it stood on a high hill two blocks south of Electric Park. Students from 14 elementary schools in Kansas City attended the high school. (Courtesy of MVSC-KCPL.)

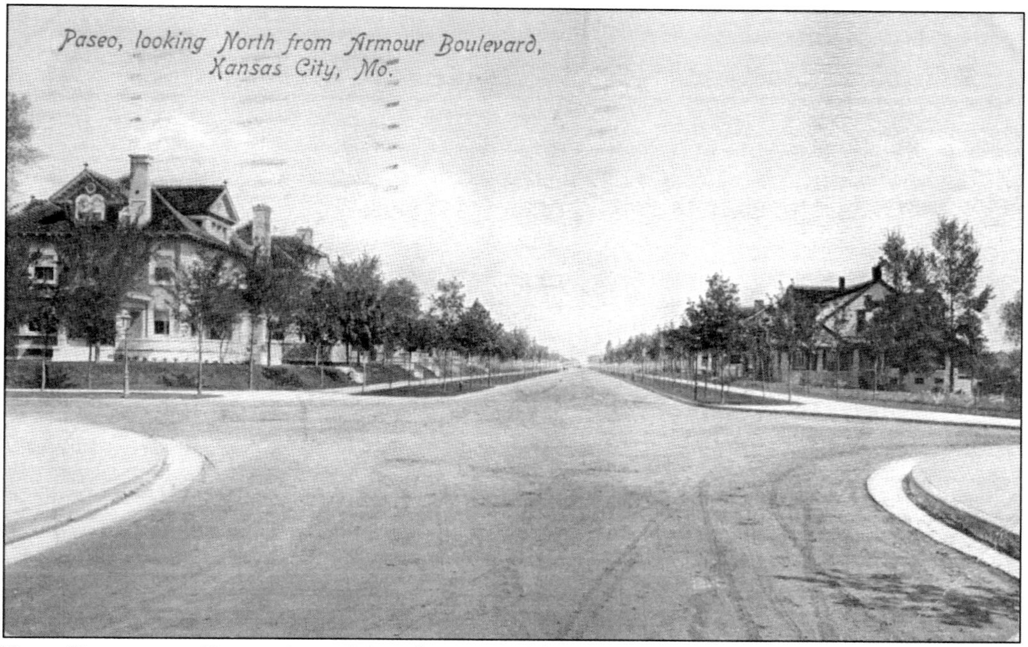

Paseo Boulevard, Early 1900s. Like other parts of the park-and-boulevard system, the construction of the Paseo resulted in the removal of several blighted areas. The idea was that new roadways would take out rundown buildings and spur higher-quality residential development. The strategy worked, and at the turn of the century, the Paseo was one of the most popular subjects for postcards, showing off the wide street and the mansions that grew up along it. These postcards show views north from Armour Boulevard, where the boulevards were attracting wealthy residents to build homes and attracting everyone else for a ride in the country along a grand avenue. (Both, courtesy of *Midtown KC Post.*)

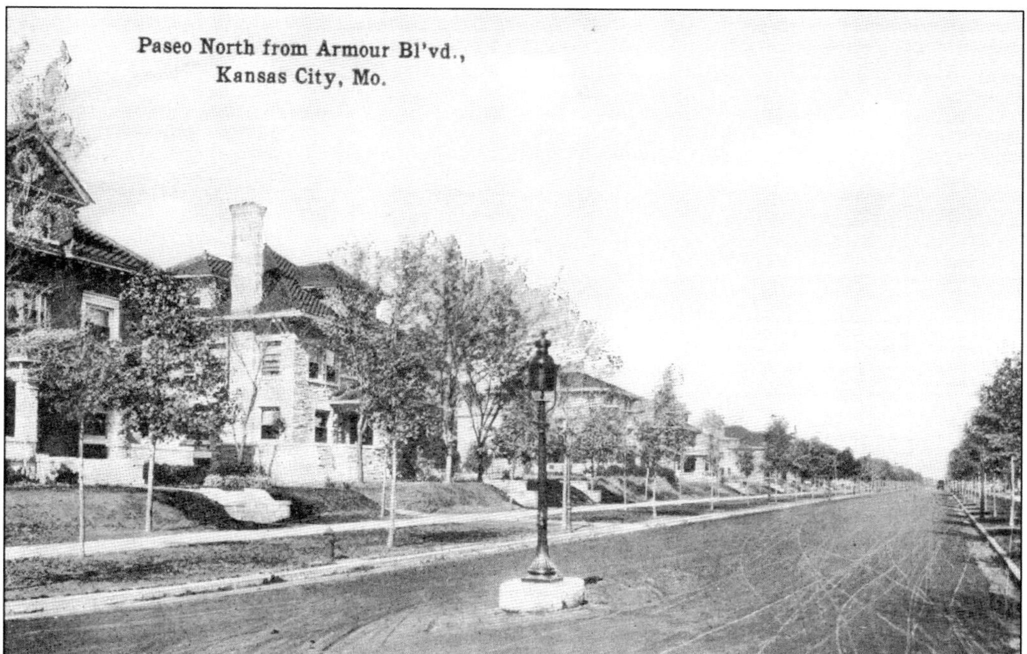

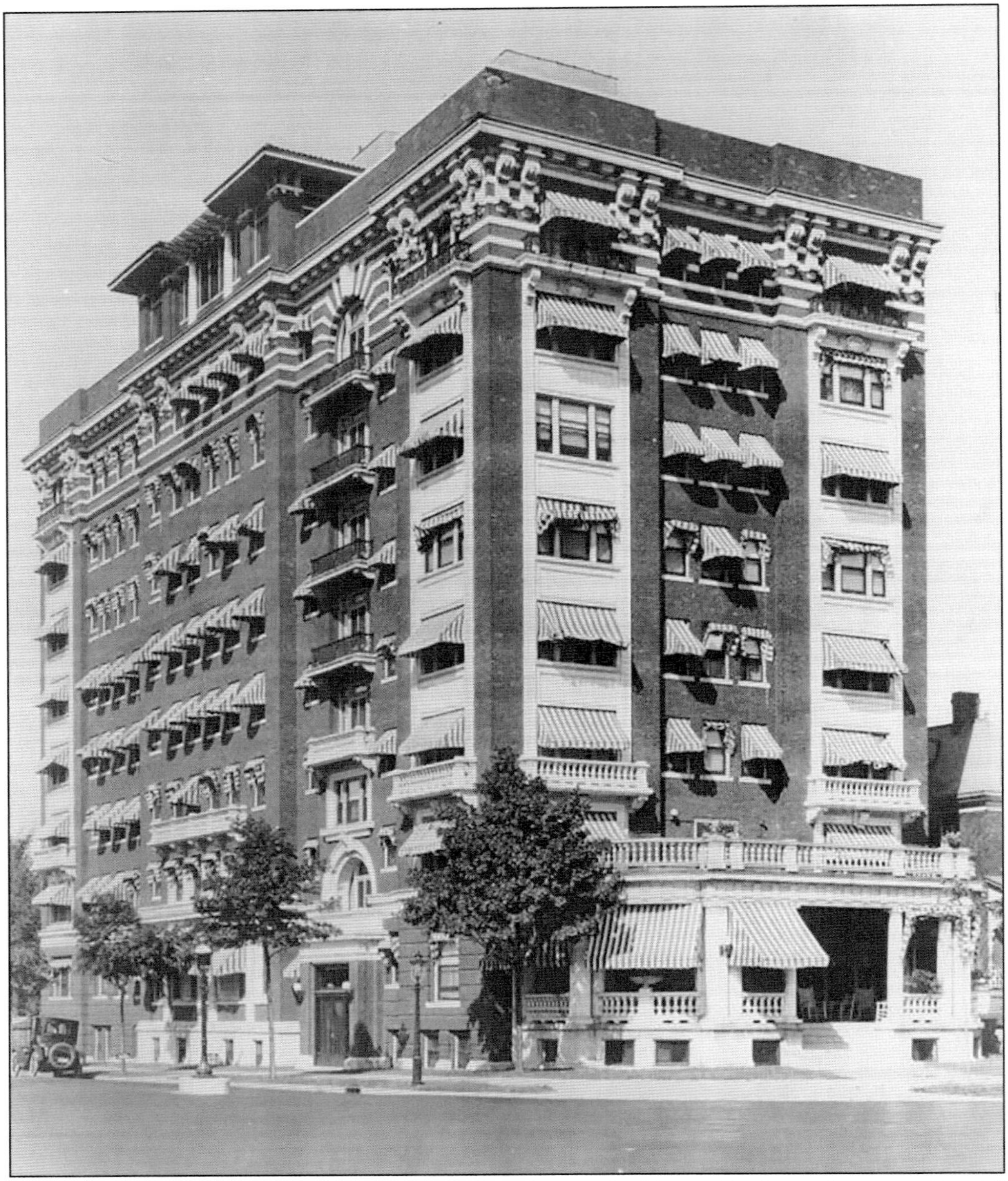

ST. REGIS HOTEL. In 1914, when the search was on for sites for Kansas City's new luxury residential hotels, no corner looked more enticing to developers than that of Linwood Boulevard and the Paseo. Real estate broker and developer Howard Vrooman and investor Henry Owen saw a chance to take advantage of the new reinforced-concrete technology to construct a nine-story building on a narrow urban lot. The St. Regis, because it stood on a hill, was called by the *Kansas City Star* in 1914 "the most conspicuous building on the skyline." Millionaire Theodore Gary was among the first to move in, but he shared the building with single folks and couples squeezed by the housing shortage. Residents entered the St. Regis through a lavish lobby with silk draperies, a piano, and intricate furnishings, according to the historical register nomination. A first-floor restaurant served both residents and the public. The basement housed a billiards room, "where a novel ventilation system granted players the luxury of smoking with impunity." The ninth floor included an elaborate ballroom. (Courtesy of MVSC-KCPL.)

Six

Armour Boulevard

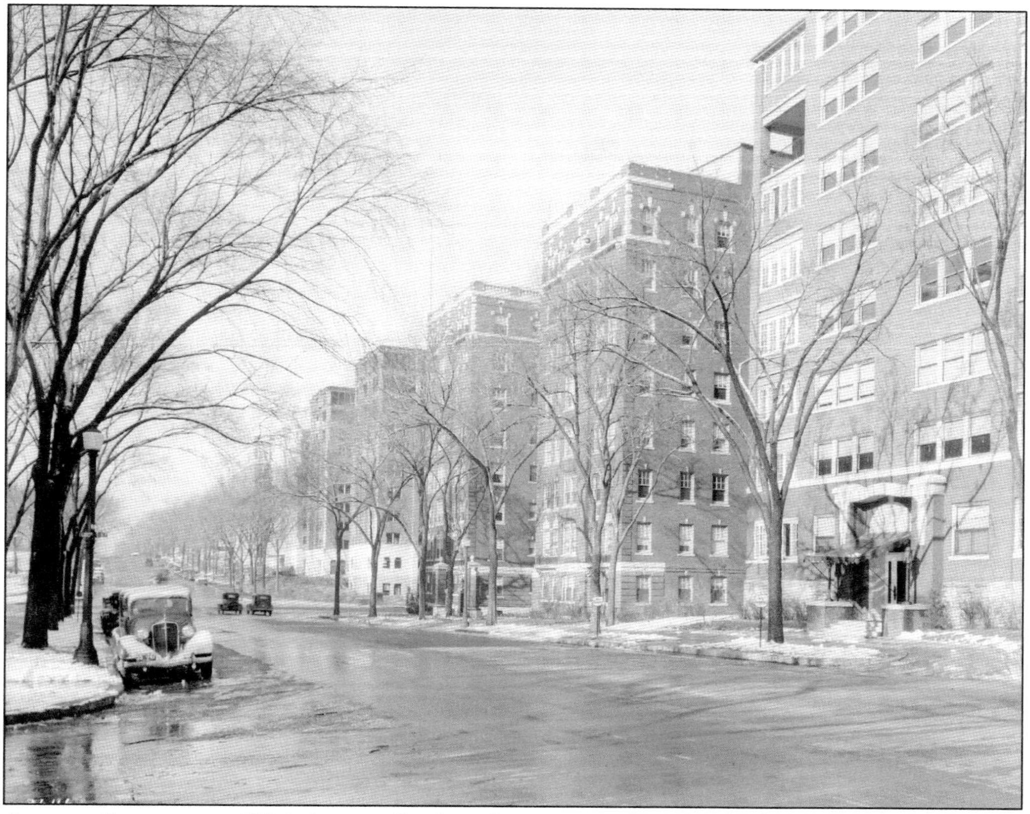

Armour Boulevard, 1934. Armour Boulevard, running only 1.25 miles from Broadway Boulevard to the Paseo, is best known today for the high-rise apartments built there between 1900 and 1930. It passes through the Midtown neighborhoods of Old Hyde Park, Hyde Park, and Squier Park. In the 1920s, Armour Boulevard filled a need for housing during a shortage. Its luxury hotels supplied living space for long-term residents and guests. The thoroughfare also had fancy restaurants and shops that served both guests and the surrounding neighborhoods. The apartments were the height of luxury when they were built, but they faded after 1940. Recently, however, many have been renovated as rental property. (Courtesy of MVSC-KCPL.)

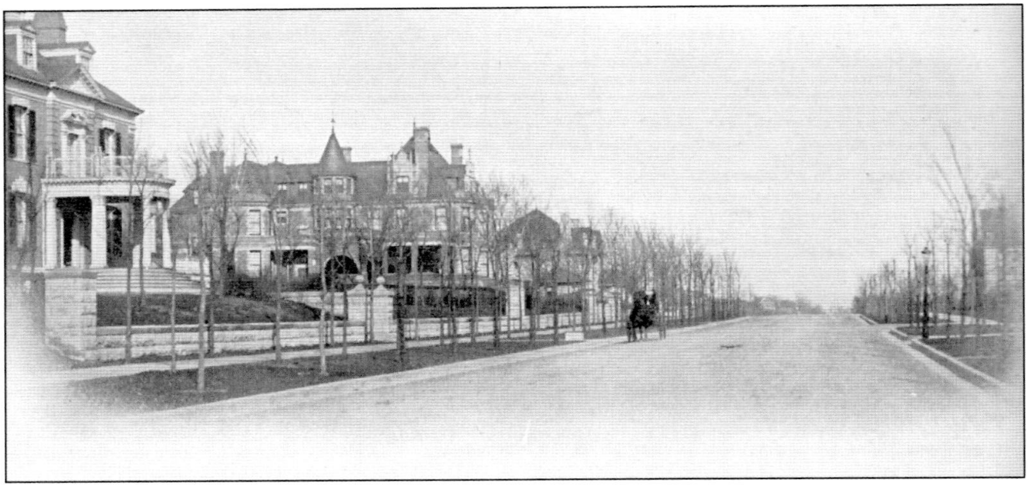

Armour Boulevard Mansions, Early 1900s. Armour Boulevard takes its name from K.B. Armour, a member of the prominent family of meatpackers, who moved south in 1893. His faith in Armour Boulevard spurred others of the city's elite to follow. Armour Boulevard was soon a tree-lined street of broad lawns and huge homes. For a brief period, Armour's grand mansions were the pride of Kansas City, but many of them do not survive. By the early 1900s, the homes were starting to share space with apartments. Some of the mansions were torn down and replaced with apartments, while others were later occupied by institutions such as the Fine Arts Institute. (Both, courtesy of *Midtown KC Post.*)

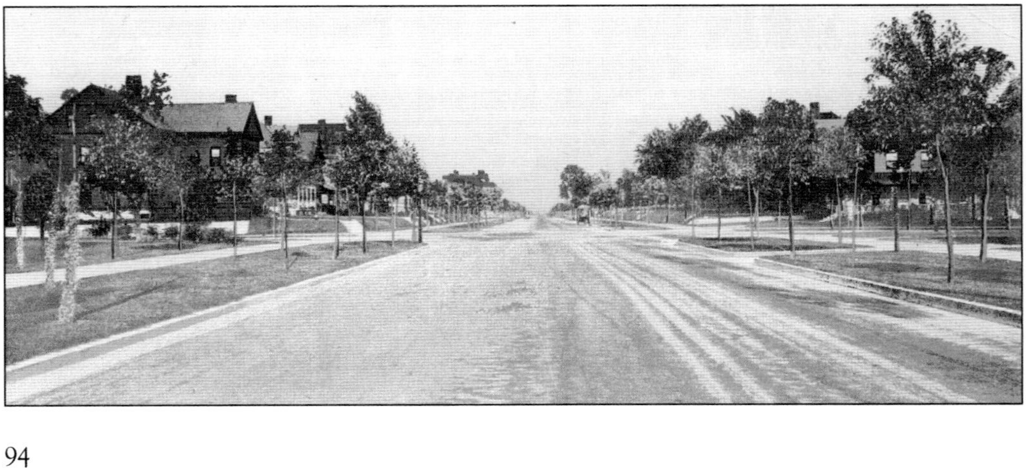

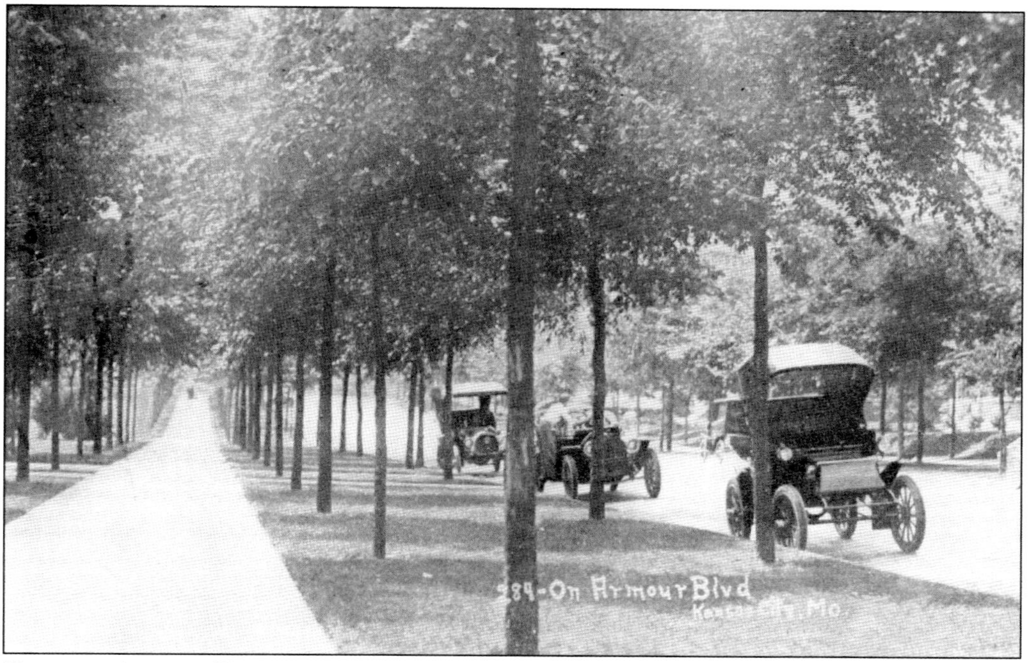

Cruising Armour Boulevard, Early 1900s. The *Kansas City Star* of July 17, 1905, said that Armour Boulevard came alive on summer evenings with pleasure-seekers on foot and in all sorts of vehicles, from "the $7000 motor car to the humble express wagon drawn by a $20 horse." Men taking their fiancés for a drive often used a buggy, and it was popular at the time for women to ride Armour Boulevard on horseback in smart riding suits. (Courtesy of *Midtown KC Post.*)

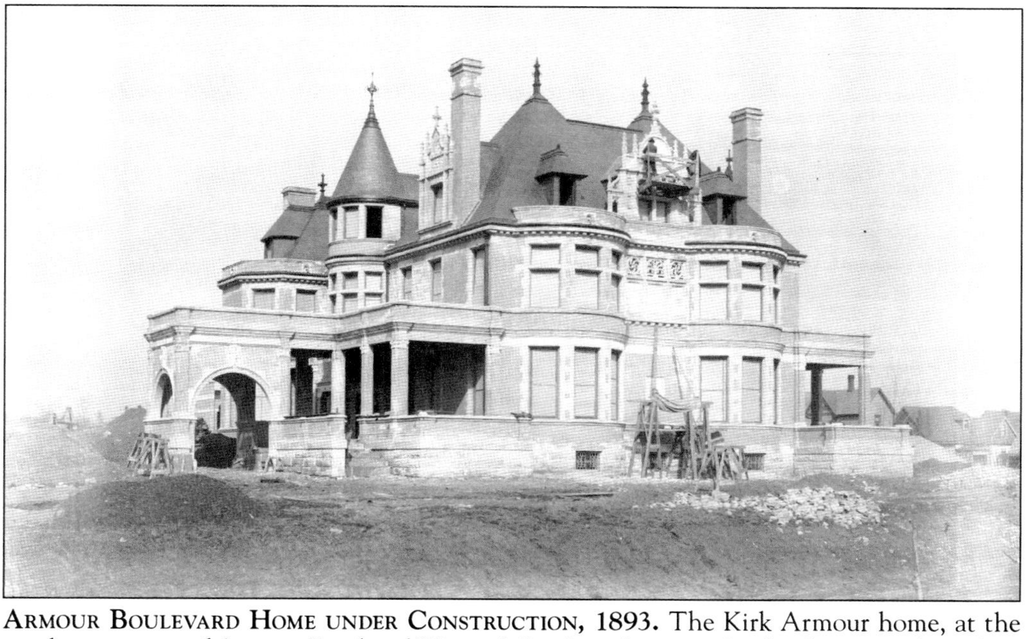

Armour Boulevard Home under Construction, 1893. The Kirk Armour home, at the northeast corner of Armour Road and Warwick Boulevard, was said to be the most admired on the boulevard. His mansion was built to last a century, especially because Kansas Citians of the day could not image the city expanding any farther south. The massive home was demolished in 1930. (Courtesy of MVSC-KCPL.)

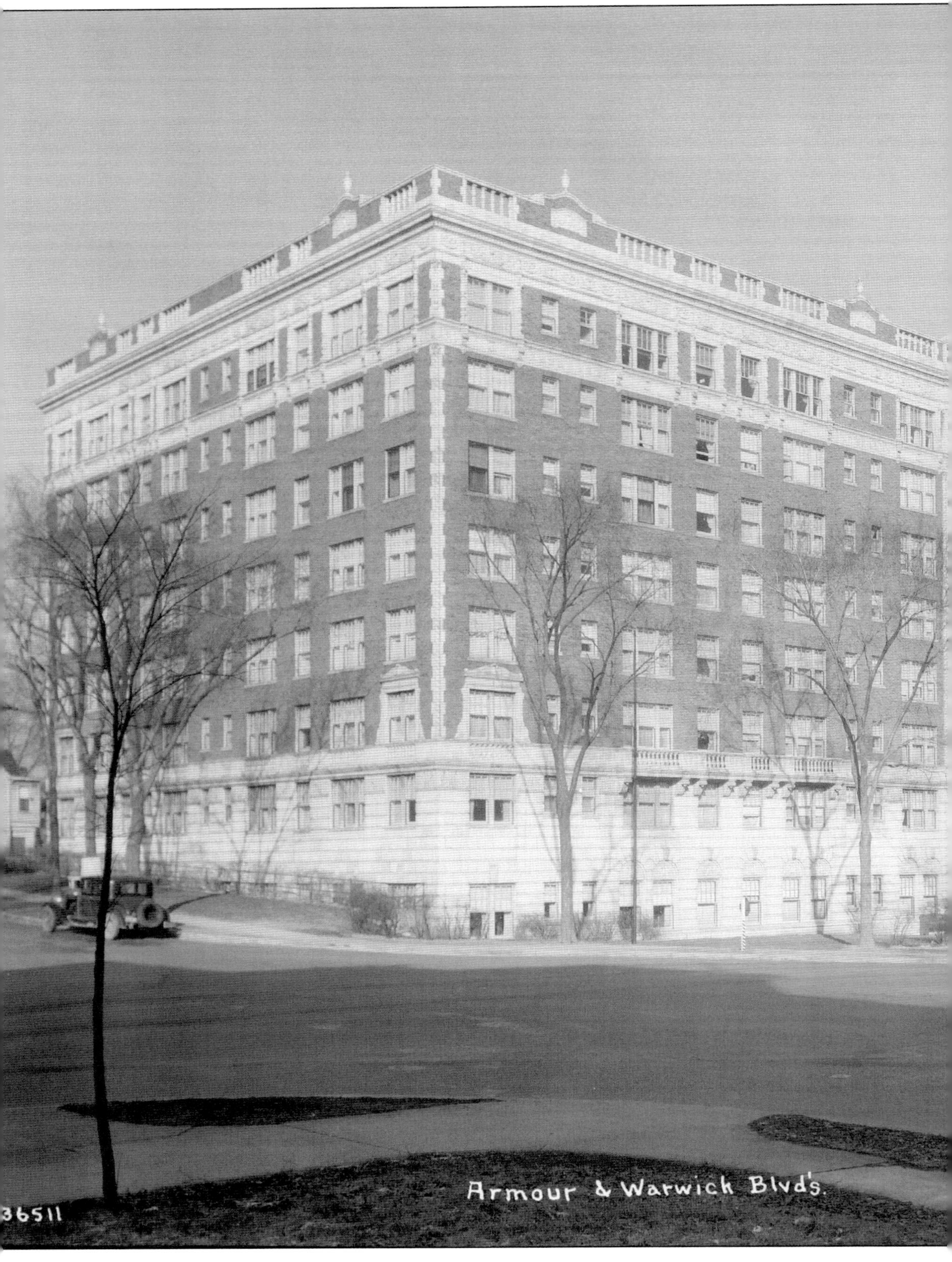
Armour & Warwick Blvd's.
36511

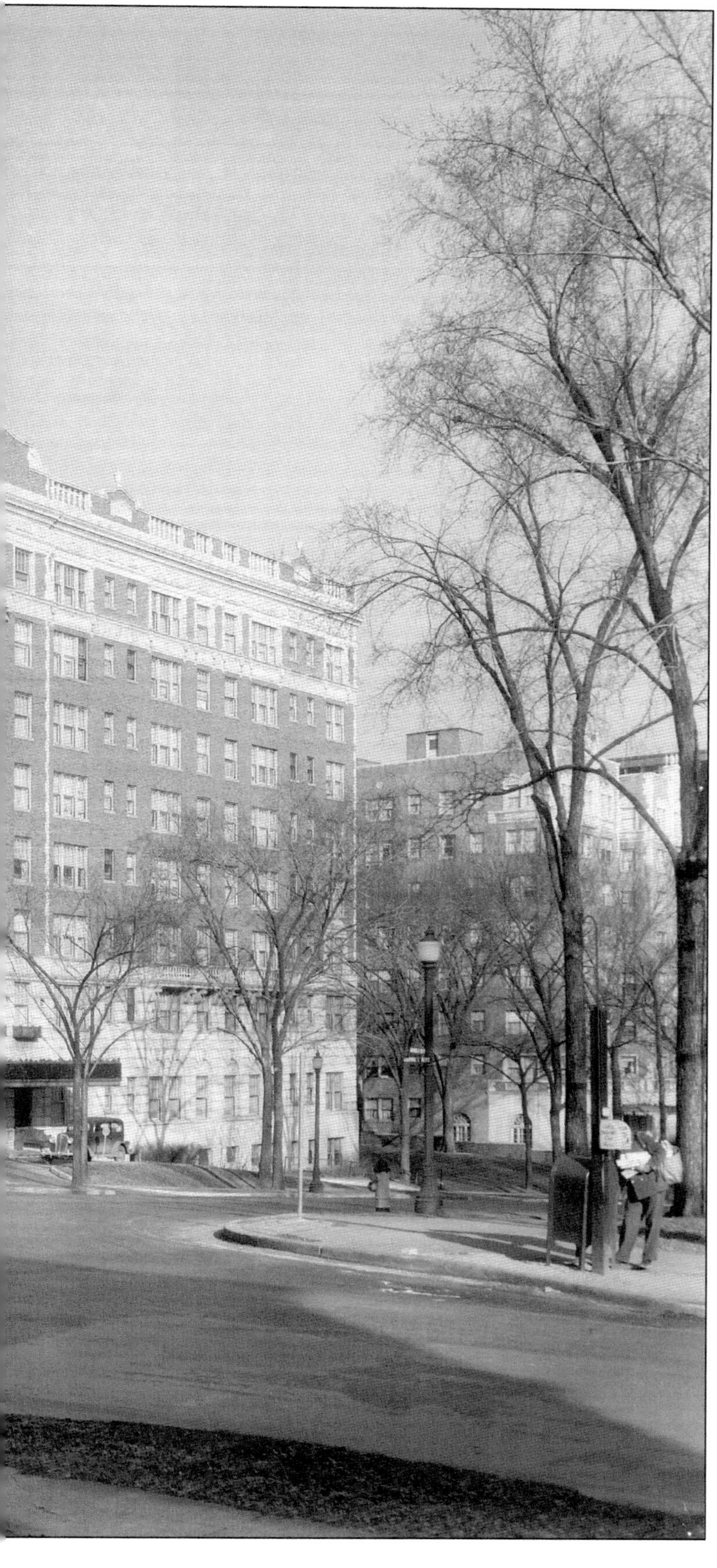

THE BELLERIVE. By the 1920s, the apartments on Armour Boulevard were becoming bigger and more luxurious. The trend among developers was away from single-family homes and in favor of multifamily high-rises. "Ground prices are reaching a point on the boulevard where the presence of large residences on a lot is a negligible item at sale," the *Kansas City Star* reported in 1904. The Bellerive was the first luxury high-rise apartment building on Armour Boulevard, constructed between 1921 and 1922. The eight-story apartment hotel was fully staffed day and night by maids, doormen, and bellmen, and it had a garage on the first floor. It had a spacious lobby and six dining rooms, one public and five private. The Bellerive became the place to stay for visiting celebrities passing through Kansas City. (Courtesy of MVSC-KCPL.)

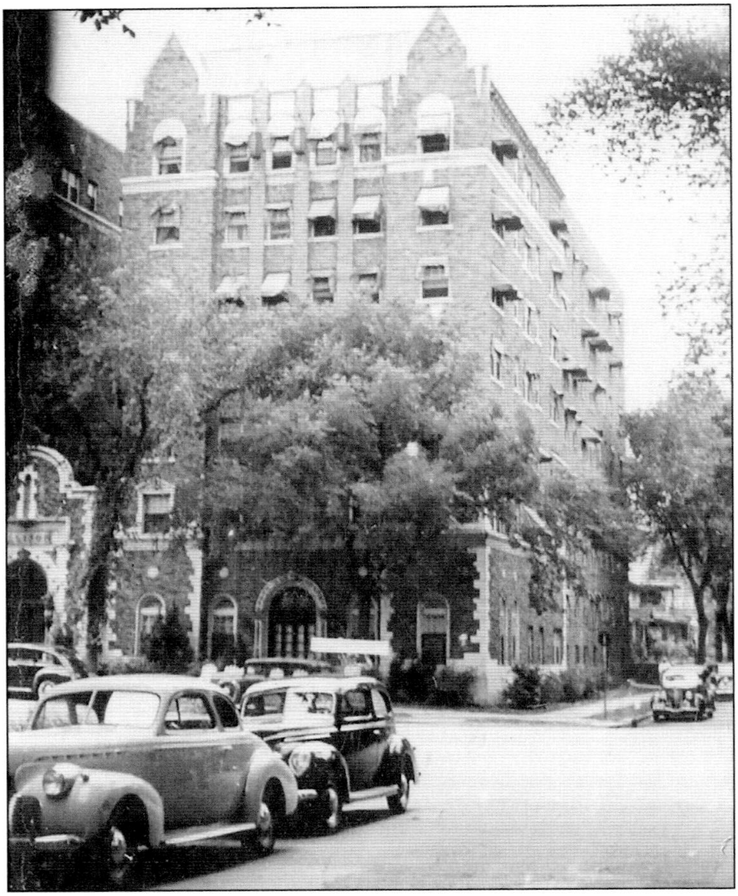

ELLISON AND BAINBRIDGE, 1940. The Ellison (left), on the corner of Armour and Broadway Boulevards, was built as a single unit. An identical tower was built later. It introduced a new style of apartment, the studio. Prolific architect Nelle Peters was involved in its design. The Bainbridge, previously known as the Armour Court Apartments, joined other tall buildings on Armour Boulevard in 1925. Shown in the 1940 tax photograph below, the building has continued to serve local residents since its opening. (Both, courtesy of MVSC-KCPL.)

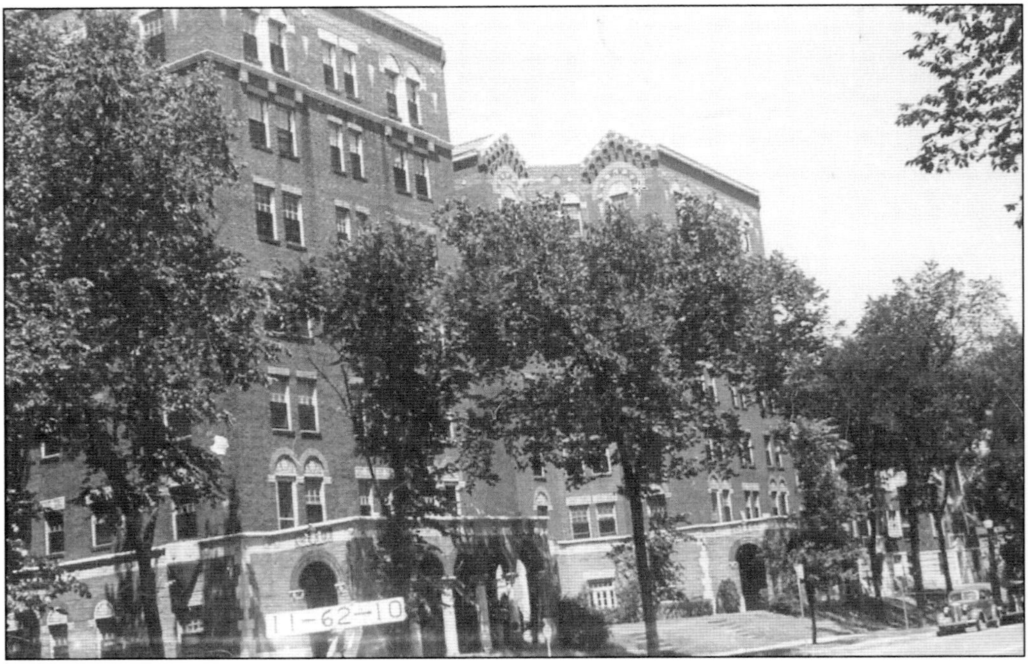

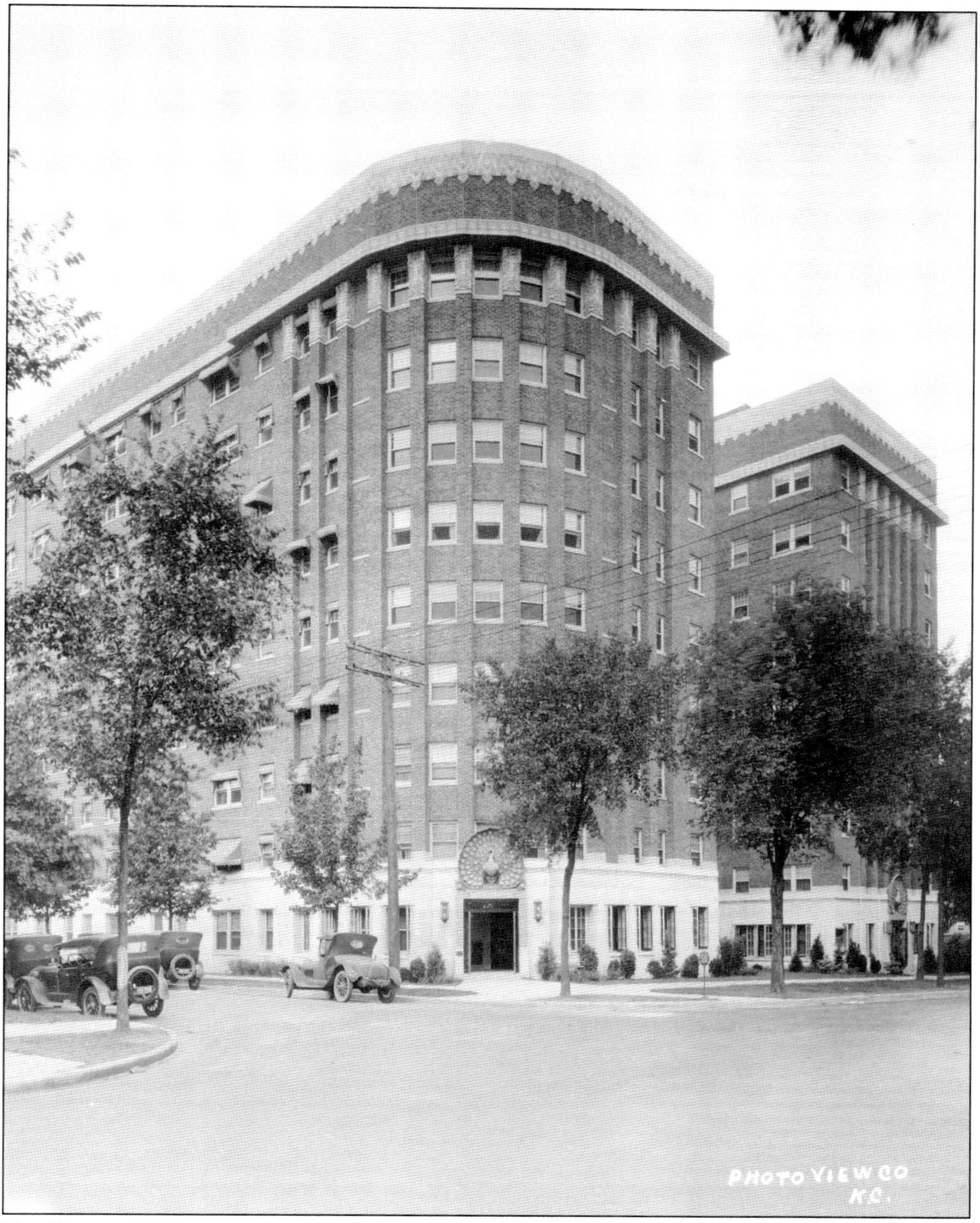

The Peacock. The Peacock Apartment Hotel (later called the Newbern Apartments) opened in 1922. The nine-story brick and terra-cotta building was advertised as a "family hotel in the exclusive South Side residential district." The *Kansas City Star* of October 8, 1922, raved about its dining room, which was open to the public as well as to residents and had become a favorite dining place for motorists. "The gorgeous appointments carry out the hotel crest. The peacock blue velvet curtains and tapestried overdrapes in peacock design, the exquisite china carrying the design, the silver hollow ware richly embossed with peacocks, the softly shaded lights, all go to make up an atmosphere of elegance and luxury that cannot be excelled." (Courtesy of MVSC-KCPL.)

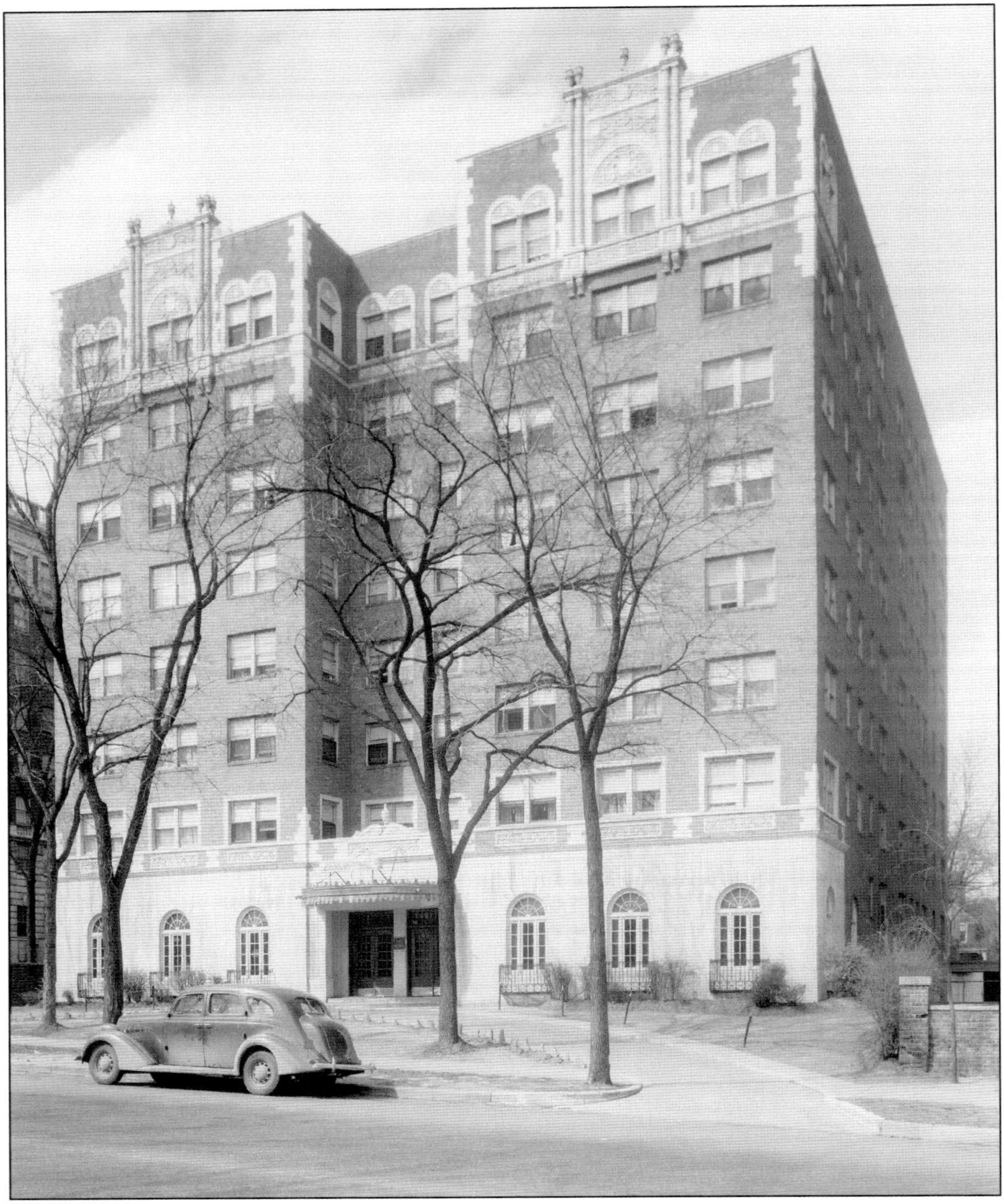

Park Central, c. 1940. By 1929, when the Park Central Hotel (above) was built, construction of the Armour Boulevard high-rises was ending. In fact, construction of the Clyde Manor, which had started in the late 1920s, was abandoned, and it sat empty until after World War II. It was not completed until 1944, when wartime housing shortages had reached a critical point in the city. The *Kansas City Star* heralded the completion, saying the Clyde Manor had stood on Armour Boulevard as a "useless monument to the depression" for too long. "For fourteen years its vacant windows have reminded the home folks and visitors of a time we would like to forget," the paper said. But the era of the luxury apartment hotels had come to an end by then. The Georgian Courts, which started the high-rise expansion in 1917, went into foreclosure, like many other apartment hotels, in the Depression. In 1935, its 36 luxury suites were converted to 114 kitchenettes. (Courtesy of MVSC-KCPL.)

Seven

Troost Avenue

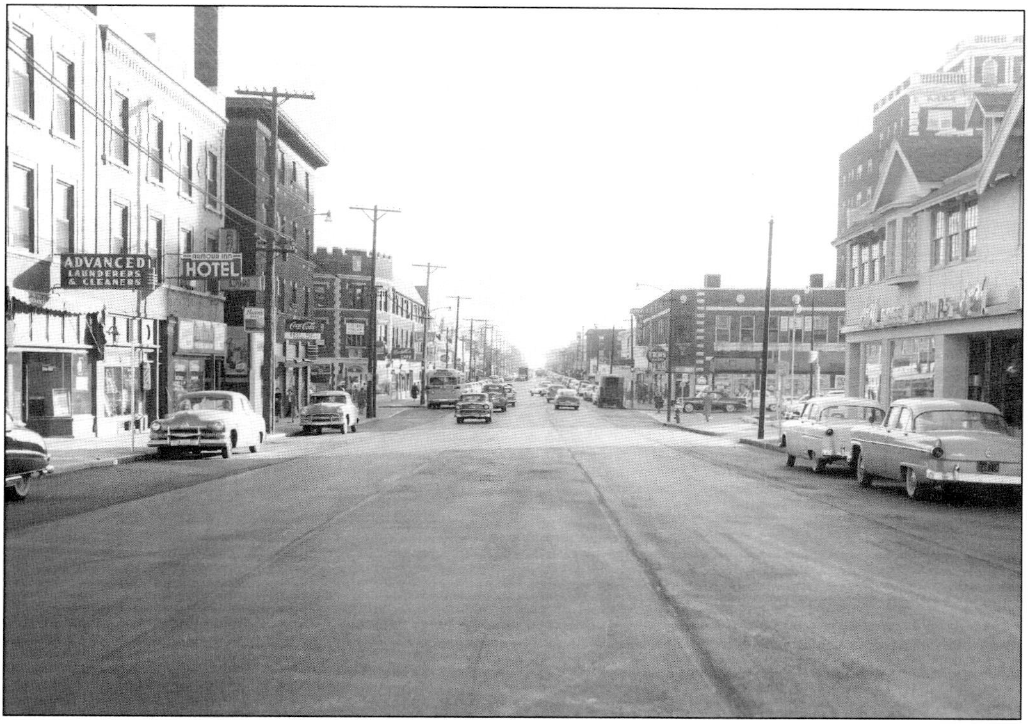

Troost Avenue at Armour Boulevard. No street in Midtown has been as important, or has undergone as much change, as Troost Avenue. Once called "Millionaire's Row," Troost Avenue was transformed from an exclusive enclave of wealthy families to a major streetcar corridor and commercial center. As Midtown neighborhoods developed, businesses and institutions such as churches and social clubs were drawn south, often finding a location on Troost Avenue. For a while after the "white flight" of the 1960s, Troost Avenue was considered Kansas City's racial dividing line, but in recent years, numerous efforts have begun to revitalize the avenue. (Courtesy of MVSC-KCPL.)

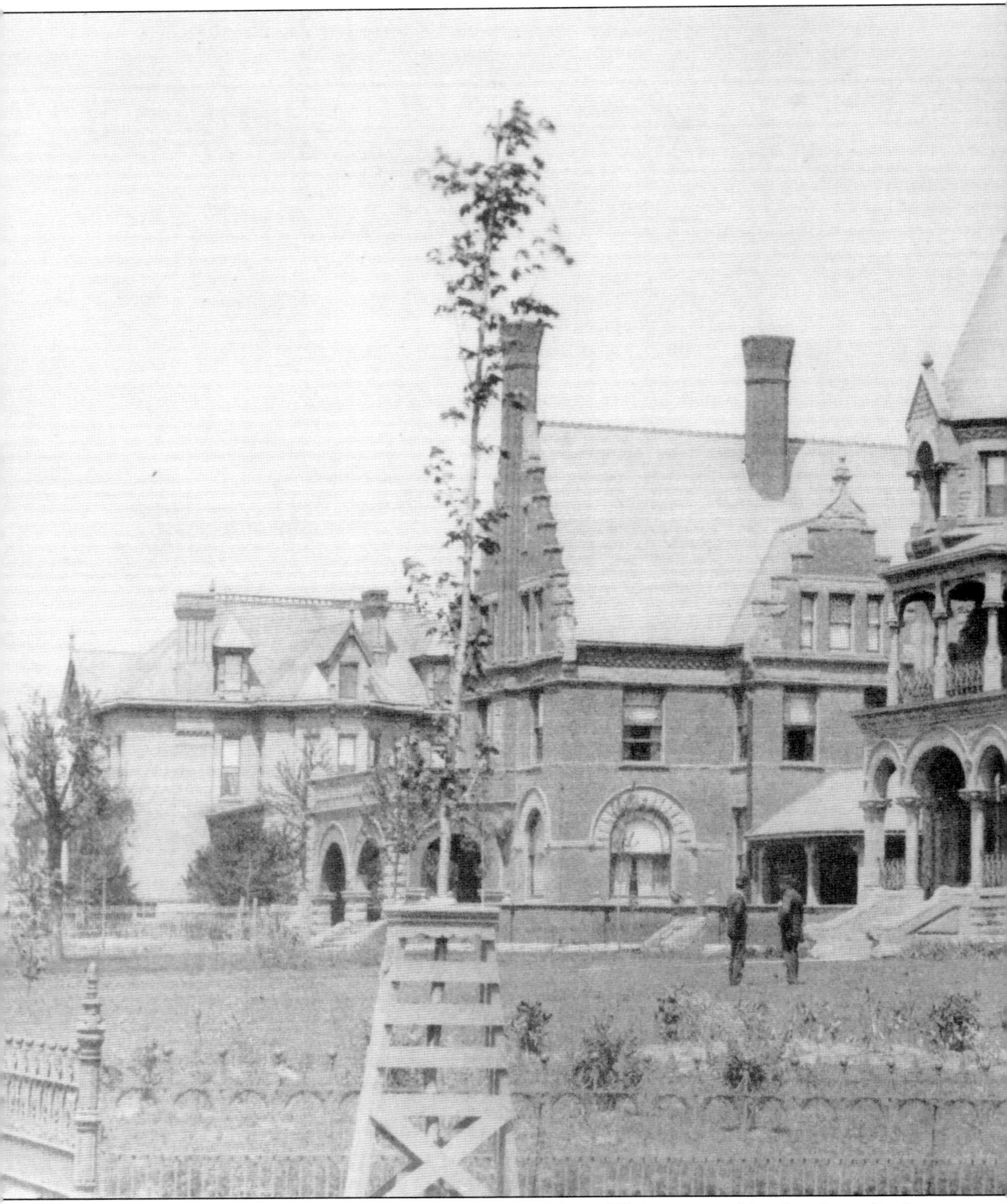

MILLIONAIRE'S ROW. When Kansas City pioneer Webster Withers moved his family to this home in 1883, he said he had decided to move to "the country." He built his mansion on 40 acres of ground on a spot few would recognize today, Thirty-first Street and Troost Avenue. "We were tired of town life," Withers's wife told the *Kansas City Star* in 1911, "and desired to get away out on a farm." The family had previously lived at Ninth and Cherry Streets. The Withers built a

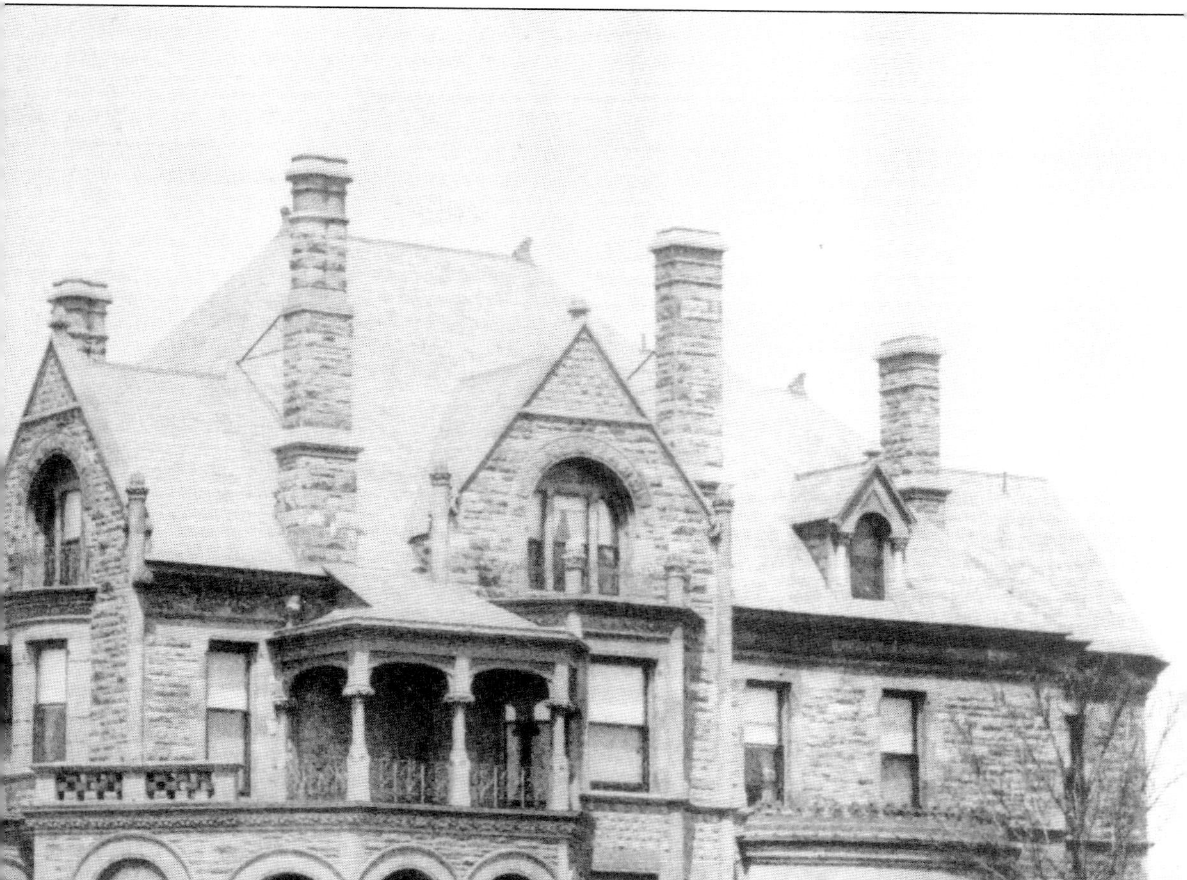

massive home featuring mahogany woodwork and hand-carved mantels on the fireplace in each room. For a while, the area must have suited them. Another newspaper story that year called Thirty-first Street and Troost Avenue "A Town Within a City," where, it said, "one could live and die without forgoing any of the luxuries or necessities of life—it has neither mayor nor council and is nameless, but there is no other lack." (Courtesy of MVSC-KCPL.)

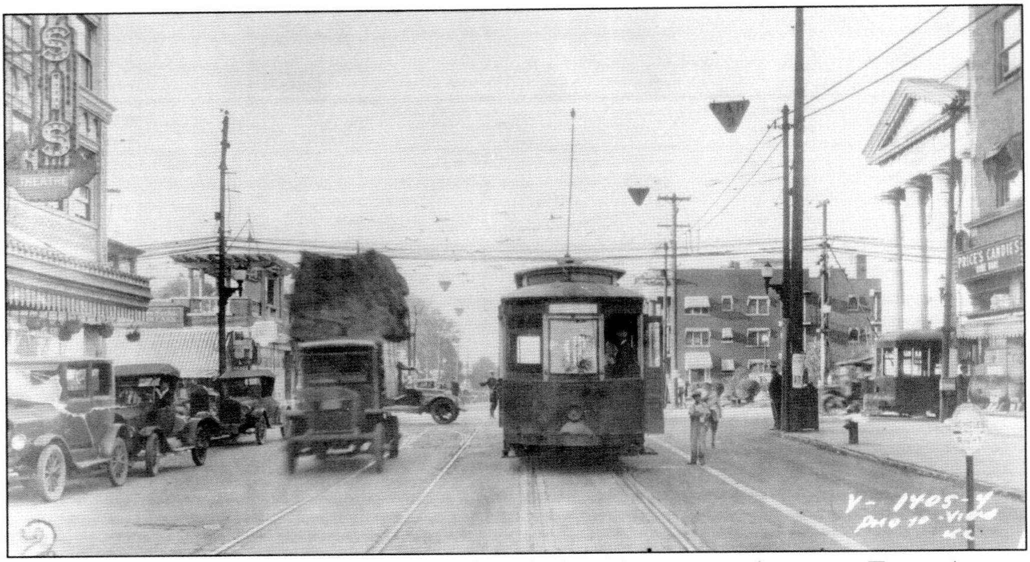

Streetcars on Troost Avenue, 1929. Those looking for peace and quiet on Troost Avenue would not find it for long. By 1911, the *Kansas City Star* reported that Withers's corner had become like a small city. It started when the Troost Avenue streetcar line, which stopped at Thirty-third Street, made that corner a meeting center. A few stores were built, and by 1926, Troost Avenue looked more urban than rural. (Courtesy of MVSC-KCPL.)

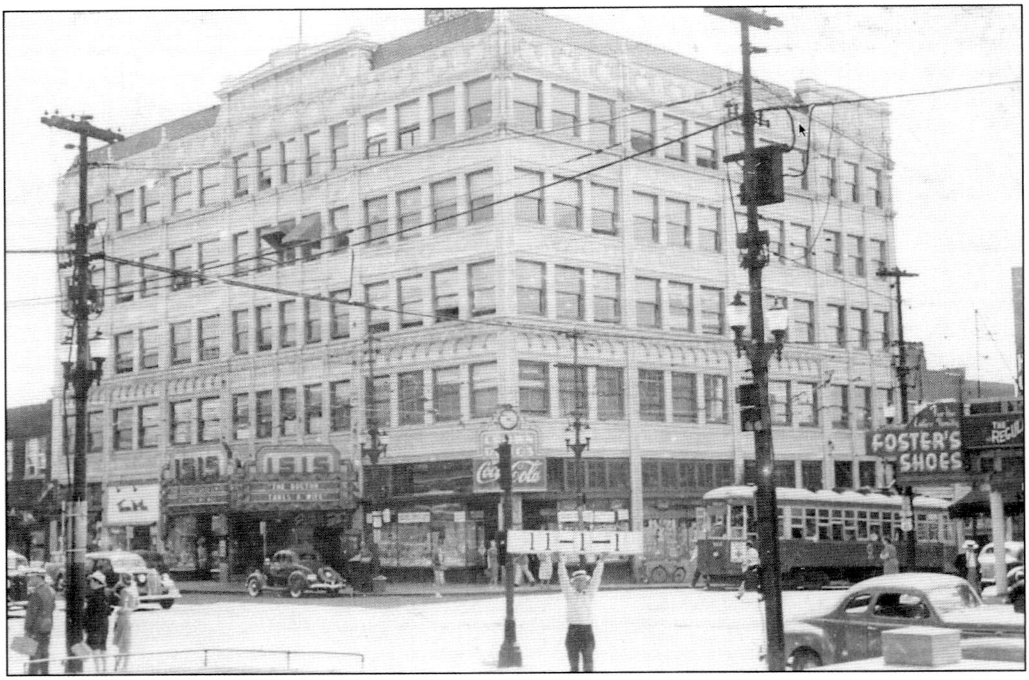

Thirty-First Street and Troost Avenue, 1940. The story of the Wirthman Building encapsulates the changes at the corner of Thirty-first Street and Troost Avenue. J.C. Wirthman, born at Twenty-seventh Street and the Paseo, built his home here in 1907. By 1918, Wirthman envisioned what he must have considered a better use for the corner. He replaced his own home with a building that bore his name. The five-story Art Deco Wirthman Building was razed in 1997. (Courtesy of MVSC-KCPL.)

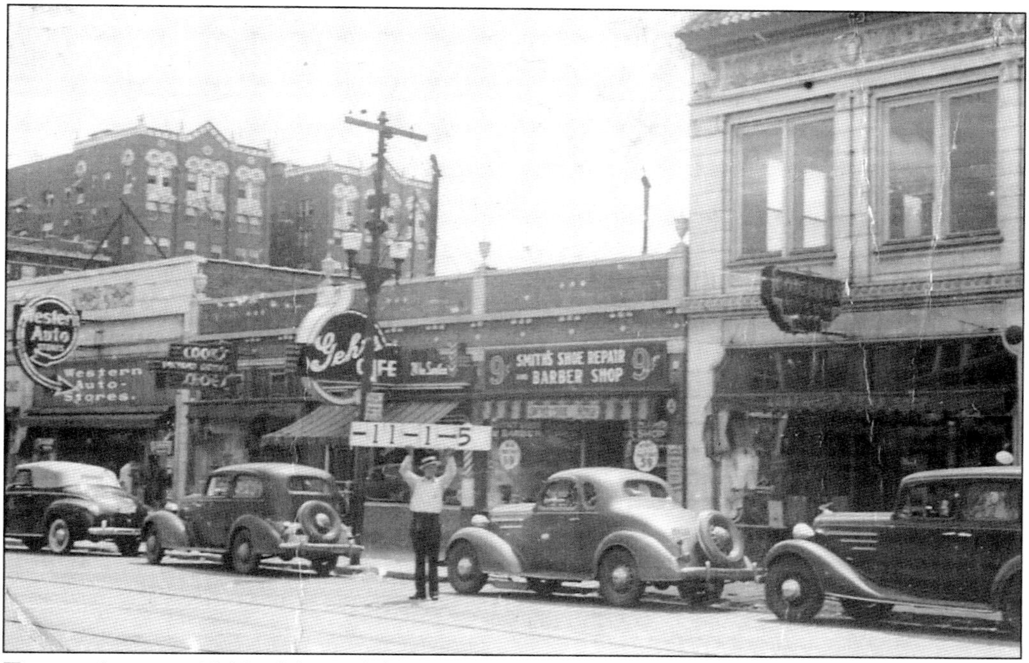

Troost Avenue, 1940s. Many of the commercial buildings on Troost Avenue were built in the early 1920s, and they included a number of small structures constructed to house local services such as butchers, restaurants, and grocers. In 1940, small businesses and services were still serving local neighborhoods near Thirty-first Street. As seen above, a shoe-repair shop, a barbershop, Cook's shoe store, and a Western Auto store surrounded Gehr's Café. Another 1940 tax assessment photograph (below) shows business activity in the Squier Park neighborhood along Troost Avenue around Thirty-sixth Street. Businesses at the time included Lee Yuen Laundry, Mobilgas, the Hensick Billiard Hall, Troostmour Garage, Spering Watch Repair, Miller Barber Shop, Bradford and Thompson Recreation Parlor, White Horse Tavern, and Armour Pharmacy. (Both, courtesy of MVSC-KCPL.)

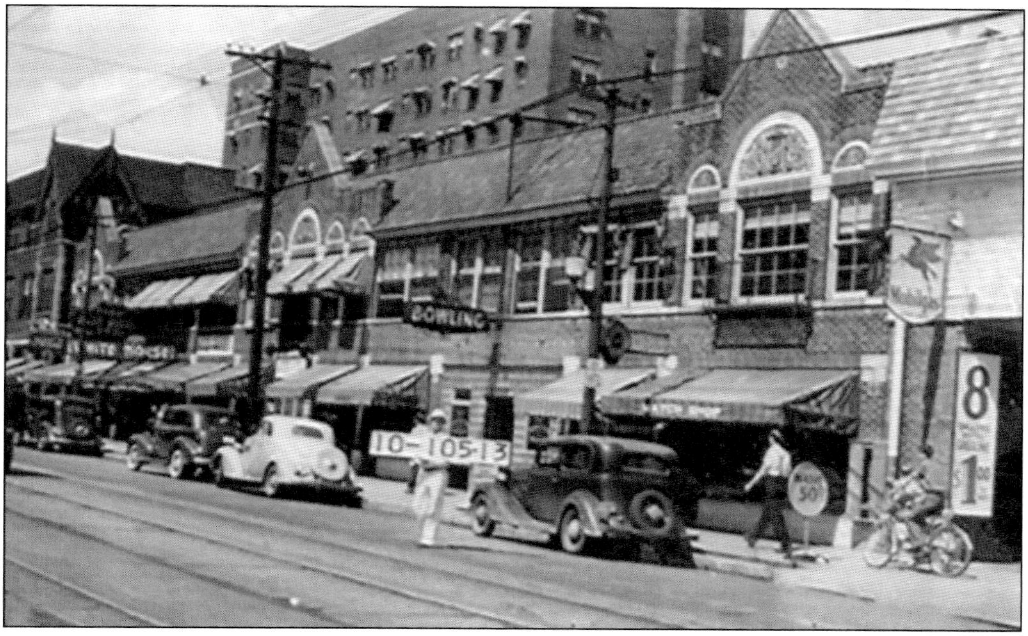

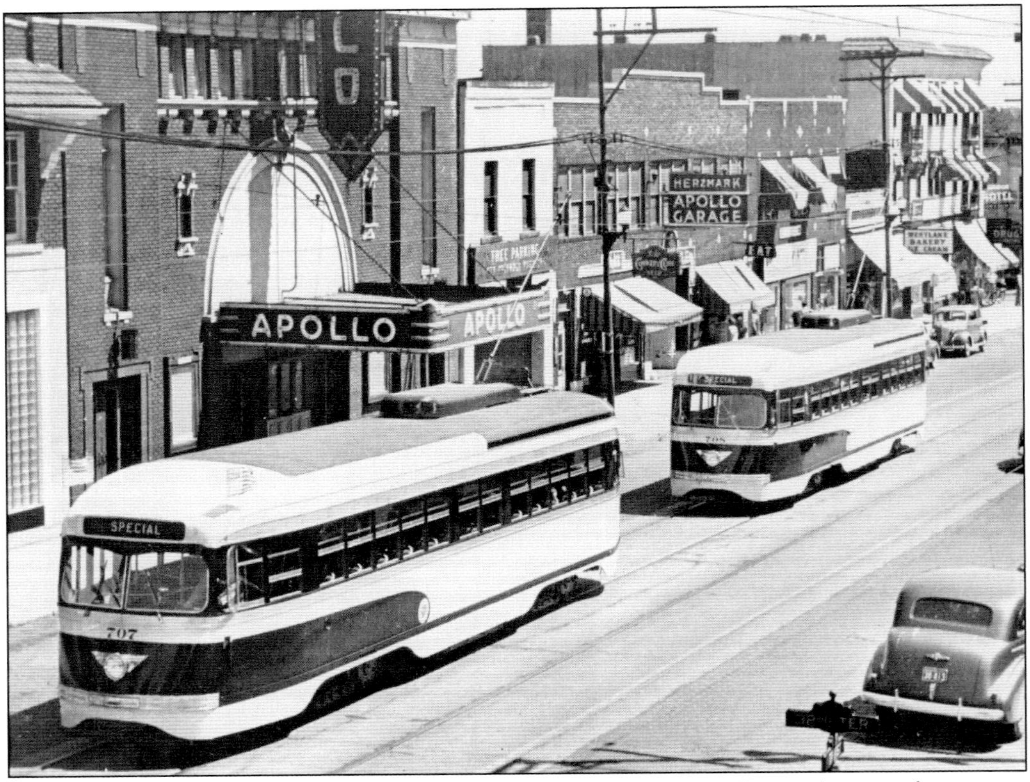

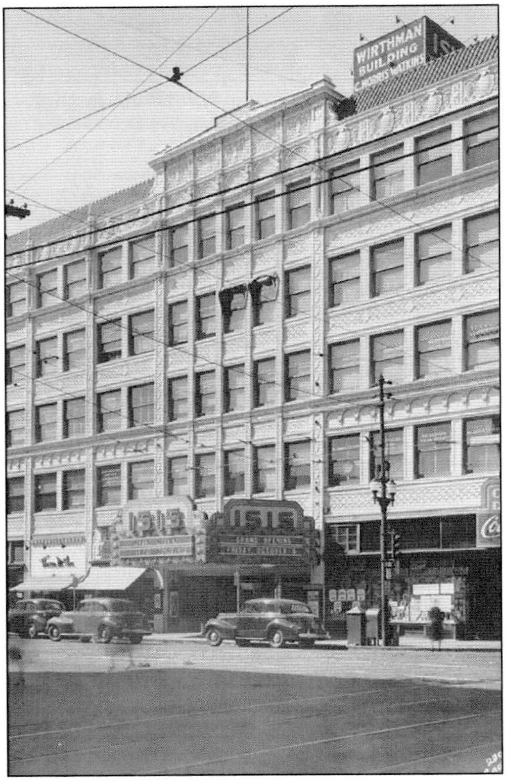

Apollo Theater. Troost Avenue also served as a center of entertainment for the neighborhoods surrounding it. For example, it had seven movie theaters, attracting residents from nearby neighborhoods beginning around 1920. One of the popular venues was the Apollo Theater at 3227 Troost Avenue, which operated from 1911 to 1958. The movies changed often, so people could go to the pictures once or twice a week and see something new. (Courtesy of Wilborn and Associates.)

Isis Theater. The Isis Theater, opened in 1918 on the southwest corner of Thirty-first Street and Troost Avenue, was considered one of the finest theaters in the city. Its marquee on the front of the Wirthman Building advertised first-run movies. In the early years, Carl Stallings, who would later come to define cartoon music at Warner Bros., conducted the orchestra and improvised on the organ. A young Walt Disney showed some of his earliest cartoons at the Isis. It was demolished in 1970. (Courtesy of MVSC-KCPL.)

Eight

Neighborhoods South of Forty-Seventh Street

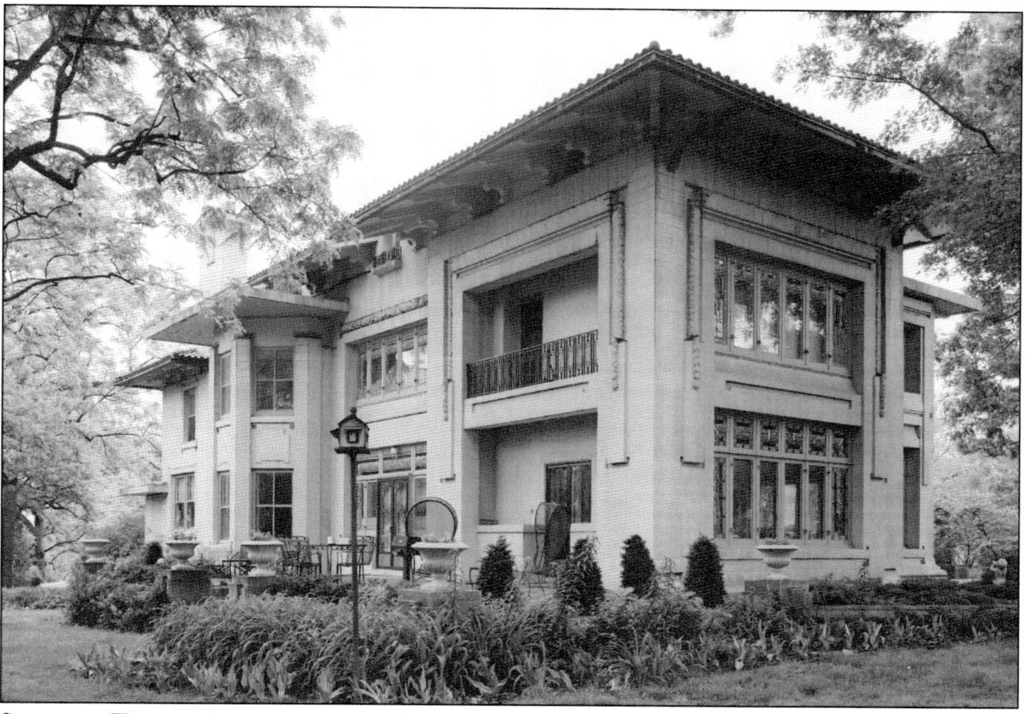

South of Troost Avenue, 1920s. The neighborhoods south of Forty-seventh Street, including South Plaza, Countryside, Sunset Hill, Westwood Park, Crestwood, and Troostwood, developed with the rest of the Country Club District between 1906 and 1920. Developer J.C. Nichols spurred the building of large homes in what he hoped would become exclusive residential areas south of Brush Creek. Some of these neighborhoods extend beyond the limits of what is now considered Midtown. The Bernard Corrigan home at 1200 West Fifty-fifth Street (pictured) was built in 1912 and 1913. (Courtesy of the Library of Congress.)

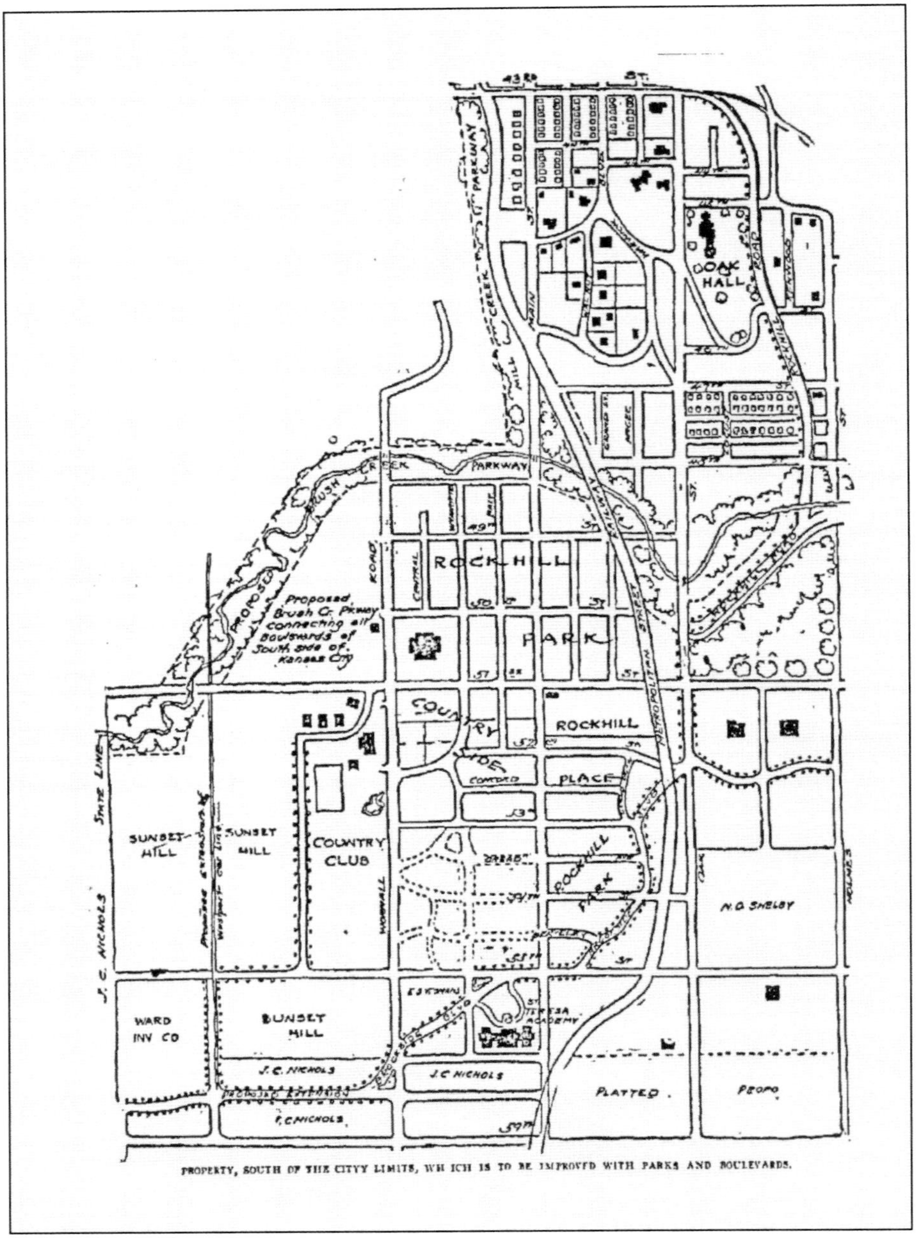

Map of Country Club District, 1908. The *Kansas City Star* published this map along with a story about plans to develop residences south of Brush Creek. It said the owners were working out "the development of a high class district" that would include boulevards, winding roads, stone walls, trees and shrubs, private parks, and streams to "work out into a harmonious whole." As neighborhoods prospered to the north, the area south of Brush Creek had been considered for a long time to be without potential. But J.C. Nichols liked the proximity to William Rockhill Nelson's Oak Hall and to fashionable Rockhill and Southmoreland neighborhoods. Many residents passed through this part of town to visit the Kansas City Country Club, which was on the site of today's Loose Park. Nichols began developing the area, opening up construction south of Brush Creek and causing many of the well-to-do homeowners from Midtown to once again move south. (Courtesy of GenealogyBank.com, a division of NewsBank, Inc.)

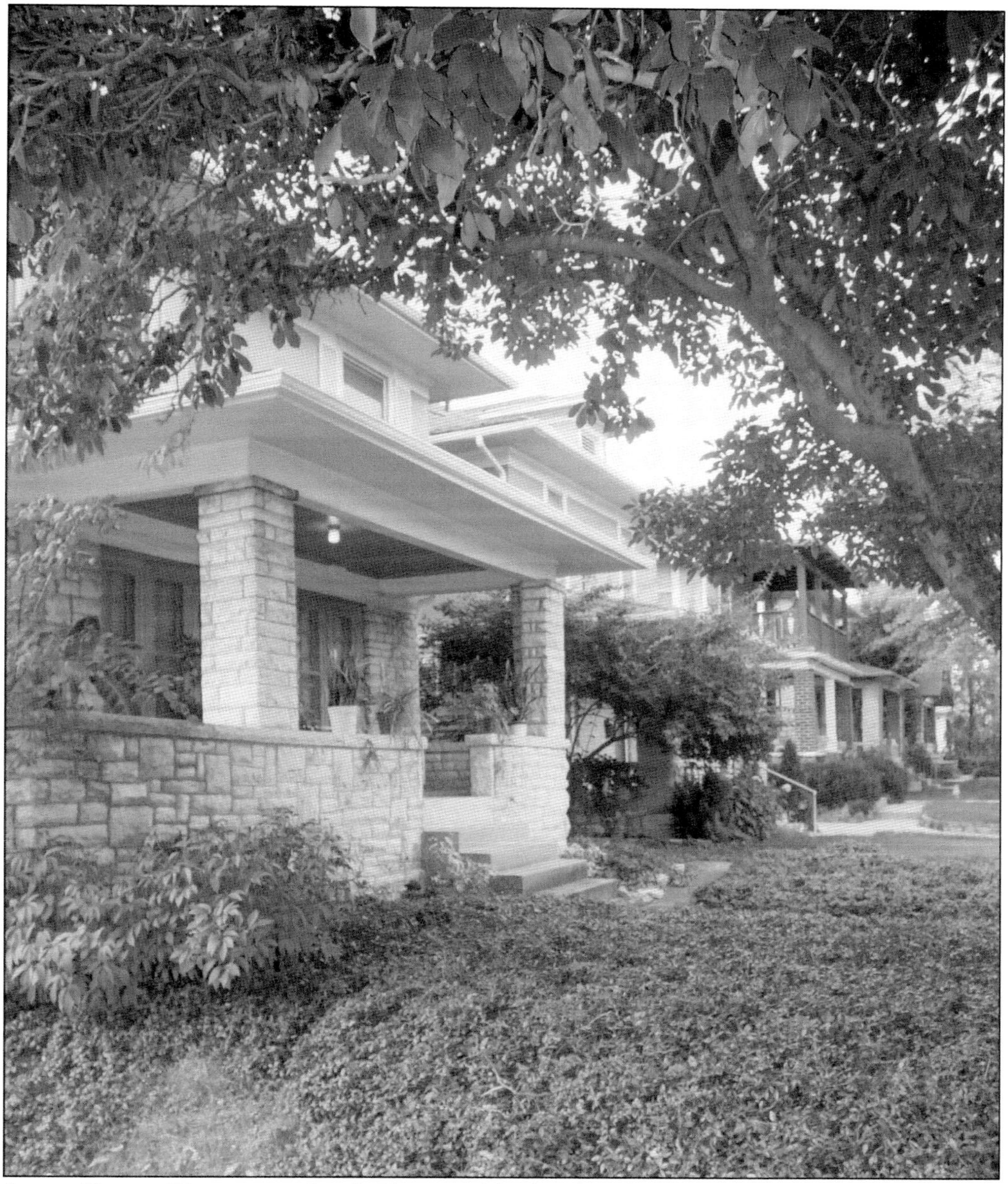

South Plaza. The current South Plaza neighborhood is the first area J.C. Nichols developed south of Brush Creek. He spurred growth by donating part of the roadway for Brookside Boulevard to extend the park-and-boulevard system into his new territory. The Dodson streetcar line ran parallel to Brookside Boulevard, and its former right-of-way has become a green space and exercise trail. Today, South Plaza is a quiet neighborhood conveniently located near the Country Club Plaza shopping district. It is home to residences and businesses that serve nearby neighborhoods, students, and visitors to Kansas City. South Plaza includes the Plaza Library at 4801 Main Street and a strip of businesses around the intersection of Fifty-first and Main Streets. Its single-family homes, most of which date from the 1920s, attract faculty and staff from nearby universities, and its apartments provide housing for students. (Author's collection.)

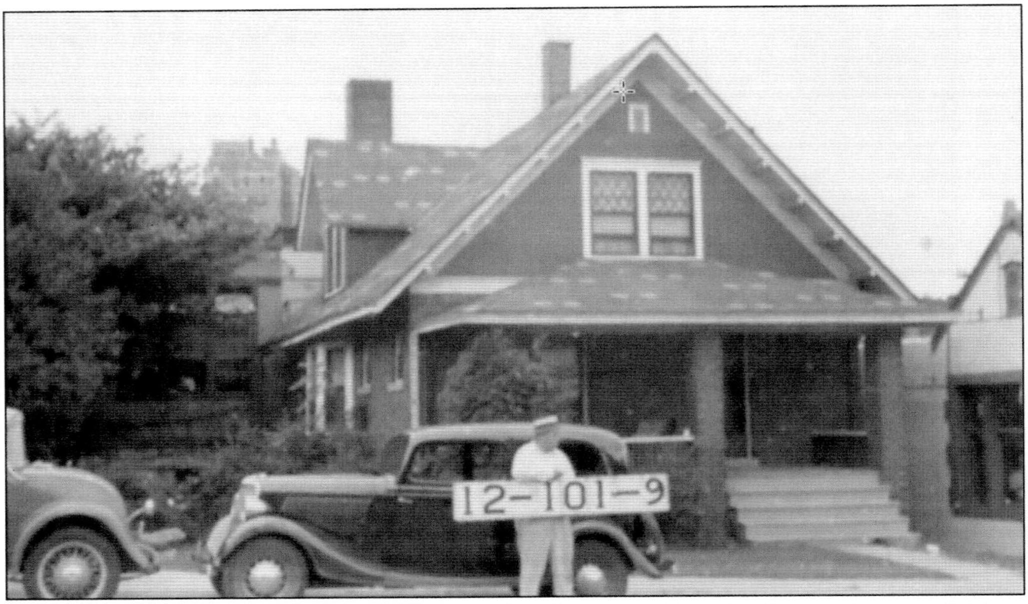

SOUTH PLAZA, 1940. In 1905, J.C. Nichols took a chance and bought 10 acres between Walnut and Main Streets, from Forty-ninth Street to Fifty-first Street, which he called Bismark Place. Although people had to cross Brush Creek on a stone bridge and the creek had a tendency to flood, Nichols began development of an area that had been considered undevelopable. Nichols opened an office at Fifty-first Street and Grand Boulevard and advised people shopping for homes to arrive early in the day to beat the crowds. He advertised his development in 1907 by extolling its "high, sightly, blue grass and trees, electric lights, city water, and sidewalks." The new residential area was also a short hop from downtown on the new Country Club streetcar line. The fare was 5¢. By 1940, the neighborhood was a mixture of homes and apartments. (Both, courtesy of MVSC-KCPL.)

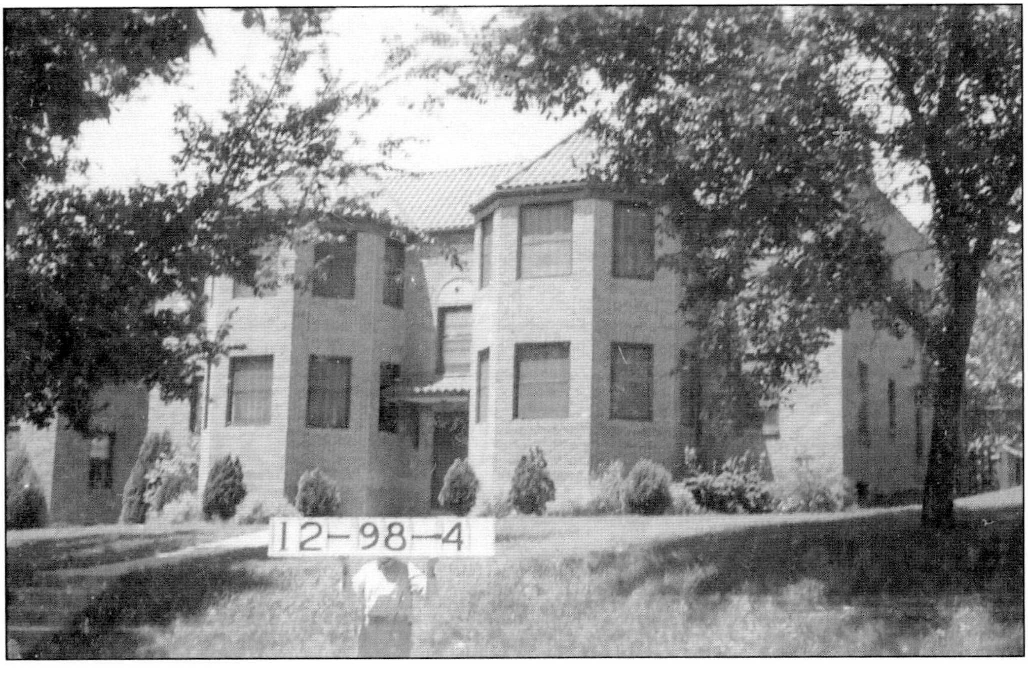

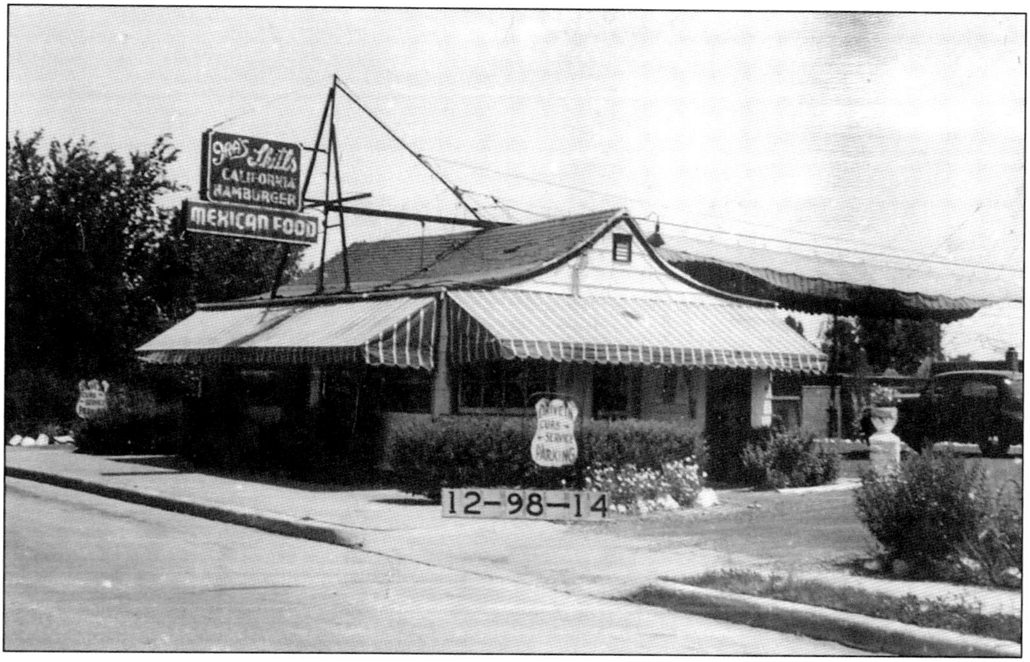

South Plaza Businesses, 1940. By the 1940s, the South Plaza neighborhood supported gas stations, dry cleaners, drugstores, and other businesses that served the new neighborhood. Ira's Skitls at Forty-ninth and Main Streets (above) offered open-air dancing on hot nights and touted its "California hamburgers." At Fifty-first and Main Streets (below), a drugstore with a lunch counter was open for business. There was also a florist, a café, and a laundry in the area. (Both, courtesy of MVSC-KCPL.)

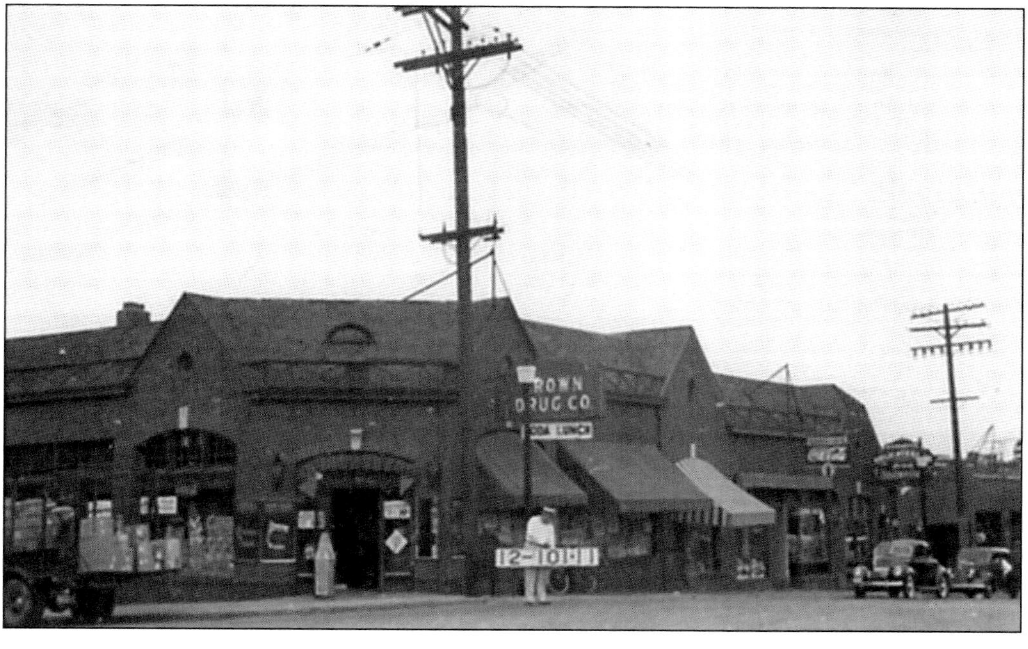

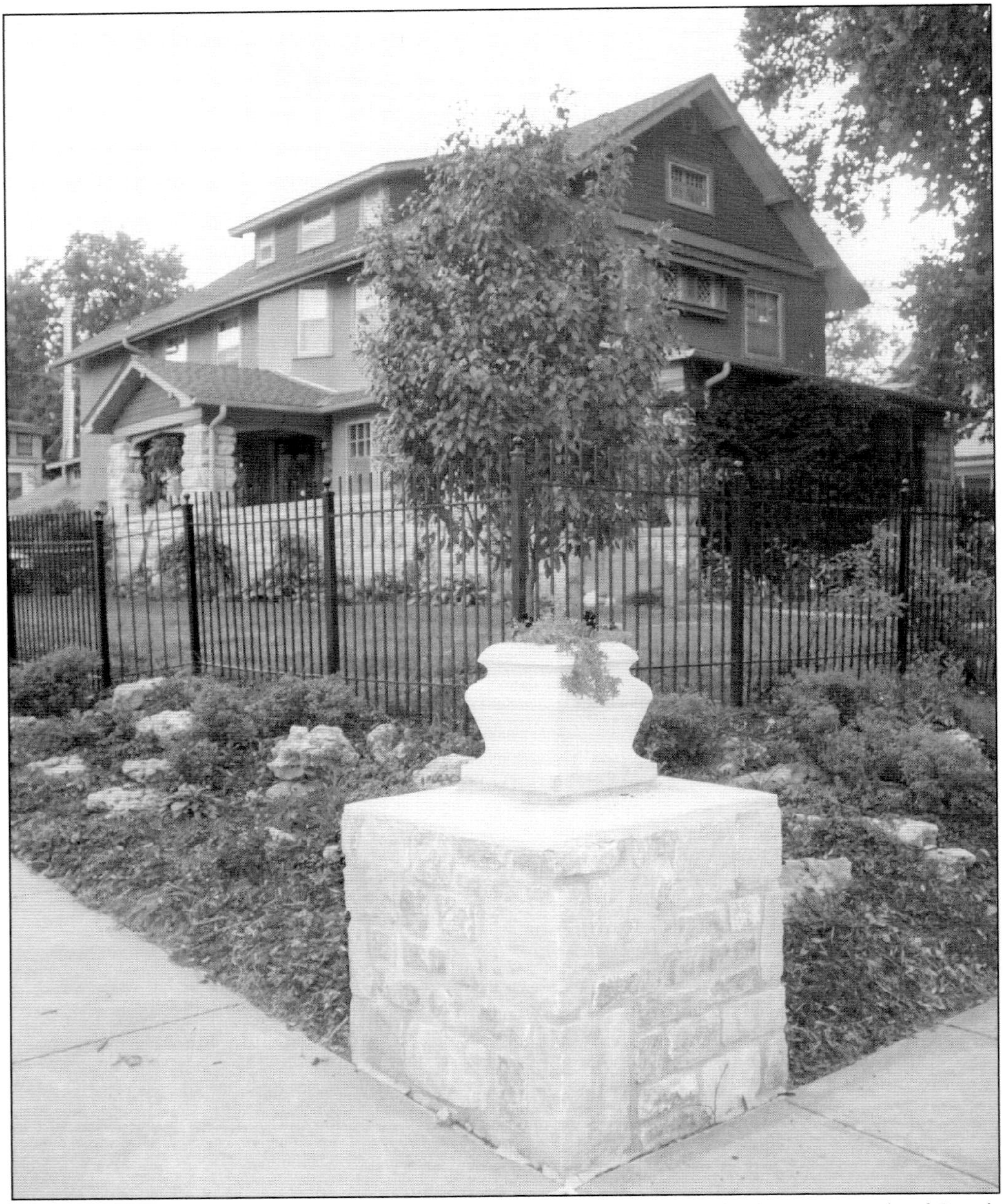

Countryside. This neighborhood (formerly known as Country Side) lies just south of South Plaza. It started out as a farm, which eventually, through inheritance, came to be owned by Catherine Simpson and her two daughters. In 1864, their farm was in the middle of the Battle of Westport, where Union forces faced the Confederate cavalry. After the war, one of Simpson's daughters married Edwin Yeomans. In 1908, the Simpson and Yeomans families filed their first plat to create the Country Side District. The area was in a prime location for development. The Kansas City Country Club had incorporated just to its south in 1896, in the current Loose Park. Nichols was also developing his Country Club District. In fact, Nichols was hired to sell lots in the Country Side District. (Author's collection.)

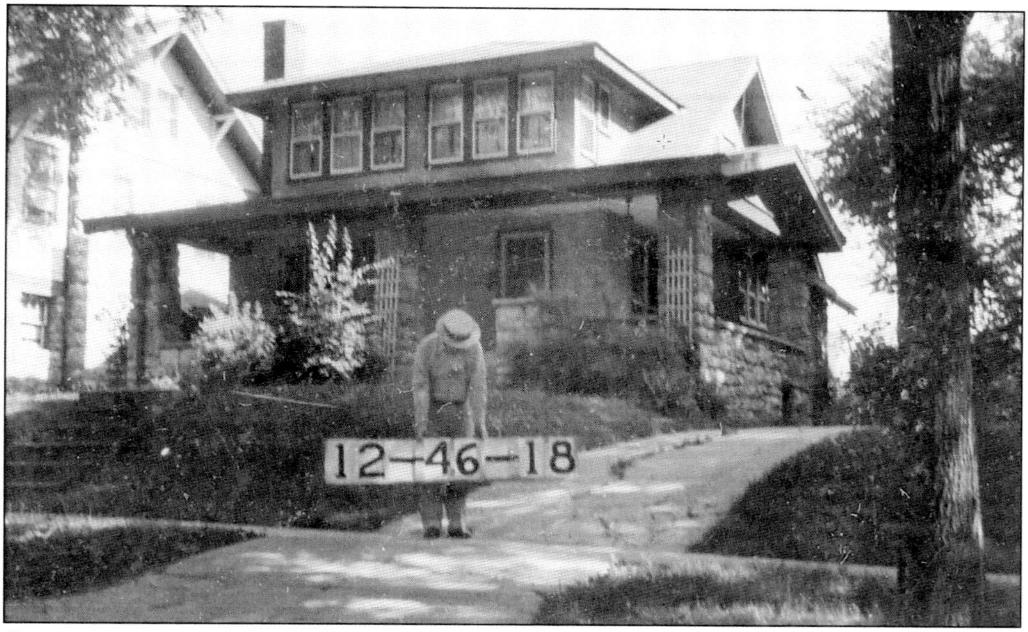

Countryside, 1940. According to its National Register of Historic Places nomination, the Simpson Yeomans Countryside District is unique for the range of architectural styles found there. "Many of the homes are distinctively 'period revival' wherein different historic styles are adopted to then contemporary taste," it says. These styles included Greek Revival, Georgian Revival, and Colonial Revival, as well as English Tudor and Cotswold Cottage, Prairie-style, and Spanish Colonial homes. Deed restrictions in place in Countryside were meant to ensure stability. They required certain setbacks from the street, a frontage of at least 100 feet, and a cost of $500 or more. The deeds also prohibited ownership or use by African Americans, a common clause in many neighborhoods. (Both, courtesy of MVSC-KCPL.)

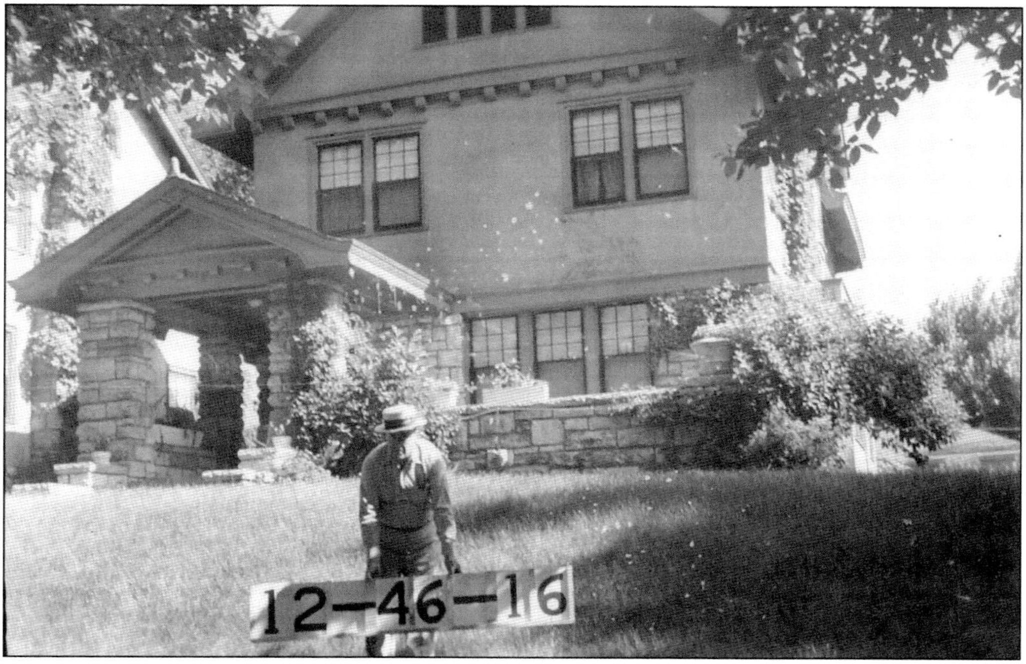

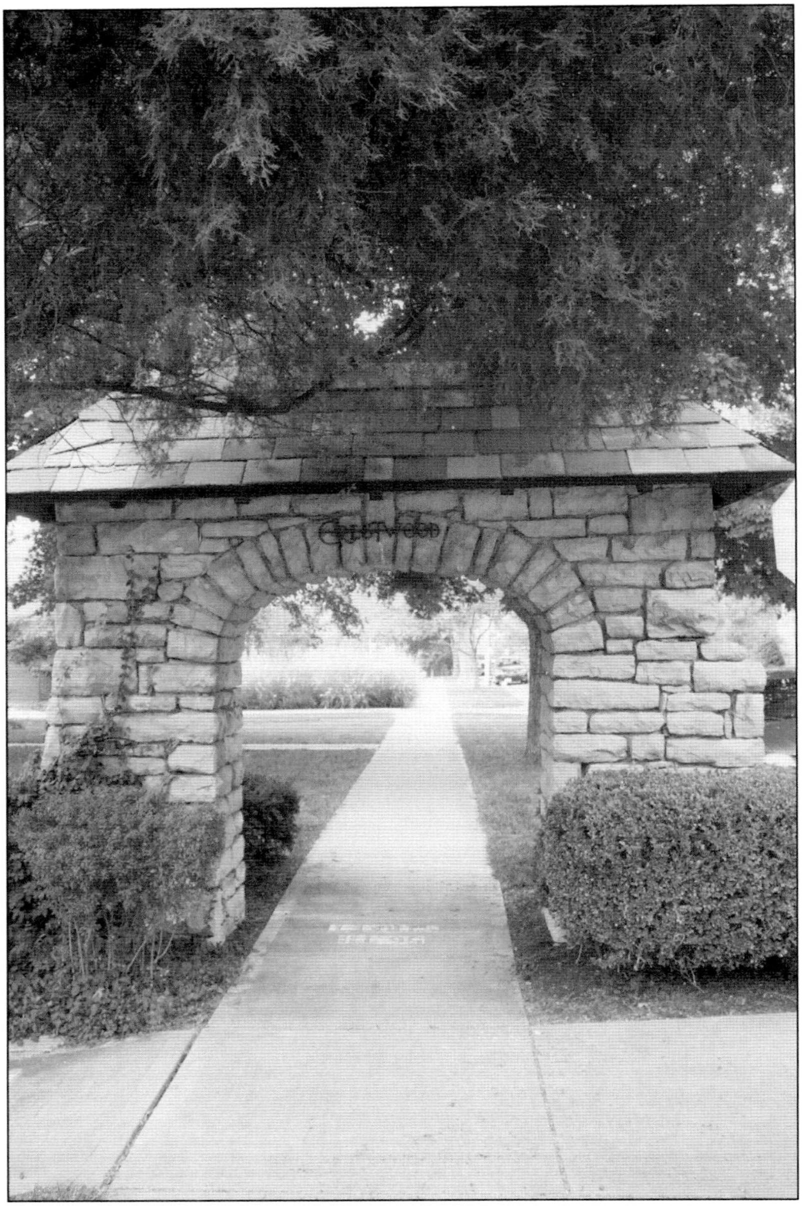

CRESTWOOD. When J.C. Nichols developed the Crestwood neighborhood beginning in 1919, it was advertised as a "garden home" district. The idea was that homes would be oriented toward the garden and the backyard rather than the street. The idea may have come from the topography of Crestwood before the first house was even imagined: it was a pasture known for its old trees. Landscape architects Hare and Hare took advantage of that when they designed the subdivision, laying out curved roads (breaking from the city grid pattern) and creating parklets with statuary or decorative touches where the roads intersected. Some blocks originally included larger parks with playground equipment. Crestwood borders the University of Missouri campus. Residents have a small shopping district, the Crestwood shops at Fifty-fifth and Oak Streets. The Second Presbyterian Church was erected in the neighborhood in 1912. Neighborhood markers welcome Kansas Citians to the residential district, where most homes were built between 1920 and 1926. (Author's collection.)

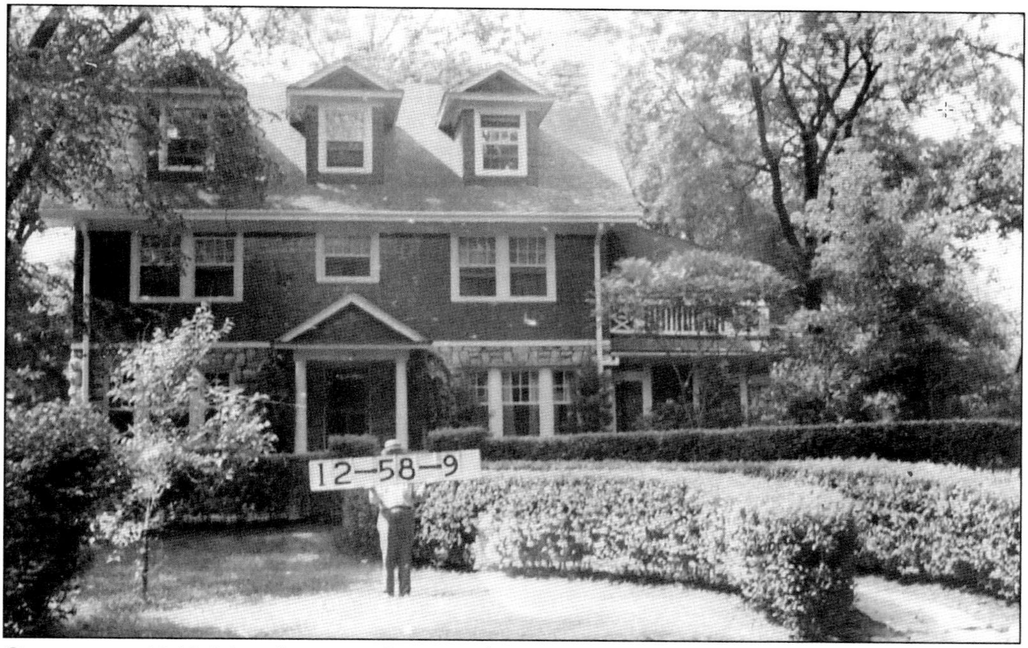

CRESTWOOD, 1940. Many homes in Crestwood incorporated into their foundations stone quarried at Fifty-fifth and Oak Streets. The architecture generally followed the post–World War I Eclectic movement in design, with the majority of homes built in the Colonial Revival or Tudor Revival styles. Although Crestwood offered some smaller bungalows for young couples, many of its homes are larger. The uniformity of size, scale, and materials gives the neighborhood its distinctive character. Frontage was often 45 to 60 feet, and lots were 100 to 120 feet deep. Photographs from 1940 show a neighborhood of well-maintained lawns and neatly clipped hedges. (Both, courtesy of MVSC-KCPL.)

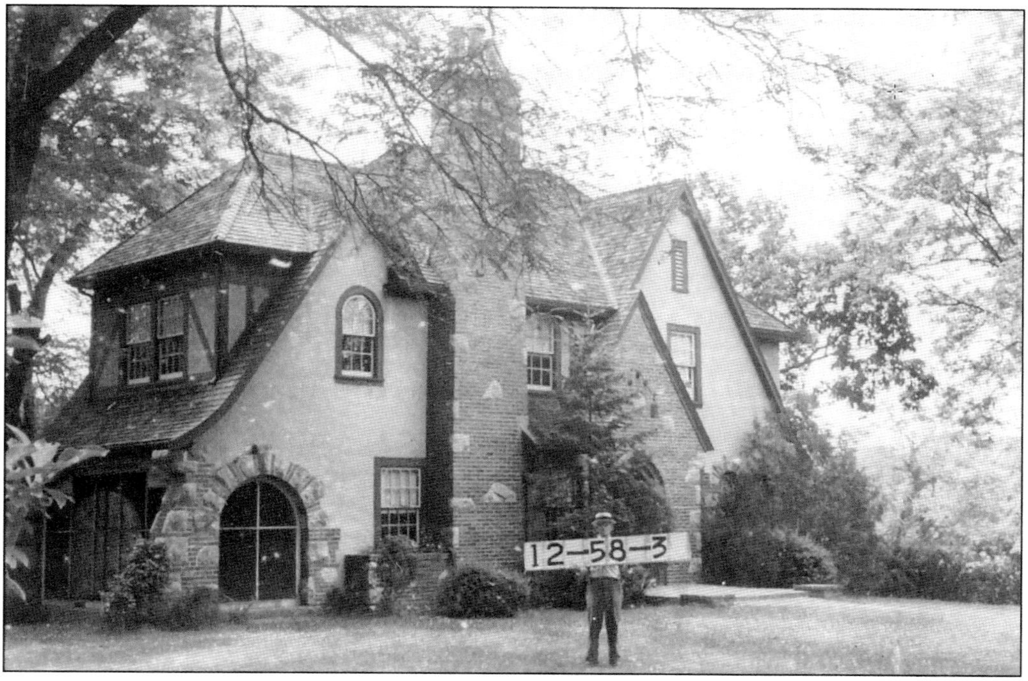

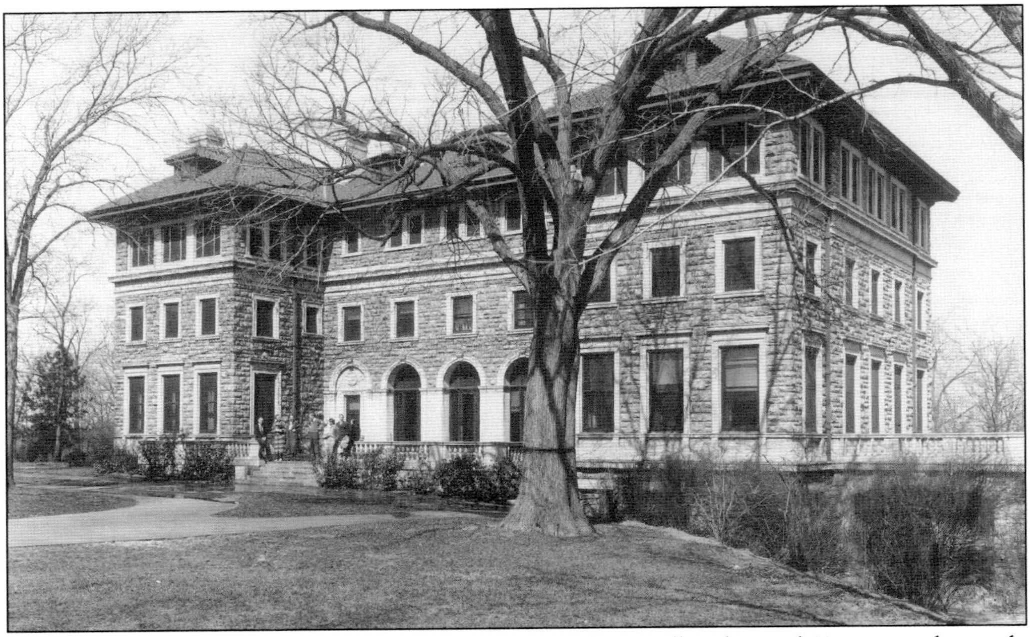

UNIVERSITY OF KANSAS CITY, 1930S. Businessman William Volker donated 40 acres to the newly established University of Kansas City in 1931. Classes began in 1933. The school grew quickly and expanded by incorporating several other institutions of higher learning. The university became the University of Missouri–Kansas City in 1963, when it joined the University of Missouri system. (Courtesy of MVSC-KCPL.)

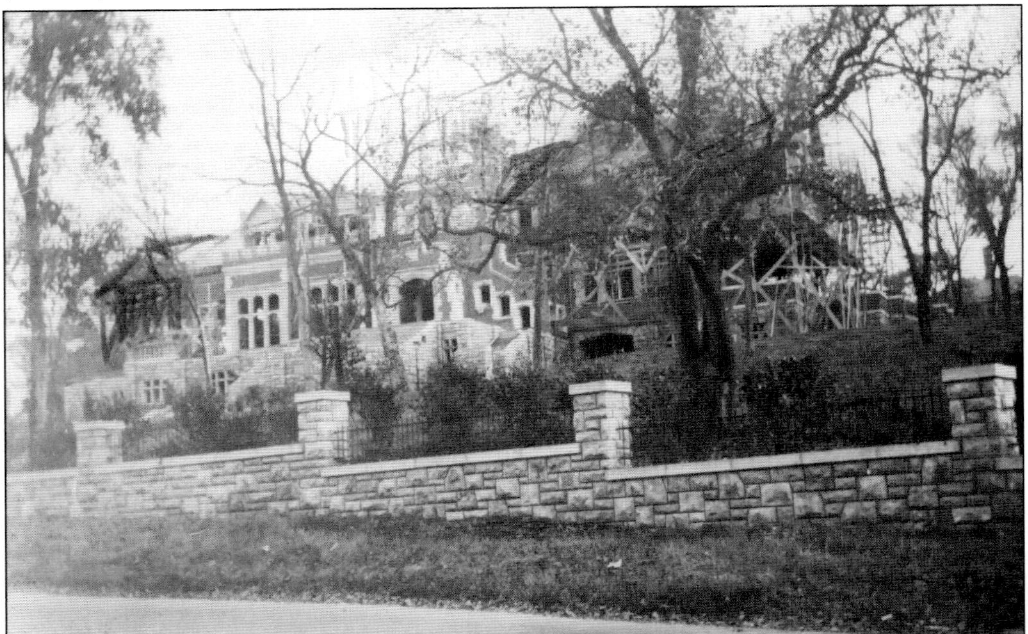

EPPERSON HOUSE. The growing school took advantage of the mansions that had been built in the area. For example, Epperson House, a 56-room former home at Fifty-second and Cherry Streets, was constructed by Uriah Epperson for $450,000 in 1919. It was donated to the university in 1942. (Courtesy of UMKC–LaBudde.)

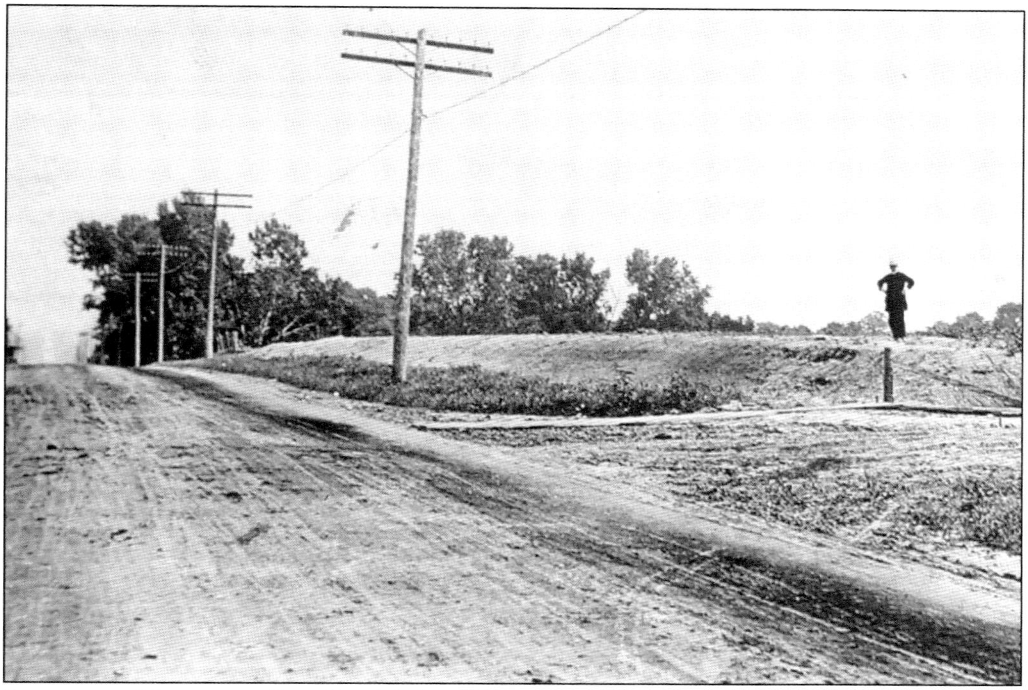

Rockhurst University Site. Rev. Michael J. Ryan, SJ, looks out over the area that would become Rockhurst College (later Rockhurst University) before construction began. Ryan oversaw the opening of the rock quarry, supervised the laborers that worked on Sedgwick Hall, and helped found the Jesuit parish at Rockhurst. Shown here looking northeast is the intersection of Fifty-third Street and Troost Avenue. (Courtesy of Rockhurst University.)

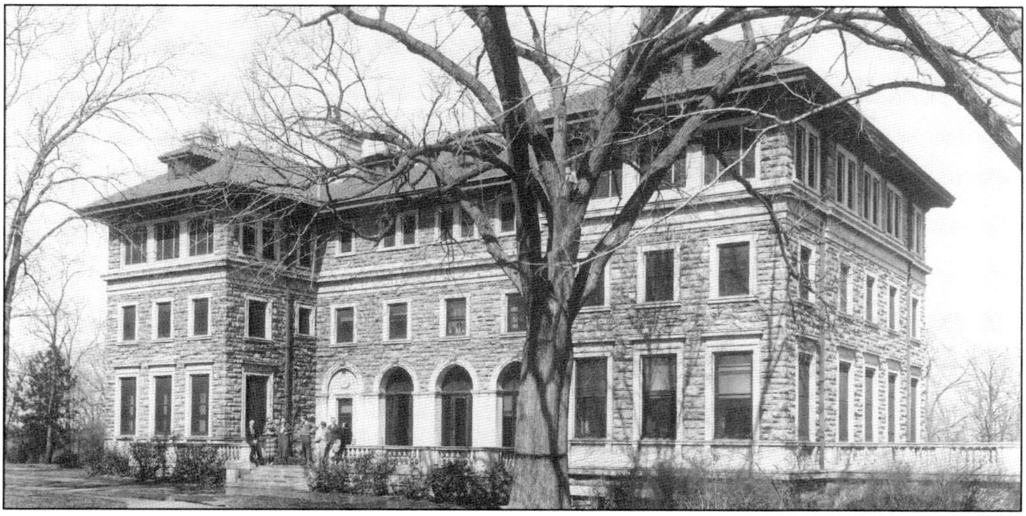

Rockhurst College. In 1909, Rev. Michael Dowling, SJ, the founder of Rockhurst, purchased 25 acres of land at Fifty-third Street and Troost Avenue for $50,000. Rockhurst College opened in 1910, and the forerunner of Rockhurst High School was located on the property until 1962. High school and college classes were taught in Sedgwick Hall (pictured), which is still used by Rockhurst University today. (Courtesy of MVSC-KCPL.)

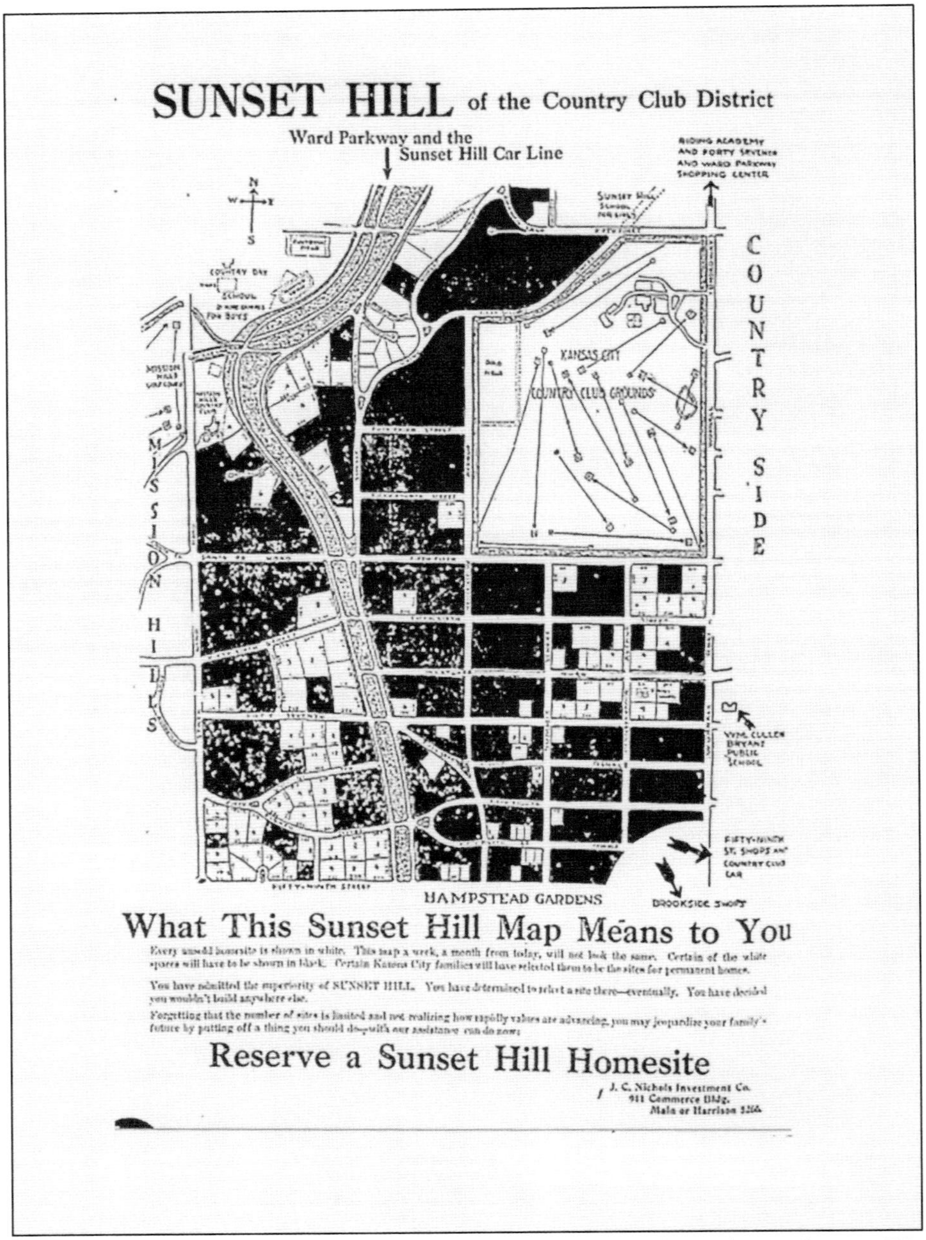

SUNSET HILL MAP, 1921. In 1906, J.C. Nichols began working with Hugh Ward, son of Kansas City pioneer Seth Ward, to develop another exclusive area, Sunset Hill. Ward had inherited several hundred acres around Fifty-first Street and Wornall Road. Working with George Kessler, Nichols had his crews take special care to protect the trees and plant new ones, as lots were laid out on the often steep slopes in what was meant to be an exclusive residential district. Nichols advertised Sunset Hill as "a picturesque woodland" where each site made the best possible use of stone ledges, slopes, and natural approaches. His newspaper advertisement showed off what Nichols considered to be the key selling points: its position between the Kansas suburb of Mission Hills and the Country Side subdivision in Missouri, transportation access via streetcar line, and the fact that the Kansas City Country Club was within its boundaries. (Courtesy of GenealogyBank.com, a Division of NewsBank, Inc.)

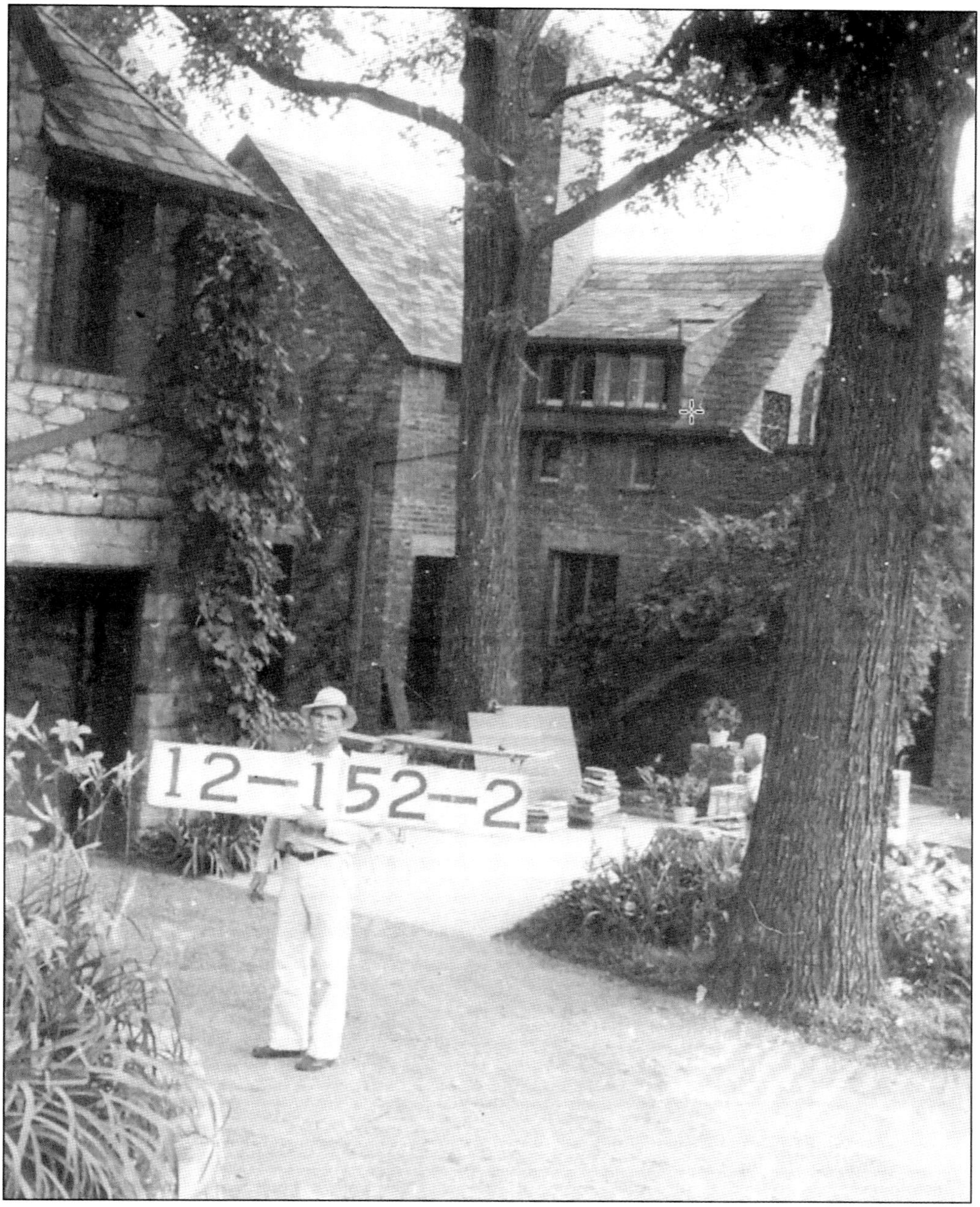

SUNSET HILL, 1940. The hilly sections of Sunset Hill provided a bigger challenge for builders, but they also offered the reward of great views to homeowners. Architect Mary Hook Rockwell specialized in fitting homes onto the hillside and incorporating native stonework. (Courtesy of MVSC-KCPL.)

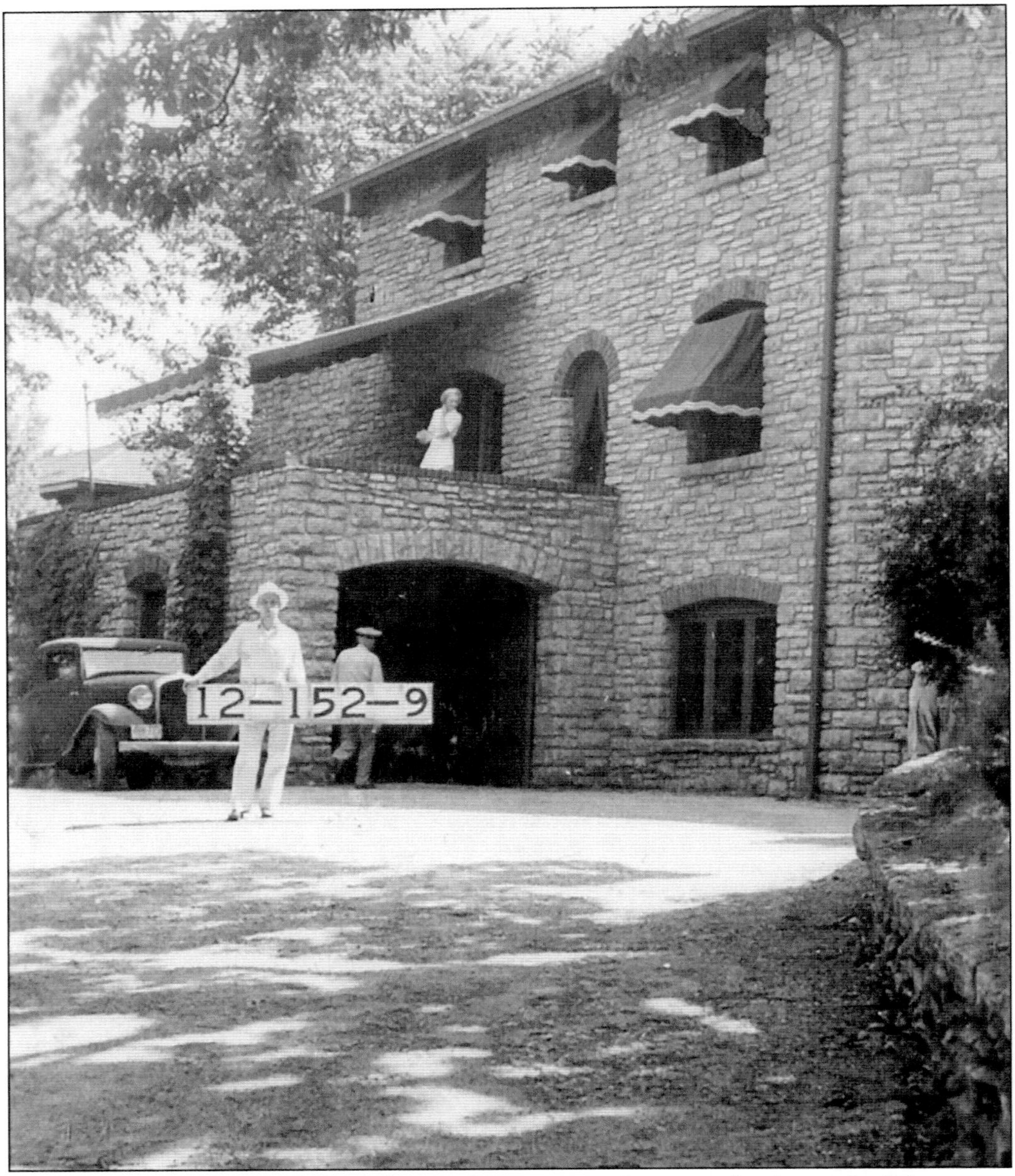

Sunset Hill. As Nichols helped the Ward Investment Company develop and sell homes on Sunset Hill, he and the firm continued practices that Nichols had begun in Countryside: the use of deed restrictions that allowed only single-family homes to be built (except for a few duplexes), requiring houses to cost a minimum of $5,000, and prohibiting sales to African Americans. (Courtesy of MVSC-KCPL.)

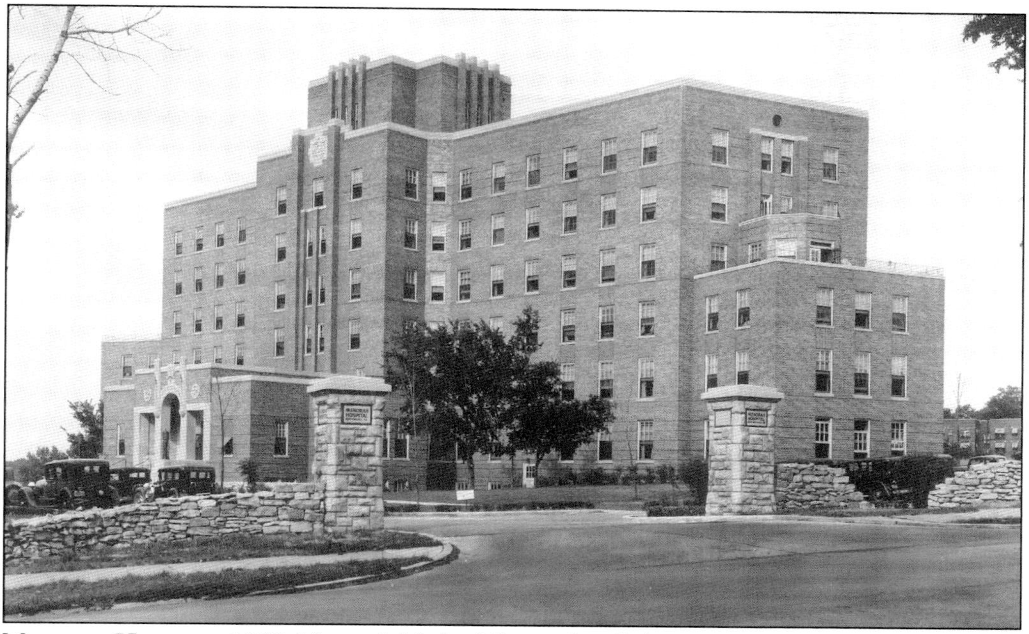

MENORAH HOSPITAL, 1930. Menorah Medical Center, briefly known as Jewish Memorial Hospital, opened its doors in 1931 at Forty-ninth Street and Rockhill Road, filling the need for more and improved hospital facilities following World War I. The hospital following the movement of its patients south to Johnson County in 1994. The Stowers Institute for Medical Research now stands on the site. (Courtesy of MVSC-KCPL.)

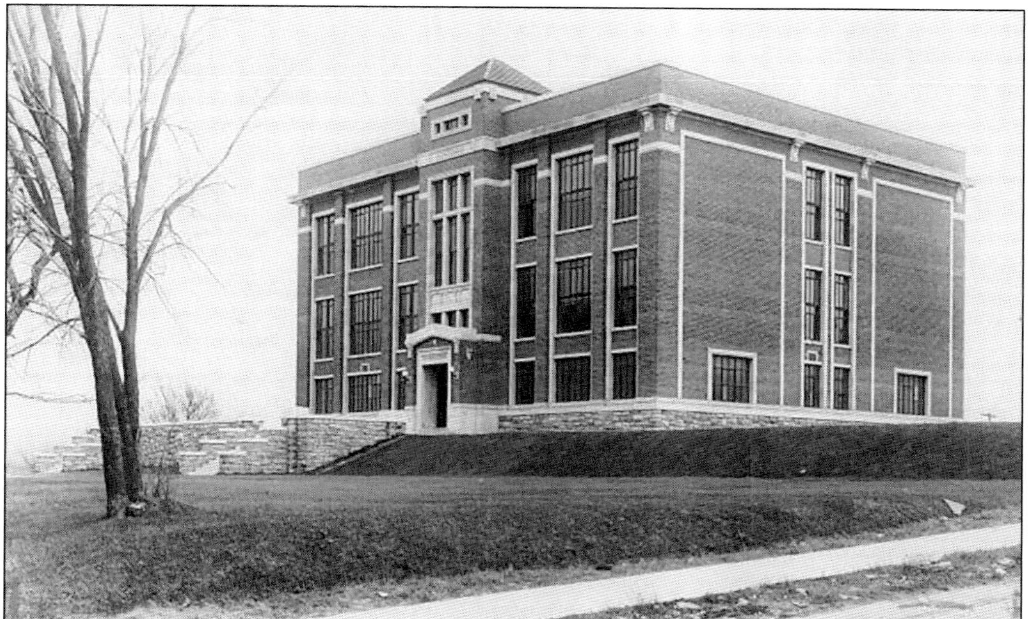

E.C. WHITE SCHOOL. As residents moved southward, the school district relocated a two-room frame building to Fiftieth and Oak Streets, which students reached by a small footbridge over a stream. In 1914, the district opened the E.C. White Elementary School at the corner of Forty-Ninth and Main Streets. It was demolished in 1965 to make way for a new plaza library. (Courtesy of MVSC-KCPL.)

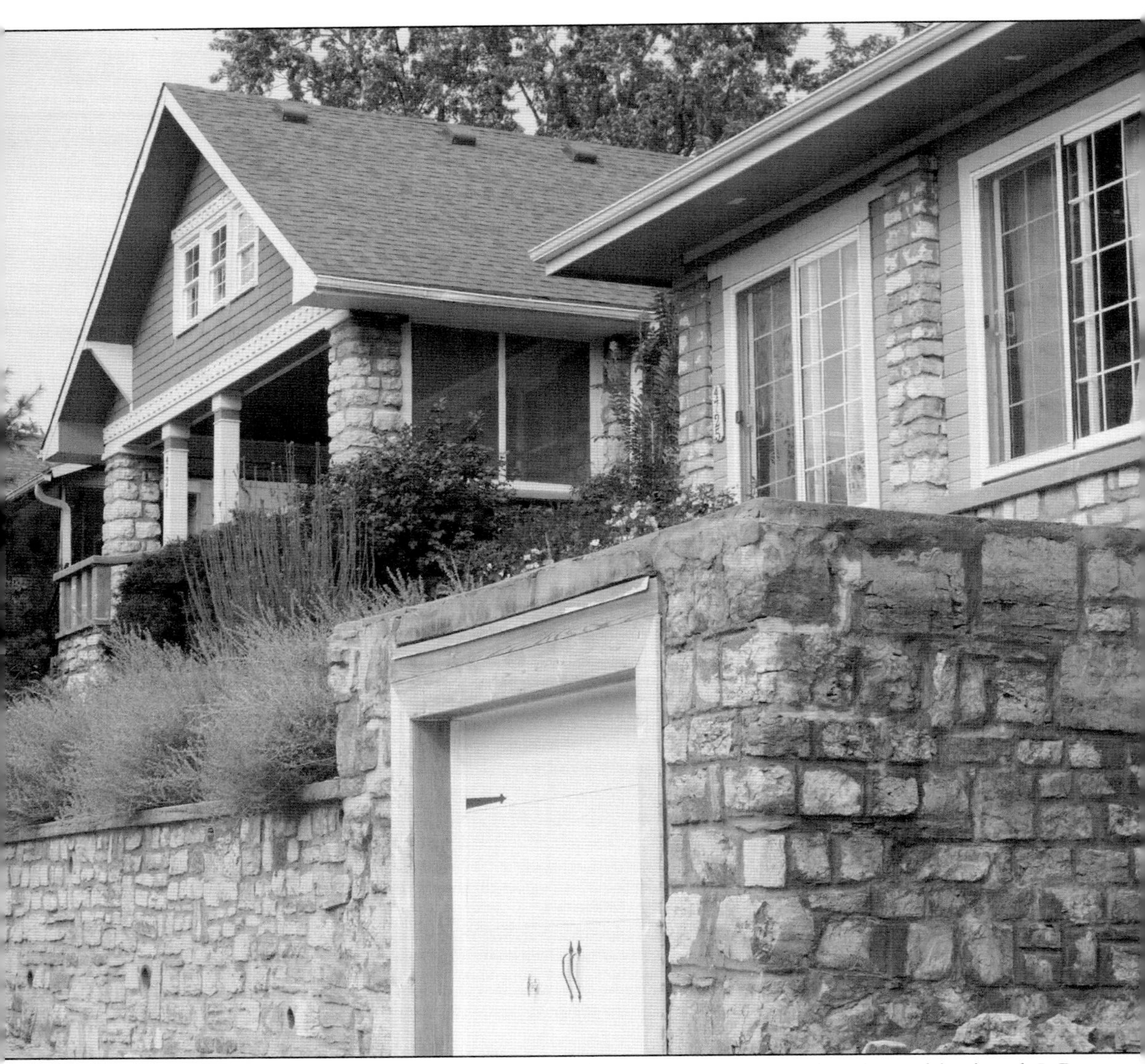

WESTWOOD PARK. Just north of Sunset Hill is the compact Westwood Park neighborhood. L.R. Wright began developing the subdivision in 1913, but sales did not really take off until J.C. Nichols bought and marketed the unsold lots in 1921. Then, Nichols boasted in newspaper advertisements, 25 percent of the home sites sold in the first week. Like Sunset Hill, Westwood Park lots took advantage of the forest trees that were incorporated into the design of the new subdivision. But here, Nichols was not marketing to the most elite buyers. He was offering the middle class a chance to be part of the Country Club District on easy monthly terms. Restrictions in Westwood Park allowed for two-story homes and "well-designed" bungalows. Outdoor activities in Westwood Park center around the 9.3-acre park after which the neighborhood takes it name. It was added to the city's park system in 1948. Westwood Park is a favorite sledding spot for area children. (Author's collection.)

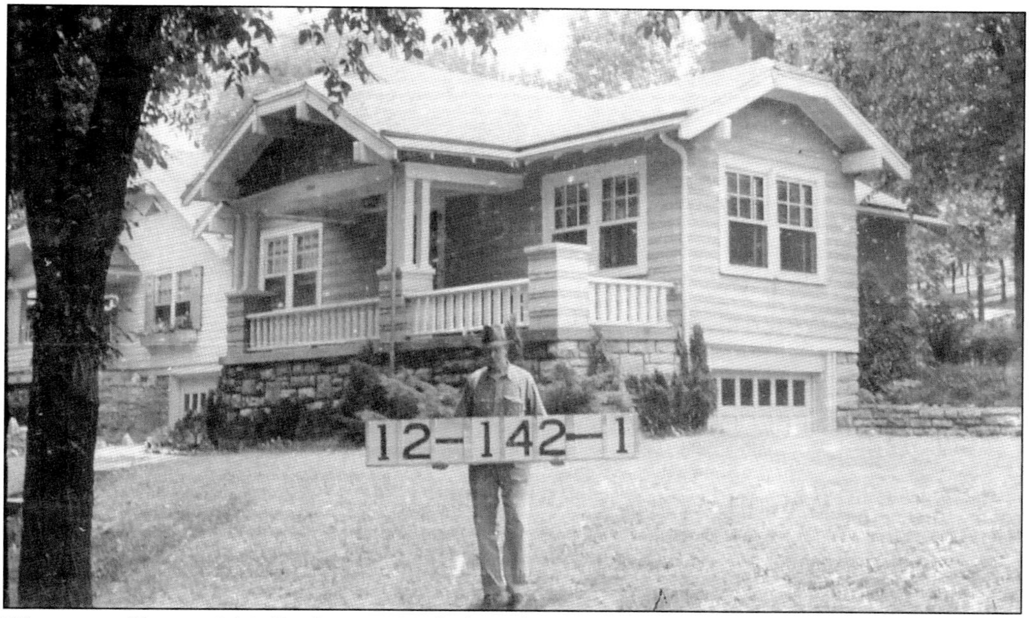

WESTWOOD PARK, 1940. By the time Nichols took over marketing Westwood Park, it had sewers, water, gas, lights, and street improvements. Residents could travel to downtown on the Sunset Hill, Ward Parkway, or Westport streetcars lines. Today, Westwood Park, like the other Nichols subdivisions, has a homes association rather than a voluntary neighborhood association. It was first organized in 1922. In Midtown, homeowners in Country Side, Crestwood, and Sunset Hill are also members of home associations. These organizations operate like the voluntary neighborhood groups in other neighborhoods, but they also have professional staff. As seen in these 1940 photographs, Westwood Park has been completely built out, with mostly compact homes that take advantage of the terrain and incorporate forest trees into their landscaping. (Both, courtesy of *Midtown KC Post*.)

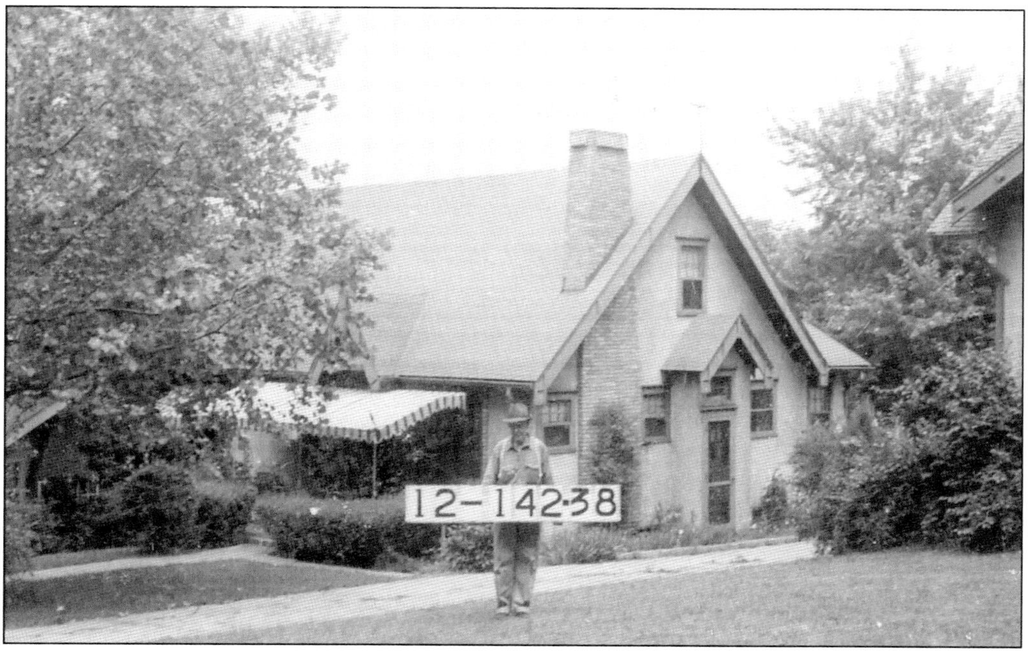

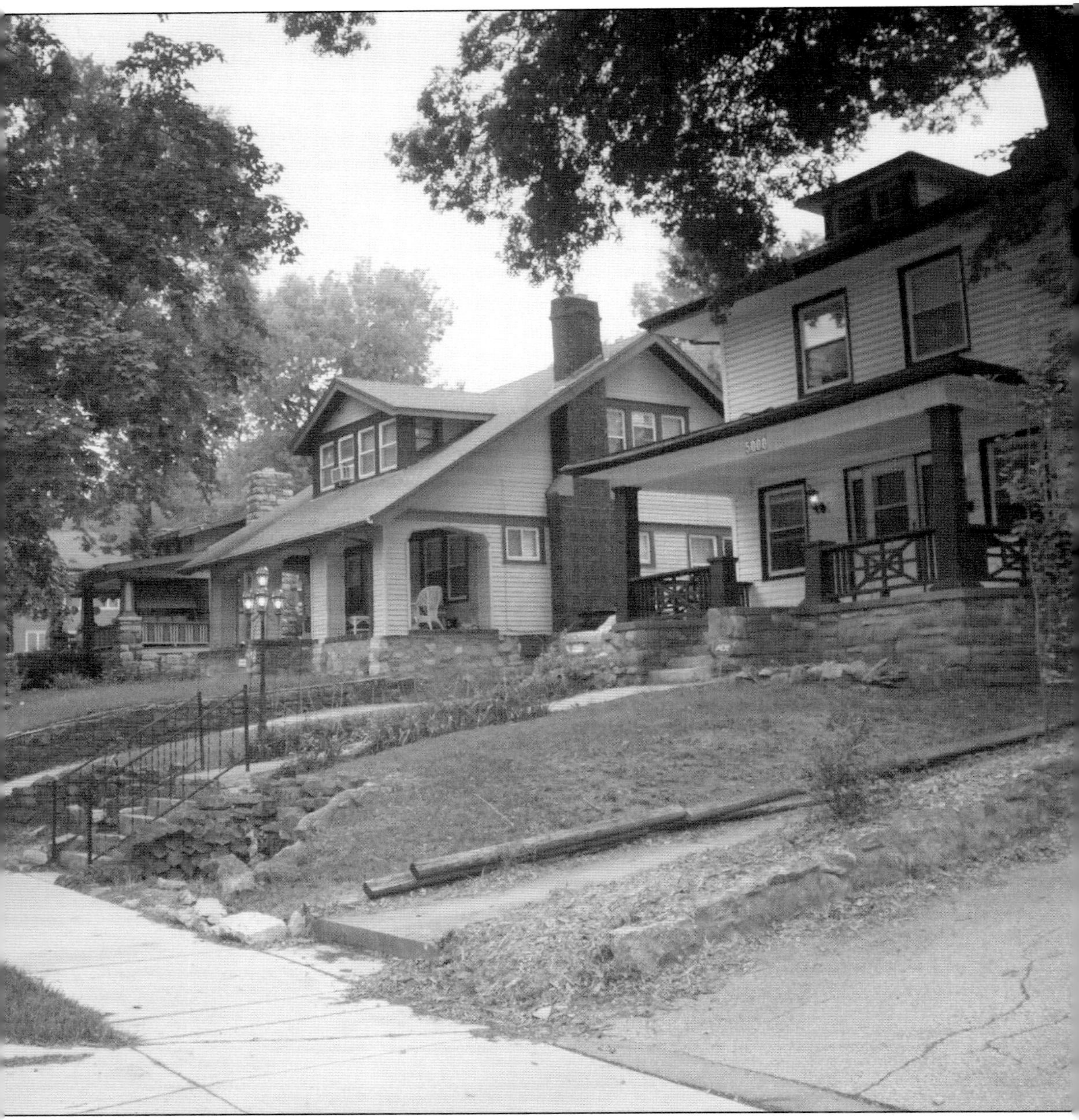

TROOSTWOOD. This neighborhood was growing on the easternmost side of Midtown as Nichols was building his subdivisions. Troostwood was the creation of James B. Welsh, a realtor who began advertising homes for sale in 1919. "Live where it's cool," Welch suggested to home buyers, offering them homes "on the crest of a shady hill in Troostwood." He had six-room and seven-room homes available for $6,500 to $10,000, close to streetcar lines, schools, and boulevards. Welsh's subdivision was built on a hill and laid out with winding roads that took advantage of views. The August L. Huber Building Company constructed mostly Colonial-style homes and bungalows. Troost homeowners organized themselves early, forming the Troostwood Improvement Society in the early 1920s. In the 1990s, Troostwood residents "reclaimed" the corner of Troost Avenue and Fiftieth Street, creating Troostwood Commons, a park that they now maintain. (Author's collection.)

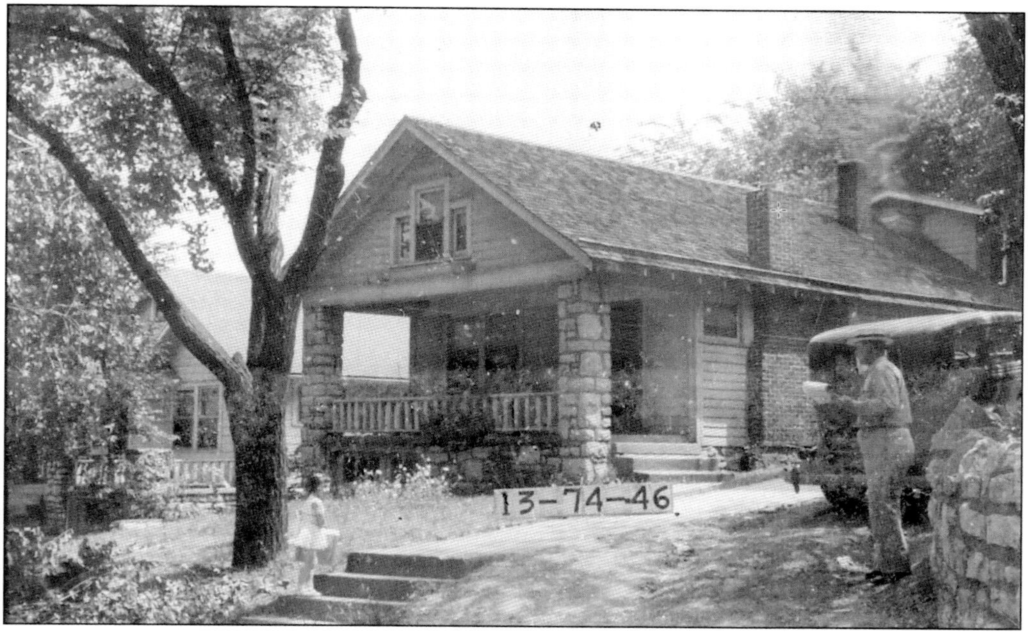

TROOSTWOOD RESIDENCES, 1940. In the 1940s, when these photographs was taken, Troostwood homes were being advertised as part of the "University District." As the new University of Kansas City and Rockhurst College began offering classes, Troostwood offered a perfect location for faculty and staff. Rockhurst High School, a Jesuit school, also operated at Fifty-second Street and Troost from 1923 to 1962. Troostwood was also conveniently located near the Nelson-Atkins Museum of Art and the Nichols' Country Club Plaza shopping district. Apartment buildings (below) lined Troost Avenue. (Both, courtesy of MVSC-KCPL.)

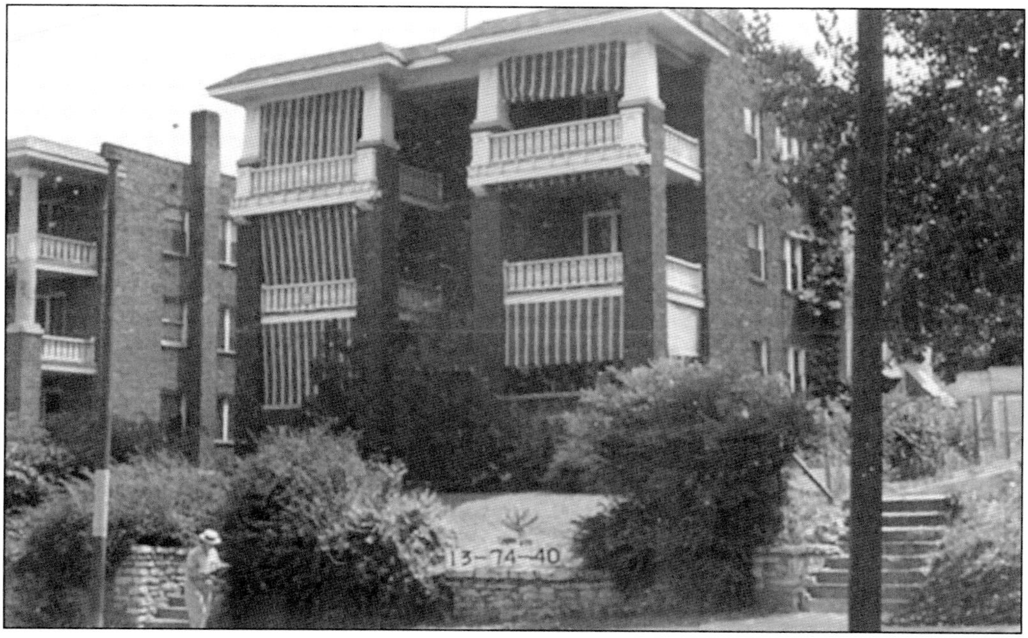

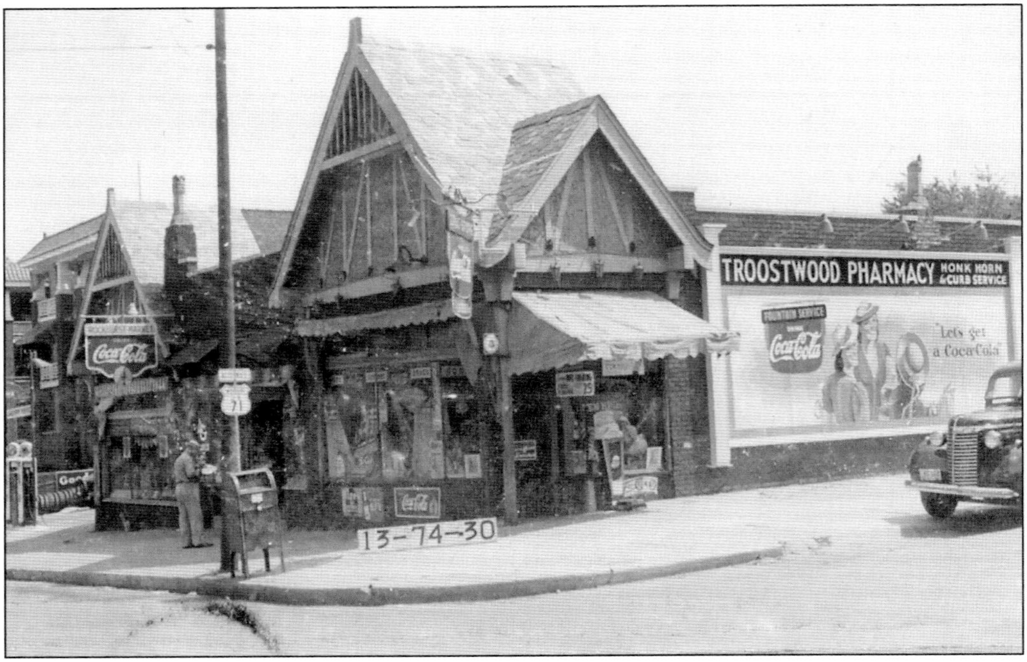

Troostwood Businesses, 1940. At the corner of Troost Avenue and Fiftieth Street, this 1940 photograph shows the Troostwood Pharmacy offering "honk horn for curb service." Next door stood a small gas station serving residents of the neighborhood and folks passing along Troost Avenue. (Both, courtesy of MVSC-KCPL.)

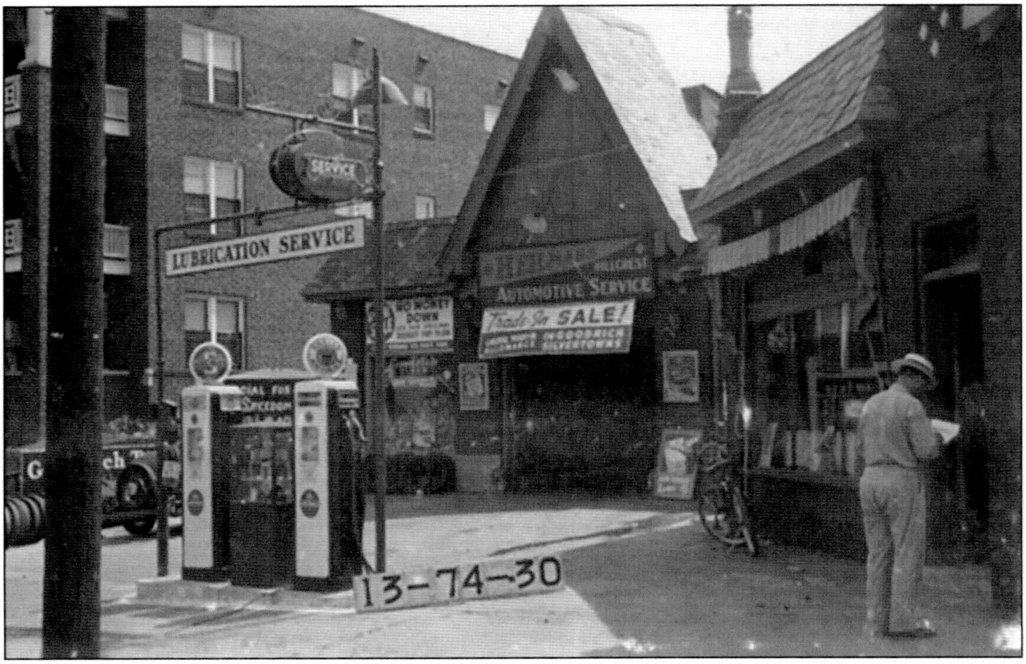

Index